THE HISTORY OF
THE COMMON LAW
OF ENGLAND

Classics of British Historical Literature

JOHN CLIVE, EDITOR

Sir Matthew Hale

—

The History of
the Common Law
of England

EDITED AND WITH AN INTRODUCTION BY

CHARLES M. GRAY

The University of Chicago Press
CHICAGO AND LONDON

ISBN: 0-226-31304-2 (clothbound); 0-226-31305-0 (paperbound)
Library of Congress Catalog Card Number: 70-155856
The University of Chicago Press, Chicago 60637
The University of Chicago Press, Ltd., London
Published 1971
Printed in the United States of America

Contents

CONTENTS

Series Editor's Preface

This series of reprints has one major purpose: to put into the hands of students and other interested readers outstanding— and sometimes neglected—works dealing with British history which have either gone out of print or are obtainable only at a forbiddingly high price.

The phrase Classics of British Historical Literature requires some explanation, in view of the fact that the two companion series published by the University of Chicago Press are entitled, respectively, Classic European Historians and Classic American Historians. Why, then, introduce the word *literature* into the title of this series?

One reason lies close at hand. History, if it is to live beyond its own generation, must be memorably written. The greatest British historians—Clarendon, Gibbon, Hume, Carlyle, Macaulay—are still alive today, not merely because they contributed to the cumulative historical knowledge about their subjects, but because they were masters of style and literary artists as well. And even historians of the second rank, if they deserve to survive, are able to do so only because they can still be read with pleasure. To emphasize this truth at the present time, when much eminently solid and worthy academic history suffers from being almost totally unreadable, seems worth doing.

The other reason for including the word *literature* in the title of the series has to do with its scope. To read history is to learn about the past. But if, in trying to learn about the British past, one were to restrict oneself to the reading of formal works of history, one would miss a great deal. Often a historical novel, a sociological inquiry, or an account of events and institutions couched in semifictional form teaches us just as much about the past as does the "history" that calls itself by that name. And, not infrequently, these "informal" historical works turn out to be less well known than their merit deserves. By calling this series Classics of British Historical Literature it will be possible to include such books without doing violence to the usual nomenclature.

When, in 1888, the great historian of English law, F. W. Maitland, delivered his inaugural lecture as Downing Professor of the Laws of England at Cambridge University, he included in it some very pessimistic remarks about the future of English legal history. Happily, time has not borne him out. Today the history of English law flourishes as never before, and by no means only as the domain of specialists. There exists an increasing awareness on the part of nearly all historians that a knowledge of legal history can often provide vital clues to the solution of historical problems which, on the surface, seem far removed from the sphere of law. Two examples come to mind. The first is the problem presented by Edmund Burke's view of the past. Here, thanks to the brilliant writings of Professor Pocock, it has become clear that in characterizing Burke's attitude to history one must refer, not merely to "romanticism" and "the revolt against reason," but also to the context of the "Ancient Constitution," guarantor of the immemorial laws of England, as the context within which Burke thought and wrote. The second example concerns the vexing question of the origin of the "Scottish Renaissance," that memorable period of cultural efflorescence in eighteenth-century Scotland. There can now be little doubt that the reason why the Scottish legal profession played such a prominent role during that renaissance is far from accidental; that it is, rather, intimately related to the fact that in eighteenth-century Scotland, in contrast to England, "civil" (that is, Roman) rather than common law prevailed.

In view of the revival of interest in British legal history, it is particularly important to make the classics in that field once again easily available. One of those classics is undoubtedly Hale's *History of the Common Law,* which Sir William Holdsworth called "the ablest introductory sketch of a history of English law that appeared till the publication of Pollock and Maitland's volumes in 1895." Like Hume's *Dialogues* and Diderot's *Neveu de Rameau,* it is one of those masterpieces that did not appear during its author's lifetime. Why this was so is one of the questions subtly answered by Professor Gray in his introduction. It is from that introduction, as well as from reading Hale's work, that the reader will come away with admiration and respect for a seventeenth-century historian who, in the course of considering the crucial problem of how the common law retained its identity in spite of the many changes it underwent, contributed, in Professor Gray's words, to "the emergence of the modern historian's art out of antiquarianism and mythmaking."

JOHN CLIVE

Editor's Introduction

Sir Matthew Hale's *History of the Common Law* is the first book
with any pretense to be a comprehensive account of the growth
of English law. There is a gap between the pretense and the performance, but the book is nonetheless a landmark in a historio-
graphic tradition. It stands out all the more because it was not
rapidly succeeded and improved on by other works of the same
sort. The tradition of English legal history, like other strands of
historical thought, has an implicit and an explicit content. On the
one hand, there is a set of attitudes, assumptions, and particular
reasoned opinions about the past—the implicit tradition; on the
other, there is the explicit perception that some segment of the
past represents a coherent whole, whose story should be told as
such. Hale was the first student of English law to have the latter
perception and to attempt a piece of writing appropriate to it.
He was also the last for a long time to come. Save for the work
of the eighteenth-century writer John Reeves (to whom Hale is
generally considered superior from a modern point of view),
Hale's *History* is virtually the only precedent for the great late
nineteenth- and twentieth-century body of explicit English legal
history. What W. S. Holdsworth, standing on the shoulders of
F. W. Maitland, achieved in the thirteen volumes of his *History
of English Law* Hale first adumbrated.

As for the implicit tradition, Hale is part of the stream. He
entered it at a crucial point, however. He contributed originally
to the body of historical attitudes connected with the law that

xi

were accumulating and changing in his time and went on doing so, despite the absence of much express interest in the totality of legal history. His book deserves attention as the pioneer of a genre, but it is even more important as a document of seventeenth-century intellectual history.

Hale was able to conceive a general history of English law partly because he lived at the end of a period during which thinking about the law in an historical dimension had flourished exceptionally. A penumbra of attitudes that can be called historical inevitably adheres to a legal system, especially a system such as that of the English, where precedent has been given conscious value and doctrine was transmitted orally and unofficially within the guild of practitioners. In that sense, the implicit tradition of English legal history has no beginning. But in another sense it can be said to have begun toward the end of the sixteenth century. The late Elizabethan generation, to which Sir Edward Coke, the greatest lawyer in English history, belonged, achieved an unanticipated consciousness of the legal past. Consciousness is not truth, historical awareness not the same as historical sensitivity. Coke and his contemporaries were mythmakers and practical men, antiquaries stronger on ancestor worship and patriotism than on realistic perspective, polemical and political users of the legal history they discovered or invented. Nevertheless, they knew about the past, talked about it, and exploited it, as earlier lawyers had not. They transformed the law from a craft to a liberal art—a focus for social thought, including historical thought.

Hale's *History* presupposes Coke and criticism of Coke. It builds on a half-century of high seriousness in the law, a seriousness of which Coke was the primary creator. It proceeds from an orientation toward history and particular historical opinions for which Coke was the great spokesman in an earlier generation. Hale was both a critic and a perpetuator of the Cokean tradition. On one side, his very attempt at a general history expresses a critical impulse—a striving for perspective and truth over against a tradition that was too "implicit," too disordered and engaged to practical ends. Ultimately, however, Hale's *History* is important, not for taking legal history out of the forum, but for giving expression to a new set of historico-jurisprudential attitudes. Implicitly, Hale was working out an alternative to Cokeanism reflective of the political and intellectual history he had lived through. The *History of the Common Law* is worthy of attention, first of all, as a document of the complex intellectual transformation of the seventeenth century. The magnitude of that transformation in science and philosophy, religion and political theory, is well recognized. The historical background of jurisprudence has received increasing attention in recent years, especially owing to J. G. A. Pocock's seminal study, *The Ancient Constitution and the Feudal Law*. Hale's *History* is possibly the most important book to come to terms with, if the legal-historical aspect of "cultural revolution" is to be more deeply understood.

The *History of the Common Law* was published posthumously. It was printed three times (1713, 1716, and 1739) virtually as it stood in manuscript and numerous times thereafter with editorial additions. The text here is reproduced from the third edition.

Sir Matthew Hale (1609–76) is a largely unstudied major figure. He stands in no need of encomia and, indeed, hardly awaits his biographer, for the simple story of his outward life has been adequately told. Hale was educated for the common law in the late twenties and thirties of the seventeenth century, succeeded as a practitioner thereafter, and rose to the Bench in 1654. Except for a brief period under Richard Cromwell, he served as a judge for the rest of his life. His place in the legal establishment and his reputation as a jurist gave him some influence in the counsels of the realm, but he was hardly a politician. He served the Cromwellian regime, then made a smooth transition to the service of Charles II. The terms of Hale's acceptance of the Commonwealth are important for his intellectual history. His acceptability to both the Protector and the restored king is evidence of his neutrality in politics rather than of the maneuvers and changes of heart of a truly political figure. He was probably perceived from all quarters as a professional whose first allegiance went to the law itself, as a scholar by nature, and as a man of unexceptionable probity.

There is evidence that Hale so perceived himself, for he translated Cornelius Nepos's life of Pomponius Atticus and is said to have taken that worthy for his model. Atticus established himself as the archetype of political neutrality by living through the Roman revolution on terms of friendship with all the major antagonists. The main point of Cornelius Nepos's sketch is to remark with praise on his subject's success in staying above the storms of politics. Like Atticus, Hale lived through a tempest without material cost to himself. The moral accounting is trickier. Atticus paid no moral price for neutralism because his sensibility was Stoic. Political flux was an analogue of passion. (True to the ideal of *apatheia,* Atticus died by self-starvation, uttering not a syllable to his entreating kinsmen beyond a sickbed oration setting forth the reasonableness of his decision.) One suspects that Hale took comfort from the example of Pomponius Atticus because his own morality did not make such easy provision for riding out the storm.

"Hobbism," in one of its senses, was the pejorative seventeenth-century word for accepting *de facto* governments on principle. Though it is unfair to Hobbes to take him as a vulgar *de-facto*ist, that implication was seen as part of the amoralism and egoism attributed to his philosophy. Hale was as far opposed as possible to a loosely conceived "Hobbism." He wrote against Hobbes in the arena of legal theory. Yet he could hardly have avoided a troubling aspersion: If a man of consequence arrives at terms with successive regimes in a revolutionary situation, must he not be convicted either of timeserving or, what is worse, of "Hobbism"? Hale's real escape from that dilemma was probably to invoke his allegiance to the law. Regimes come and go, the common law abides. The duty of men called to the law is to keep it running, to preserve its continuity and quality when, despite political vicissitude, that remains a possible endeavor. Though these propositions have their complexities, they probably define Hale's basic posture and self-justification. They make sense abstractly, and they made sense in context, for the antagonists in the English revolution largely shared an interest in maintaining the common law. Levellers who would have reformed it drastically and religious zealots to whom temporal tradition was of no consequence were exceptional. So was Hobbes, the original mind on the right with certain leftward affinities. Continuity of civic order as such mattered to Hobbes; the unbrokenness of positive legal tradition did not. For Hale, legal continuity was vital for

xiv

civic identity. Unlike Pomponius Atticus, whose plan of life was to remain a private man, Hale was a public figure, though not a fully political one. The English Christian lawyer may have looked on the Roman Stoic knight with a certain yearning.

It is Hale's inner history—the course and coherence of his thought as expressed in a large body of writings and in his judicial opinions—that is largely unwritten. This brief introduction to his *History of the Common Law* does not claim to supply the want. I shall only essay (in the most literal sense of the word) a sketch of Hale's intellectual character.

Hale was undoubtedly a great common-law judge, though it should be noted of him (as of most other seventeenth-century judges, including Sir Edward Coke himself) that we lack a judicial biography and hence a real basis for gauging the special quality and influence of his judicial work. He was also an indefatigable scholar and writer on law, jurisprudence, legal history, religion, and science. His public life was led on the Bench and to some extent in the affairs of the community; his private studies absorbed a large share of his energy. They were private studies in a specific sense. In his lifetime, Hale published two scientific tracts. Shortly after his death, and so presumably in accord with his intentions, four other works were published: a third scientific tract, the translation from Cornelius Nepos, a book of religious contemplations, and a brief abstract of criminal law. Save for the last of those, all of Hale's legal writings, as well as numerous further works on the other subjects he was interested in, were left in manuscript. He requested that none of these manuscripts be published. To the breach of his desires we owe the *History of the Common Law* and the other works (entirely legal) on which Hale's fame as an intellectual figure depends.

In a sense, then, Hale did not set up for an author. To the extent that he did, it was mostly as an amateur of natural philosophy and as a pious Christian, impelled, perhaps reluctantly, to share his meditations as a reasonable service to God. He did not burn to teach law outside the courtroom, to make known what he so extensively knew of legal history, or to communicate his thought about the law in dimensions more philosophical than those of cases and controversies. We cannot tell what accidents or reticences explain Hale's silence. Perhaps he was simply a busy man with many interests who worked at this and that, failed to finish things or revise them to his satisfaction. At the end, he may simply have preferred that work which he regarded as imperfect should remain unpublished. Many of his writings, including the *History of the Common Law,* are fragmentary.

Alternatively, or additionally, there may be reason to imagine Hale as a man whose main literary impulse was to write for himself. Perhaps one should expect such a bent in a psychological Puritan, which Hale plainly was. (It is doubtful whether he was ever a programmatic Puritan, in any of several senses, as opposed to a tolerant son of the Church of England.) His austere, studious, self-driving, and self-critical temper was confirmed and given shape by a religious culture of high seriousness that transcended ecclesiastical and political party. In that culture, rendering an account of oneself to God could easily pass over into accounting intellectually to oneself. The public performance needed to be offset by an internal struggle for clarity and perspective.

To the Puritan sensibility, the world was a dubious enterprise, a scene of confusion. Yet it was not to be fled. A Christian man must do his work in the place to which he was called. The work was witness to the faith; and, within limits, the working of Christian men could impress a moral quality on the world's business. The dream that the saints could subdue the world and reshape nature was the excess and perversion of Puritanism. In more and less controlled forms, that disease had troubled Hale's times. The more orthodox and enduring thrust of Puritanism was to circumscribe the potentiality of works and to balance action with inwardness. Christian energies should go out, then flow back. To act on the world effectually, a man needed to pull back into critical consciousness of self. Part of that consciousness must be renewed awareness that only so much is possible within the structures provided by a working Christian's place and opportunity; that nature is only impressible, never transformable by grace; that our best, with which our consciences must learn to rest, is always questionable when the perspective within which it is examined is enlarged, and only improvable as its questionableness is opened and reopened.

The private life of the mind, even the professional mind, is implied in such double sensibility. Moral introspection and prayer were the heart of Puritan inwardness. Hale was much given to that kind of reflection. But the impulse to study and think can also be reinforced and shaped by a Puritan sense of life. Because of it, a man may need to understand more about the segment of worldly life he deals with than mere use requires, to ask more searching questions than must be asked in immediate situations, to criticize what must be assumed in action, and to seek justification for one's assumptions. He may perceive his intellectual life as part of that spiritual realm where conscience and faith hold sway and works are set at a distance. Perhaps Hale saw his life as a legal scholar and writer more as the background of his work as a judge than as a second legal career or additional way of putting his impress on the world.

If Hale's personality and religio-cultural tradition made for a certain privatization of intellectual life, so did the character of his intelligence and the state of his subject matter. Besides being a learned man, Hale was a clear-minded one. He valued, and was capable of, logical cogency and precision. With a mind of that quality, he confronted an enormous body of material—the sources of English legal history and, intermixed if not synonymous therewith, the authoritative sources of English law. He also confronted a contemporary awareness of worlds beyond the insular common law—the tradition of comparative law and institutional history with which the names of John Selden and Henry Spelman are associated. (To both of those scholars Hale was obligated in his work, and Selden was influential on him through personal friendship.) Finally, Hale faced a babble of tongues *about* the common law and the English polity—claims for the common law and criticisms of it, uses and abuses of legal learning, historical speculation and philosophical dissent from the relevance of history. To an environment over-full of knowledge and half-knowledge, widened perspectives and false perspectives, theories, resistance to theory, and partisanship dressed up as thought, Hale brought a powerful impulse to digest and control. His mind sought order and system, while recognizing at the same time the incompatibility of order and system. That is to say, Hale recognized that putting particular rooms in order

xvii

draws off the energy that might go into architecture. Yet those clear, prehensile minds that refuse to be fooled by the *esprit systématique* are likely to be just the minds that on another level surrender to its aspiration. The strength that can achieve clarification of particulars stretches for an integrating clarity, discovers new ranges of difficulty, settles for glimpses of the whole, yet never ceases to look upward. The almost-achieved monograph seems to crave some further perfection, and the projected general work is a fragmentary series of approaches to general questions.

Hale seems to fit the type. He wrote but did not publish several effectively finished works on particular legal subjects (most notably his treatises on the Pleas of the Crown and the jurisdiction of the House of Lords). He was the first man to attempt a general history of English law. His *History of the Common Law of England* bears the impress of the analytic mind, rather than of the instructorial or synoptic. Its mere incompleteness may be an accident. Its character as a series of discrete essays or problems would seem to point to the author's needs and non-needs, powers and incapacities. Some concrete problems Hale solved to his satisfaction, some abstract principles he articulated. Yet the philosophic history he was reaching for eluded him, and unphilosophic history failed to hold his interest. His impulse to find a jurisprudence in legal history and to write legal history through the categories of jurisprudence was focused on the *History of the Common Law,* but the focus did not hold. Other projects emerged as apter approaches to the issues Hale was trying to clarify. He undertook a tract on the principles of law reform and their application and a refutation of Hobbes' diatribe against the common-law mentality. Both of those works are fragmentary, both thrusts at system and achievements of partial order. Consummation of Hale's design did not come.

Perhaps it did not much matter to him. To speak of the privatizing tendency of Hale's intellectual character and situation is not to deny that he aspired, in time, to give the fruits of his study to the public. He was working on a body of *opera* through which a new understanding of the English legal tradition and a way to dispel misunderstandings would become available. Behind the *persona* of the judge, a second public *persona* was, no doubt, in preparation. Yet, after allowance for self-abnegation and perfectionism as personal qualities, there is something to be said for the view that those who need to publish will publish. Perhaps Hale's drive to grasp general principles and clarify particulars was primarily a need to make sense to himself, to render a private accounting of the intellectual milieu of the law in which he passed his worldly life. Was confusion about the law something that could be or need be publicly dispelled? Were there dangers in setting forth historical facts and ideas about the law in less than wholly clear and wholly integrated form— dangers of adding to the contrary winds of doctrine that had blown hard during the revolutionary decades and perhaps only subsided with the Restoration? Was it perhaps the surer way to public benefit for the conscientious judge to struggle privately for as broad and lucid a professional intelligence as he could reach? One can only wonder whether these were explicit or semi-explicit questions for Hale. However that may be, the first general history of the common law was not intended for our eyes.

In the sense of "antiquarianism," legal history was massively available to Hale's generation. Hale himself was an extensive collector of legal manuscripts. He participated in the blend of passion and practicality that defines the seventeenth-century antiquarian spirit. The passion for having and handling monuments of the legal past was part of a wider phenomenon—a spectrum that includes the art collector and the almost indistinguishable curio collector; the traveler and the indefatigable traveloguist; Baconian–Royal Society data-gathering; the first wave of romantic appreciation for the half-consumed victims of time. The world was newly perceived as "a number of things," in temporal layers choked with dust as well as in the amplitude of places and products, information and inventions, available at the time to European experience. The hunger to gather and arrange interesting treasures became an intellectual appetite—a cousin to more fundamental accumulative instincts, but one who kept her distance from vulgar relatives. Toward material acquisitiveness, Hale took an attitude of careless austerity. He was uncomfortable with the rewards of his profession, gave his money away, made do with old black suits worn threadbare. His only monumental benefaction was a clock donated to his native village church. To Lincoln's Inn he bequeathed a valuable collection of manuscripts, another emblem of time. Time's power to corrupt Hale recognized, but the evidences of legal history were worth the gathering.

On the other side, English antiquarianism was often practical in its motives and application. The interest in legal antiquities, in particular, served professional and political purposes. From the last two decades of the sixteenth century, lawyers greatly extended the use of documents from the relatively remote past in their practices. They took a major step toward the modern assumption that legal argument is centrally based on research. At another level, extended knowledge of the legal past served an increasingly important legitimating purpose and was the more pursued for that reason. Historical awareness was put to the ahistorical use of establishing the immemorial character of the common law and hence its title to represent the ultimate in achievable social wisdom. The test of time was exalted as against the claim of the living to evaluate laws and institutions wisely, and the English past was studied to show that infinite ages had validated and revalidated the normative structure of English society. The prevailing jurisprudence and the historical information and misinformation that sustained it played, in turn, into the political conflicts of forty years that led to the Great Rebellion. The parties contended on the common ground of loyalty to the ancient constitution. The arsenal of records furnished both sides with live ammunition, though propensities to doubt the prescriptive standard of right were occasionally woven into the texture of debate.

Hale's participation in the antiquarian spirit was qualified by the perspective of his generation and the frame of his mind. By the time he wrote, restraints had been imposed on mythmaking in legal history. Scholarship had extended the range of information and scrutinized uncritical conclusions. Civil war had called attention to the danger of polemical history. The prescriptive standard of right had been challenged openly. Hale's instinct was to defend that standard from a tenable base in history and theory. Such a defense was the need and opportunity of his generation of common lawyers, but it was equally the tendency of his mind. Hale was an analyst. He was not, like a true antiquarian, awed by the mere presence of monuments, nor, like a mythmaker, apt to shape the fragments of the past into figments of self-justification. Sentimentally, no doubt, he approached the English past with patriotic reverence and conservative piety. Intellectually, he sought to get on top of his material. He took documents and asked precisely what could be said on the basis of them. He framed historical questions and deployed the evidence and inferences that would support an answer. There is no better example of a firstly-secondly-thirdly mind than Hale's, and the logical appropriateness of his enumerated points is always clear. On a higher plane of abstraction, his capacity to evolve satisfactory categories was limited by the difficulty of the attempt, but his impulse was philosophical. He wanted to say what the process of law formation over the continuum of history is like. He sought to use a grasp of process to justify the institutions of English government and the characteristic attitudes and activities of common lawyers. Hale's theoretical and normative interests took him outside the antiquarian sphere and, in a way, beyond the historical. He was devoted to reading records and to reasoning and imagining from them to projections of past situations. The accuracy and restraint with which he did so associate him with the emergence of the modern historian's art out of antiquarianism and mythmaking. But he was in the end too involved in the drift of seventeenth-century intellectual life into the light of general principles to be headed into the chiaroscuro of historical consciousness.

One of Hale's metaphors to embrace the history of English law was the Ship of the Argonauts. The ship went so long a voyage that eventually every part of it decayed and was replaced; yet (says the paradox of identity in spite of change) it remained in a meaningful sense the same ship. The metaphor might be applied to Hale himself in relation to Sir Edward Coke, for they were predecessor and successor in one tradition, though sundered by differences of character and generational experience. Both were guardians of the common law's claim to legitimacy based on immemorial continuity and of usage's title to personate reason. Speaking from a common platform of training, professional pride, and legal-historical learning, they were in many ways saying the same thing. Some of the superficial ways of contrasting the two lawyers may tend to dissociate them too much. It is true that Hale was a saintly, cool-headed man, while Coke was a Titan—a political battler, rashly confident of whatever he chose to assert, as passionately proud and ambitious for himself as for the common law. It is true that Hale was an historian as Coke was not. Hale had the advantage of a more mature scholarly tradition and the greater advantage of an objective mind. Coke, by contrast, was credulous, ancestor-worshiping, and addicted to advocacy. His learning was the instrument of his presuppositions, his ego, and his causes. Yet such contrasts, though valid, risk unfairness to Coke. Coke is easily caricatured. (There is no comic Hale.) But underneath the exaggerated features of his public life Coke was a serious intellectual figure. A great deal of the credit for giving a new value to documented knowledge of the legal past belongs to him, though his historical consciousness was foreshortened and unordered. With the tools and materials at his disposal, he was working toward a jurisprudence. He saw the need for a body of social thought drawn from the experience of the lawyer but transcending the narrow certitudes and skills of the practitioner's craft. In his style, he worked one out and launched it into the open waters of his intellectually creative and politically troubled generation.

Hale was working toward the same end, seeking to secure the same values. But it is misleading to take him simply as a later, smoother representative of the Cokean tradition—as if the Ship of the Argonauts remained the same ship save for the installation of a motor. Hale was a trained young lawyer when Coke died, and the short trip between them is not to be compared with the common law's Argonautical voyage from Anglo-Saxon times. Even so, there is a way in which Hale's picture of English legal history and the jurisprudence associated therewith were fundamentally different from Coke's—the same ship, yet not the same.

Numerous passages in the *History of the Common Law* testify that Hale recognized the fact of legal change straightforwardly. The Ship of the Argonauts is a strong metaphor for acknowledging it. The problem in Hale's use of the metaphor concerns the sense in which he thought the law retained identity in spite of change. It may be useful to distinguish the following possibilities: (1) The law has changed over its history in every feature that can be considered optional. As between two widely spaced points on the time line, substantive rules governing the same situation will usually be different, as will the procedures by which rights and liabilities are enforced. Change, however, has been extremely gradual. The closer together any two points on the time line are, the fewer differences in the legal system there will be as between those points. (2) Although the law has changed very considerably over the course of its history, it has retained some identifying features of substance and procedure. Even as between widely spaced points, some optional *and important* features can be recognized as at least generally the same, though they may be altered in detail. (3) Substantive rules and civil and criminal procedure have changed, perhaps totally, over the system's history—with steady gradualness or by jumps, as the case may be. But one essential thing has remained unchanged throughout: the basic political frame, or the constitutional rules by which other rules can be authoritatively recognized as binding. Specific features on the constitutional side of law may have changed, but those changes will themselves have been made by underlying and unaltered procedures for amendment. These three models differ from each other in emphasis, but they are not logically incompatible: change might be consistently gradual but less than drastic; substantive continuity, as well as constitutional continuity might characterize the system's history; the abiding constitution might permit sudden change, yet change might in fact have been entirely incremental.

With the three models in mind, let us try to place Hale in relation to Coke. All the models are meant to allow for a high degree of change. Coke would probably have denied the need to account for change of such extremity. One must beware of parodying him. He did not inhabit a fool's eternity, wherein the law of seventeenth-century England looked simply indistinguishable from Anglo-Saxon law. He recognized the fact of change but tended to see it as degenerative on the one hand and restorative on the other. There was such a thing as the ancient common law—a describable system which did indeed operate in Anglo-Saxon times, even in pre-Roman Britain. There had been many departures from that system, largely for the worse, but these could be and had been reversed. Degeneration was primarily the effect of unwise legislation and equitable interference with the common law. Two specific examples, the entail and the use, were especially influential on Coke's general thinking. The statute *De Donis,* which created the entail, was in Coke's opinion a blot on Edward I.'s record as the English Justinian. Anciently, every fee was a fee simple; that is, the aboriginal legal system recognized only one kind of hereditary interest in land, the freely alienable, undevisable interest that passed to lineal and then to collateral heirs by the primogenitary rules of inheritance. The legislative attempt to introduce another kind of hereditary interest was ill advised from a utilitarian point of view (by bringing in many technical complications and interfering with the free circulation of land). But the legislature did not get away with it. Lawyers discovered and the courts endorsed means of disentailing tied-up land. Indirectly, the common law found its way back to its beginnings. The degenerative pattern was offset by a restorative one.

The history of the use was different. In the beginning and forever after, the common law took note of only one kind of land-ownership—the proprietary right that rested ultimately on seisin or on notorious acquisition of seisin from another having it. For motives Coke regarded as fraudulent, landowners went about to detach the right to the economic benefit of land from the legal property—in other words, to create uses or trusts. Their efforts would have come to nothing had the chancellor not provided an equitable remedy for the beneficiary, who thus became the equitable owner. The evil, in Coke's eyes, of this system of double ownership (again, such practical evil as uncertainty as to who was the effective owner of anything) was swept away by the intention of the Statute of Uses. Coke saw the statute as a drastic restoration of the common law. He also saw the danger that it would be perverted to a different effect—to introduce into the common law new forms of conveyancing, unheard of types of interest, and new versions of the defeated entail. He was over-optimistic about the courts' power to frustrate such perversion and bring back the ancient order.

I dwell on these points to emphasize that Coke's thinking was not wholly general or mystical. His picture of an aboriginal law —from which men in their weakness fall away and to which men of law in their wisdom come back—was historically imaginary. But in one aspect it was projected from realistic paradigms and served a pragmatic and even reformist purpose. Like most premodern utopias, Coke's ideal legal system had a fantasy existence in the past, but it also had a straightforward content: Simplicity would be its main characteristic. There would be a limited range of legally possible interests and means of transferring them. Litigation would be minimized by substantive simplicity and also by limiting the forms of action, so that the winner of a suit concerning one thing could rarely be defeated in another kind of suit for the same thing.

On the other hand, Coke's vision of the ideal was limited by the prescriptive and romantic elements in his thought. He was more than satisfied with the simplicity and serviceability which he saw in medieval English law (as opposed to some higher degree of those qualities one might dangerously dream of and propose to enact). The test of time was what legitimated the law, not the rationality available at any moment in time. Behind the visible advantages of medieval law lay the more portentous guarantee of immemorial usage.

Moreover, reaction-reform was built into the system. Coke did not need to call for effort to overcome the corruptions he saw in modern law, because he believed then they would be overcome anyway. The courts and the legislature would cooperate to bring back the old, normal order. Legislation was a necessary technique, not a suspect human interference with the workings of time and the judges' guardianship of the common law. The judges could and should check degenerative propensities in legislation by interpreting it as restorative of, or consonant with, the common law whenever possible. Yet, though the judges were usually reliable guardians, they were not always blameless. Some degenerations (for example, the erosion of the real actions, hence of the limited range of procedures to protect interests in land, by action of ejectment on fictitious leases) could only be blamed on the judiciary. The High Court of Parliament existed to right such wrongs. The ancient statutes (Magna Carta through Edward i.) were the authoritative text of the common law because Parliament had done its job of restoration and preservation in the old days.

On the other hand, Coke could hardly conceive of the need for legislation to create law for novel situations. The common law was good for specifiable reasons, but (more mystically) it was also "copious." As the product of limitless time, it was like an infinitely experienced man; it never really confronted a problem it could not solve by the direct authorities or analogies in its horn of plenty. By and large, therefore, judicial means for developing the law were sufficient. Across history, judge-made change—in the sense of elaboration, exposition, and refinement —could be observed. In that sense, there was progress, as opposed to the rhythm of degeneration and restoration, but progress was toward a richer and more perspicuous gloss on the pre-existent law, not toward better law. The judges expound, they do not create. The richer gloss was a blessing if rightly understood, but not an unmixed blessing. Coke saw the danger in too elaborate a tradition, in confronting the courts with farragoes of authority and analogy. He praised the absence of frequent citation in the Year Books, preferred argument from principle to precedent-shuffling (interested though he was in precedents), and trusted the sages of the law too implicitly to handle the law's simple principles correctly. Coke compared his own day to a better past, echoing the familiar classico-Christian idea that this world's tendency, after all, is to run down. At the same time, he felt in touch with that better past. The optimism implied in his sense that the law of today was in living communion with its ancestry outweighed the conventions of gloom.

At almost every point, Hale's thinking bears a complex relationship to Coke's, sometimes agreeing, sometimes pulling away quite radically (though perhaps not quite consciously), sometimes concurring on separate grounds. Hale reflects the degenerative-restorative model at times, but it is not basically his. For the picture of an infinitely ancient system from which subsequent times tended to fall away and to which they could and should return, he substituted a generalized skepticism about remote origins. The skepticism represents a gain for realistic historical thinking. Coke could see in a sentence from Caesar's Commentaries proof positive that a still familiar institution of English law existed when the first conqueror set foot on British soil. Hale recognized the absurdity of such inferences, the paucity of evi-

dence about ancient law (Anglo-Saxon and twelfth-century, not
to mention Druidical), and the indications in the extant sources
that early institutions were largely different from later ones.
There is a sense, however, in which Coke had the greater interest
(albeit an ideological, distorting one) in making what could be
made of the fragmentary ancient sources. In his way, he asked
"What can be known about the law of pre-Roman Britain?"—
misleading as the conclusion that it was written in Greek may be!
Hale was not much interested in asking such questions, even of
the sources at his disposal substantial enough to justify the effort
(for example, the Anglo-Saxon dooms). The search for recog-
nizable origins was pointless, tempting to credulity, and danger-
ous to the legitimating purpose of legal history. Positive state-
ments about remote law invited refutation. Refutation invited the
conclusion that historically well-known or current features of
English law had no immemorial basis, and therefore that they
were either wrongful impositions (typically, in Leveller thought,
the impositions of William the Conqueror, who enslaved the
English and gave them law fit for slaves), or else the perfectly
rightful fiat of sovereign authority, in no way dependent on a
pedigree for their validity or putative wisdom (as Hobbes and
other royalists maintained).

For Hale, the irrelevance of positive inquiry into remote times,
and hence of the errors begotten on its tenuousness, was the vital
point to establish. He swung, accordingly, toward the third of the
models of legal change outlined above—toward (the language is
his own), the "formal" continuity of the English system. Though
he thought an occasional identifying feature (such as trial by
jury) could be placed before the Conquest (cf. the second model
above), only one feature of the system was clearly immemorial
so far as could be or need be known: the constitutional frame
(or, more abstractly, the mere fact of being one political society
with a continuous set of criteria for recognizing the validity of
rules).

The Norman Conquest is carefully analyzed in the *History of
the Common Law*. Hale's main point is that the transition to the
Norman dynasty was in no way a constitutional break. William
came as a claimant, not as a conqueror properly so-called, and
even if he had not pretended rightful succession to Edward the

Confessor (says Hale's ahistorical argument from international law), he could still not be taken as a true conqueror. Be that as it may, he came to win the crown he claimed as his and won it without the least intent to alter English law in its underlying, constitutional aspect. Therefore the Conquest could have been accompanied by any amount of substantive legal change without detracting from the continuity of English law in the crucial sense. William was bound by the actual, indeed necessary, nature of his accession to do what he did: permit English law to be administered as before, except insofar as the new regime changed it by existing procedures for making changes. In the event, Hale thought, there was not a great deal of substantive alteration. Under pressure from the English, William drew back from the innovations he may originally have meant to introduce, or was at least willing to suffer his Norman-dominated courts to admit, and expressly confirmed the laws of Edward the Confessor, except for a few deliberate changes. In the upshot, Hale's picture of the Conquest is like Coke's: the greatest apparent trauma in English history was hardly a tremor in the history of English law. Only for Hale nothing really depended on that contingent, perhaps unreliable, historical truth. Any amount of material change would have been compatible with the "formal" continuity of the *Grundnorm.*

About the content of the abiding constitutional framework Hale is almost silent. The predicament of his thinking gave him a motive to avoid hard questions about constitutional history. Coke thought that Parliament existed long before the Conquest. Hale agreed, though without facing the question head-on. He insists that William I. proceeded by Parliament both in confirming and in amending Anglo-Saxon law. He does not say what "Parliament" means in eleventh- or twelfth-century contexts. If he was skeptical, for example, as to whether the Commons were represented, he reveals no doubts. His formalism was perhaps sophisticated enough to leave room for maneuver: Why should lawmaking procedure not have changed over time as well as the rest of the law—provided always that such changes were made by the lawmaking procedure in existence beforehand? Since, however, most early legislative documents show signs of consultative procedure of some sort, it was not necessary to push the formalism so far. It was easier to project an unchanging mode of parliamentary government.

In Hale's view, the legal history of the twelfth and thirteenth centuries was highly progressive. The law did not advance by restoring an ancient order interfered with by the Conquest, much less fall away from apostolic purity. It simply advanced, from barbarism to civilization. Hale's language for describing progress is markedly neoclassical: rude law was "polished" and "perfected." Its becoming more intelligible to Hale sometimes counted, a little dangerously, as becoming better, though he is often explicit on the superiority of new institutions to old. He is impressed by the pace and degree of improvement, not its gradualism. Legislation, far from being an ambiguous character, is the hero of the piece. Hale's human hero, Edward I., is presented as a law reformer. Not only does Hale recognize the role deliberate legislation actually played in the Middle Ages; he hypothesizes it in the absence of evidence. Lost statutes are his preferred explanation for changes not accounted for by known legislative acts. He speaks occasionally of "insensible" change and acknowledges judge-made law in a somewhat stronger sense than the Cokean text-gloss model allows for. But for Hale the basic changes of the crucial medieval centuries pointed to conscious general legislation. In part, that was only the simplest theory to explain the facts. In part, it probably reflects what Hale wanted to believe.

Taking "legislation" to mean "law changing"—in contradistinction to the restorative, declaratory, explicative, and implementary roles that acts of Parliament can play or be seen as playing—Hale's bias was prolegislative, as Coke's was antilegislative. For one thing, Hale was a law reformer himself. His essay "The Amendment of the Laws" is a masterpiece of conservative liberalism. Its final tendency is to support legislative alteration of the common law. The conservatism has two sides. On the one hand, Hale sounds the note of caution—the danger that law reformers will start from an inaccurate picture of the law to be reformed and give too little consideration to the inconveniences that may ensue from superficially desirable changes. On the other hand, he insists that reformers stay away from constitutional law. The law had been reformed in the past, Hale's history assured him. There was no reason to suppose that England had moved into a post-historical never-never land, where the law needed only to develop by the expository application of a fundamentally perfect body of principles. But legislated reform in the past had taken place within the stable constitutional framework which gave Hale his primary assurance of continuity. Only in the very recent past had the rules been broken. Substantive law reform had been broached under the Commonwealth, and Hale had been involved in the project. The attempt came to little, partly because politicians were obsessed with the frame of government—so concerned with settling the state and divided over the form it should take that they could not settle down to the sober business of legislation. Writing after the Restoration, Hale tried to keep a cautious version of the reformist spirit alive, perhaps to stay in contact with his own past. The prerequisite was accepting the Restoration settlement as a settlement indeed, distinguishing between ordinary law, which remained open to responsible change, and constitutional law, which should not be tampered with. The political constitution was the nation's identity. Identity crisis was incompatible with constructive activity.

Hale's history, in short, was influenced by his Restoration liberalism. That attitude was compounded of rejection and affirmation of the English revolution. It appreciated the price tag on the progress and pluralism that the revolution had liberated as ideals. Outside the law, Hale's associations were with men who in their sphere occupied the same "extreme center" that he held in jurisprudence. He was close to a number of churchmen who, in different ways, held out against religious narrowness (Wilkins, Stillingfleet, Baxter, Ussher, and others). To such men, as to Hale himself, the Church of England represented or came to represent the same values of settlement and national identity as the traditional secular constitution. Yet, whether because they had been through Puritanism themselves, or only because, in spite of party, they were not blind to the values Puritanism was getting at, they resisted Restoration neo-Laudianism and Clarendon-Code conformity. With his clerical friends, Hale went on working for the cause of comprehension that had failed at the Restoration.

Within the law, Hale kept the meliorist spirit alive by setting it in a foil of political conservatism. He had collaborated with a revolutionary regime to steady the ship of the law through a tempest. Continuity in the ship's personnel and daily routine had been vital when utopianism and preoccupation with political reform stultified the very hopes for improvement they expressed. As its liberal loyalists saw it, the Restoration did not infuse artificial life into a dead past. The Commonwealth's failure did not legitimate every corruption and stupidity the revolution raged against (including the pedantry and selfishness of lawyers, which, as Hale was well aware, had a recurrent tendency to impede the law's efficiency and justice). The common law itself was not to be set up like an idol, cherished for every intricate twist in its carving that bespoke the hand of antiquity. For all his prestige as a champion of the law and his influence as a teacher, Sir Edward Coke was not to be high priest of such a Baal. To its liberals, the Restoration brought back the structures within which an indigenous gift for progress and reform could operate effectually—as it were, the living God.

On the one hand, then, Hale wanted to encourage reflection on the law's improvability and the will to intelligent action. It was useful to provide historical warrant for the legislative spirit. On the other hand, he wanted to discourage the belief that judges make law and ought to. That was important to Hale for several reasons. The common-law tradition, with Coke's imprimatur, so insisted. In addition, the experience and debates of the revolutionary period and the emergent political orthodoxy of Hale's day made the sovereignty of Parliament prominent in a new way. The Cokean model of interplay between Parliament and the courts within a common intent to conserve the ancient law entailed role switching—now Parliament, now the judiciary, checking each other's ill-considered moves—though that picture did not impair the solemn fiction of Parliament's ultimate power as "the whole body of the realm" to estop everyone, including the judges. (One might compare the conception of marriage as ideally and realistically mutual, though finally predicated on male dominance.) A sharper awareness of the distinct roles of the branches of government emerged in the seventeenth century. Commanding, expressing one's will, being in constant control, making the big decisions: by stages and zigzags, Parliament came to be regarded as the expected and rightful locus of those attributes of dominance (mainly at the expense of the King-out-of-Parliament). A clearer subordination of the courts was implied, a realization of their role as servant-agent-executor-trustee. Those alternative words indicate the continuing flexibility and indefiniteness of the court-legislature relationship. Servility in the sense of "non-responsibility for absurd results provided orders are followed" is not implied. Neither is the freedom of the strongest type of trustee to pursue his beneficiary's interest irrespective of his instructions. All the words hint at what none conveys. All contrast to "partner," even "secondary partner." As was often argued in the seventeenth century, and as Hale indirectly urges in the *History of the Common Law,* subordination of the courts to Parliament does not morally entitle the legislature to usurp the judicial function. Differentiation of roles can accent the autonomy of the subordinate one. But the effect of both phenomena—a clearer sense of "who's boss" and a surer sense that bosses should stick to bossing—was to reinforce the separation of lawmaking from law applying.

That reinforcement came when the old assurance that courts do not make law was under stress. Thomas Hobbes asserted the fact and the desirability of judicial legislation, by which he meant that decisions cannot and should not be drawn out of a reservoir of positive law (as opposed to the fund of general moral rules with which we are all provided by nature). He did so in a tone and a setting of political doctrine that Hale felt bound to dispute. Hobbes was contemptuous toward the ideas characteristic of common lawyers, especially as Coke had expressed them: Owing as much to the muddledness of their thinking as to the flaws in their premises, lawyers had been mischievous contributors to the revolution. Their mischief-making potential had not been destroyed by the experience of civil disruption. As against Hobbes's hyperbole and arrogance, Hale's impulse was to defend the tradition of social thought connected with the law. The philosophic iconoclast was in fact vulnerable at the hands of a clear-minded modern lawyer, for Hobbes's notions of the judicial process were simplistic, at least as stated, entitled as he may have been to triumph over the Cokean mentality as such.

Hobbes at least appeared to commit two errors: (1) The fallacy of excessive realism: He was aware that judges do not and cannot settle cases merely by applying rules given them by the legislature or by tradition, without reference to the reasonableness of the result. He concluded that the reasonableness of the result according to the judges' lights is the only thing that judges can or do really inquire into. Hale thought that there was a large area in which the judicial function was truly applicatory, though he conceded a periphery where judges must go by the "mere reason." (2) The compensating fallacy of excessive faith in natural-law adjudication: Apart from and because of the *de facto* relevance of reasonableness alone, Hobbes thought that judges ought only to ask what solution would be reasonable. They should of course obey the sovereign's orders, reasonable or not. But short of the limiting case of an *ad hoc* command, they should consider only the requirements of universal natural law. The ideal society would be governed by natural law, subject to the consequences of that law's highest imperative, "Seek peace"—subject, that is to say, to the duty to obey one sovereign regardless of the justifiability of his commands. Judges should act as they would in ideal society—do justice and equity—subject to being overruled by the sovereign. They should not excuse wrong decisions by pretending to be foreclosed by general instructions, which can never unambiguously dictate a concrete act. Above all, they should not excuse and perpetuate error by invoking the custom of the community or the decisions of prior judges, which, in addition to indecisiveness, lacked authority, save in the perverse sense in which an irrational compulsion to act habitually or imitate may be said to have "authority" when it has usurped the seat of natural reason and rationally necessary government.

To this second part of Hobbes's argument, Hale could oppose an experienced judge's awareness that natural-law adjudication is more easily embraced than practiced. If one seriously asks only, "What is just in this case?" the difficulties of answering the question close in. Real legal problems usually fall in the zone of moral ambiguity, where there are legitimate values to be served by deciding either way. If judges are encouraged only to weigh the equities, infinitesimal differences of judgment as among even the wisest men will eventuate in inconsistent lines of cases, hence in a low degree of legal predictability. To Hale, the conventional lawyers' canon, "Apply the law as it is, not as it ought to be," was the path to certainty, the value of which would ordinarily override the marginal disadvantages of some rules embedded in the system. Hale probably underestimated the degree of *legal* ambiguity in problematic situations, hence overestimated the possibility of certainty. There are nevertheless great advantages in encourgaging judges to look for the "is" and defer seeking the "ought" until the primary quest fails, as Hale admitted it sometimes will. The essential advantage lies where Hale and the Cokean tradition behind him put it, though it is best expressed in different language: "Legal positivism" is a useful myth to lead judges to an appreciation of the marginal moral choices typical of the historic community they are serving.

Good decisions need to reflect those choices, even though the wisest of judges might make better ones. Hale, unlike Coke, knew that such communal choices are not aboriginal, not literally authenticated by infinite experience, hence guaranteed superior to the highest legislative wisdom. He knew that time-testedness was only a contingent merit of rules that had happened to survive for a long time, and not always a net merit. Change was real and good. The community could and should reevaluate and perfect its choices from time to time. But the central Cokean idea survived "Argonautically" in Hale. Authority did not inhere solely in reason and in the political sovereign who personifies reason and actualizes its power to secure peace and civilization. Those potentates must share authority with the subrational forces that make us communal animals as opposed to merely political ones—with the values shared by people who identify with each other across the barriers of individuality and class, values learned by imitation, confirmed by habit, transmitted through national history. Intellectually as well as politically, Hale defended a "mixed constitution" against Hobbes. As against Coke, he demoted the legal tradition from "artificial reason"—the *persona* of ultimate rightness in as strong a sense as Hobbes's sovereign— to the conservative side of a complex balance. The judiciary was to hold down that side of the balance so far as possible and insofar as the judges were not simply executors of the living community's legislative judgment. That seemed to Hale to have been its role in history, especially in the best periods. A model of legal change as entirely incremental (cf. the first of the three models above), conceivably and desirably effected by judicial decisions alone, extreme over centuries and progressive, would have offended Hale's normative ideas of balance even if it had been accessible intellectually. Such a model probably becomes accessible only when extensive social and economic change and awareness of it become realities (so that judges have to be perceived as adapting old principles to radically new circumstances), and when romantic preference for legal development along the unconscious paths of folklore and language has produced an anti-legislative bias stronger than Coke, Hale, or Hobbes could have imagined.

Closer to home, in the relatively microscopic world of English legal history since 1300, Hale's thinking was in some ways nearer to Coke's than it was on the plane of general principles and total history. For practical purposes and specifiable reasons, high medieval law was normative for Coke. So it was for Hale to many intents. Progressive change was rapid and clear up to Edward 1. In his reign, the common law achieved perfection such that later change was reduced in scale and rendered more ambiguous in value. Through most of the fourteenth century, Hale saw continued progress, especially in the art of pleading, which was central to his judgment of the quality of legal practice and the clarity and utility of the law. Thereafter, Hale saw degeneration toward the prolixity and oversubtlety that afflicted pleading in his own day. Substantive law after 1300 is virtually omitted from the *History of the Common Law,* ostensibly because it was well known from the Year Books and other sources. In another place, Hale wrote a succinct summary of the extensive changes that had taken place in the last three centuries. He was in fact perfectly aware of Edward 1. did not bring the interesting part of the story to a close, true as it was that he had created or perfected numerous features of the system that still survived.

One might speculate that Hale left out the final period partly because it was an embarrassment: a history of judge-made change, largely for the worse. There are hints in the *History of the Common Law* to suggest that Hale assessed the latter days pretty much as Coke did, as a falling-off from the simplicity and workability of our fathers' law, as it were, though not our great-great-grandfathers'. Hale is not so explicit as Coke on the points where they agreed (most notably, the virtues of the ancient real actions to recover land and the old presumption in favor of possession in property disputes). The complexity of modern property-law and the consequent range of opportunity it afforded men to settle their estates and effect their private purposes was probably less objectionable to Hale than to Coke. In any case, it was not attractive as a stick to beat the legislature with. The equity which, in Coke's eyes, had corrupted the law with uses and necessitated clumsy legislative surgery goes unmentioned by Hale. Among other differences, the equity Hale had to deal with the daily life was a tamer rival than the chancery Coke had struck at with the pains of praemunire. By and large, however, Hale's immediate values were closer to Coke's than the general set of his thinking. With respect to the latter, the trip between them, though short in time, was "Argonautical" in character.

Many more facets of the *History of the Common Law* deserve note than those that I have singled out in this attempt to locate its author as an intellectual figure. It is a tribute to Hale's writing that his straightforward presentation of legal history and inferential arguments, though worthy of comment, do not urgently require it. It has often been recognized that the *History of the Common Law* is good history within the limits of evidence and scholarship available to anyone in the seventeenth century. If it is read for information, it must of course be supplemented and corrected by modern learning. Detailed correlation of what Hale knew and how he grasped it with what we positively know and how we typically arrange and express it would be a useful exercise. It would be well to remember that our measurable advantage over Hale has been almost entirely gained since the late nineteenth century; that for a long time the *History of the Common Law* was something like the standard work; that until the advent of academic history Hale's familiarity with the sources was not rivaled; that his advantage in rationally controlled knowledge over his predecessors of circa 1600 represents one of the biggest jumps in English legal history's development. In this introduction, I have tried to deal with the limits of Hale's history in a wider sense: the boundaries of situation that confine, direct, focus, and distort the perceptions of all historians at all times.

Bibliographical Note

For Hale's life, see the *Dictionary of National Biography* and W. S. Holdsworth, *History of English Law*, vol. 6, pp. 574–95, both of which draw on the major contemporary memoir, Bishop Burnet's *Life and Death of Sir Matthew Hale* (1682).

Although such older writers as Holdsworth make valuable observations on Hale's quality of mind and place in the development of legal-historical consciousness, there are only a couple of discussions of him which reflect a more modern style of intellectual history. One is chapter 7 of J. G. A. Pocock, *The Ancient Constitution and the Feudal Law* (1957). My debt to Mr. Pocock will be evident to those familiar with his book, as will the mixture of concurrence and dissent as between his treatment of Hale in the common-law tradition and mine. Barbara J. Shapiro, in "Law and Science in Seventeenth-Century England" (*Stanford Law Review*, vol. 21 [1969], pp. 727–66), relates Hale to general intellectual tendencies in interesting ways and makes use of his scientific writings.

The essay above is for the most part an interpretation of the *History of the Common Law* itself, with some assistance from Hale's other works in print, especially his "Considerations Touching the Amendment or Alteration of Lawes" (*Hargrave Law Tracts*, 1787, pp. 249–89) and the "Reflections by the Lrd. Cheife Justice Hale on Mr. Hobbes His Dialogue of the Law" (printed as appendix 3, vol. 5, in Holdsworth, *History of English Law*). My points on Coke are drawn from many places in his writings, especially the prefaces to the first eleven volumes of his *Reports*. For an introduction to Coke's general thinking, I would recommend those prefaces, plus his opinion in Calvin's Case in contrast with the concurring opinion of Lord Ellesmere (*Howell's State Trials*, vol. 2, pp. 559–696). Hobbes's views of the judicial process are an aspect of the vexed problem of his general meaning. The former, a useful route into the latter, are best pursued by comparing Hobbes's *Dialogue of the Common Laws* (English Works, vol. 6, pp. 3–100) with Hale's "Reflections" (*supra*). Hale's brief account of relatively recent changes in English law is in his introduction to Rolle's *Abridgment* (quoted by Holdsworth, vol. 6, pp. 624–26).

CHARLES M. GRAY

THE HISTORY OF
THE COMMON LAW
OF ENGLAND

I

Concerning the Distribution of the Laws of England into Common Law, and Statute Law. And First, concerning the Statute Law, or Acts of Parliament

The Laws of England may aptly enough be divided into two Kinds, *viz. Lex Scripta,* the written Law; and *Lex non Scripta,* the unwritten Law: For although (as shall be shewn hereafter) all the Laws of this Kingdom have some Monuments or Memorials thereof in Writing, yet all of them have not their Original in Writing; for some of those Laws have obtain'd their Force by immemorial Usage or Custom, and such Laws are properly call'd *Leges non Scriptæ,* or unwritten Laws or Customs.

Those Laws therefore, that I call *Leges Scriptæ,* or written Laws, are such as are usually called *Statute Laws,* or Acts of Parliament, which are originally reduced into Writing before they are enacted, or receive any binding Power, every such Law being in the first Instance formally drawn up in Writing, and made, as it were, a *Tripartite Indenture,* between the King, the Lords and the Commons; for without the concurrent Consent of all those Three Parts of the Legislature, no such Law is, or can be made: But the Kings of this Realm, with the Advice and Consent of both Houses of Parliament, have Power to make New Laws, or to alter, repeal, or enforce the Old. And this has been done in all Succession of Ages.

Now, *Statute Laws,* or Acts of Parliament, are of Two Kinds, *viz.* First, Those Statutes which were made *before Time of Memory;* and, Secondly, Those Statutes which were made *within* or *since Time of Memory;* wherein observe, That according to a juridical Account and legal Signification, *Time within Memory*

3

is the Time of Limitation in a Writ of Right; which by the Statute of Westminster 1. cap. 38. was settled, and reduced to the Beginning of the Reign of King Richard 1. or *Ex prima Coronatione Regis Richardi Primi,* who began his Reign the 6th of July 1189, and was crown'd the 3d of September following: So that whatsoever was before that Time, is *before* Time of Memory; and what is since that Time, is, in a legal Sense, said to be *within* or since the Time of Memory.

And therefore it is, that those Statutes or Acts of Parliament that were made before the Beginning of the Reign of King Richard 1. and have not since been repealed or altered, either by contrary Usage, or by subsequent Acts of Parliament, are now accounted Part of the *Lex non Scripta,* being as it were incorporated thereinto, and become a Part of the Common Law; and in Truth, such Statutes are not now pleadable as Acts of Parliament, (because what is *before* Time of Memory is supposed without a Beginning, or at least such a Beginning as the Law takes Notice of) but they obtain their Strength by meer immemorial Usage or Custom.

And doubtless, many of those Things that now obtain as Common Law, had their Original by Parliamentary Acts or Constitutions, made in Writing by the King, Lords and Commons; though those Acts are now either not extant, or if extant, were made before Time of Memory; and the Evidence of the Truth hereof will easily appear, for that in many of those old Acts of Parliament that were made before Time of Memory, and are yet extant, we many find many of those Laws enacted which now obtain merely as Common Law, or the General Custom of the Realm: And were the rest of those Laws extant, probably the Footsteps of the Original Institution of many more Laws that now obtain meerly as Common Law, or Customary Laws, by immemorial Usage, would appear to have been at first Statute Laws, or Acts of Parliament.

Those ancient Acts of Parliament which are ranged under the Head of *Leges non Scriptæ,* or Customary Laws, as being made before Time of Memory, are to be considered under Two Periods: *Viz.* First, Such as were made before the coming in of King William 1. commonly called, The Conqueror; or, Secondly, Such as intervened between his coming in, and the Beginning of the

Reign of Richard 1. which is the legal Limitation of Time of Memory.

The former Sort of these Laws are mentioned by our ancient Historians, especially by Brompton, and are now collected into one Volume by William Lambard, Esq; in his *Tractatus de priscis Anglorum Legibus,* being a Collection of the Laws of the Kings, Ina, Alfred, Edward, Athelstane, Edmond, Edgar, Ethelred, Canutus, and of Edward the Confessor; which last Body of Laws, compiled by Edward the Confessor, as they were more full and perfect than the rest, and better accommodated to the then State of Things, so they were such whereof the English were always very zealous, as being the great Rule and Standard of their Rights and Liberties: Whereof more hereafter.

The second Sort are those Edicts, Acts of Parliament, or Laws, that were made after the coming in of King William, commonly named, The Conqueror, and before the beginning of the Reign of King Richard 1. and more especially are those which follow; whereof I shall make but a brief Remembrance here, because it will be necessary in the Sequel of this Discourse (it may be more than once) to resume the Mention of them; and besides, Mr. Selden, in his Book called, *Janus Anglorum,* has given a full Account of those Laws; so that at present it will be sufficient for me, briefly to collect the Heads or Divisions of them, under the Reigns of those several Kings wherein they were made, *viz.*

First, The Laws of King William 1. These consisted in a great Measure of the Repetition of the Laws of King Edward the Confessor, and of the enforcing them by his own Authority, and the Assent of Parliament, at the Request of the English; and some new Laws were added by himself with the like Assent of Parliament, relating to Military Tenures, and the Preservation of the publick Peace of the Kingdom; all which are mention'd by Mr. Lambert, in the Tractate before-mentioned, but more fully by Mr. Selden, in his Collections and Observations upon Eadmerus.

Secondly, We find little of new Laws after this, till the Time of King Henry 1., who besides the Confirmation of the Laws of the Confessor, and of King William 1. brought in a new Volume of Laws, which to this Day are extant, and called the Laws of King Henry 1. The entire Collection of these is entered in the Red Book of the Exchequer, and from thence are transcribed and published by the Care of Sir Roger Twisden, in the latter End of Mr. Lambart's Book before-mention'd; what the Success of those Laws were in the Time of King Steven, and King Henry 2. we shall see hereafter: But they did not much obtain in England, and are now for the most Part become wholly obsolete, and in Effect quite antiquated.

Thirdly, The next considerable Body of Acts of Parliament, were those made under the Reign of King Henry 2. commonly called, *The Constitutions of Clarendon;* what they were, appears best in Hoveden and Mat. Paris, under the Years of that King. We have little Memory else of any considerable Laws enacted in this King's Time, except his Assizes, and such Laws as related to the Forests; which were afterwards improv'd under the Reign of King Richard 1. But of this hereafter, more at large.

And this shall serve for a short Instance of those Statutes, or Acts of Parliament, that were made *before Time of Memory;* whereof, as we have no Authentical Records, but only Transcripts, either in our ancient Historians, or other Books and Manuscripts; so they being Things done before Time of Memory,' obtain at this Day no further than as by Usage and Custom they are, as it were, engrafted into the Body of the Common Law, and made a Part thereof.

And now I come to those *Leges Scriptæ,* or Acts of Parliament, which were made since or within the Time of Memory, *viz.* Since the Beginning of the Reign of Richard 1. and those I shall divide into Two General Heads, *viz.* Those we usually call the *Old* Statutes, and those we usually call the *New* or later Statutes: And because I would prefix some certain Time or Boundary between them, I shall call those the *Old* Statutes which end with the Reign of King Edward 2. and those I shall call the *New* or later Statutes which begin with the Reign of King Edward 3. and so are derived through a Succession of Kings and Queens down to this Day, by a continued and orderly Series.

Touching these later Sort I shall say nothing, for they all keep an orderly and regular Series of Time, and are extant upon Record, either in the Parliament Rolls, or in the Statute Rolls of King Edward 3. and those Kings that follow: For excepting some few Years in the Beginning of K. Edward 3. *i.e.* 2, 3, 7, 8 & 9 Edw. 3. all the Parliament Rolls that ever were since that Time have been preserved, and are extant; and, for the most Part, the Petitions upon which the Acts were drawn up, or the very Acts themselves.

Now therefore touching the elder Acts of Parliament, *viz.* Those that were made between the First Year of the Reign of K. Richard 1. and the last Year of K. Edward 2. we have little extant in any authentical History; and nothing in any authentical Record touching Acts made in the Time of K. Rich. 1. unless we take in those Constitutions and Assizes mentioned by Hoveden as aforesaid.

Neither is there any great Evidence, what Acts of Parliament pass'd in the Time of King John, tho' doubtless many there were both in his Time, and in the Time of K. Rich. 1. But there is no Record extant of them, and the English Histories of those Times give us but little Account of those Laws; only Matthew Paris gives us an Historical Account of the *Magna Charta,* and *Charta de Foresta,* granted by King John at Running Mead the 15th of June, in the Seventeenth Year of his Reign.

And it seems, that the Concession of these Charters was in a Parliamentary Way; you may see the Transcripts of both Charters *verbatim* in Mat. Paris, and in the Red Book of the Exchequer. There were seven Pair of these Charters sent to some of the Great Monasteries under the Seal of King John, one Part whereof sent to the Abby of Tewkesbury I have seen under the Seal of that King; the Substance thereof differs something from the *Magna Charta,* and *Charta de Foresta,* granted by King Henry 3. but not very much, as may appear by comparing them.

But tho' these Charters of King John seem to have been passed in a kind of Parliament, yet it was in a Time of great Confusion between that King and his Nobles; and therefore they obtained not a full Settlement till the Time of King Henry 3. when the Substance of them was enacted by a full and solemn Parliament.

I therefore come down to the Times of those succeeding Kings, Henry 3. Edw. 1. and Edw. 2. and the Statutes made in the Times of those Kings, I call the *Old Statutes;* partly because many of them were made but in Affirmance of the Common Law; and partly because the rest of them, that made a Change in the Common Law, are yet so ancient, that they now seem to have been as it were a Part of the Common Law, especially considering the

7

many Expositions that have been made of them in the several Successions of Times, whereby as they became the great Subject of Judicial Resolutions and Decisions; so those Expositions and Decisions, together also with those old Statutes themselves, are as it were incorporated into the very Common Law, and become a Part of it.

In the Times of those three Kings last mentioned, as likewise in the Times of their Predecessors, there were doubtless many more Acts of Parliament made than are now extant of Record, or otherwise, which might be a Means of the Change of the Common Law in the Times of those Kings from what it was before, tho' all the Records of Memorials of those Acts of Parliament introducing such a Change, are not at this Day extant: But of those that are extant, I shall give you a brief Account, not intending a large or accurate Treatise touching that matter.

The Reign of Henry 3. was a troublesome Time, in respect of the Differences between him and his Barons, which were not composed till his 51st Year, after the Battle of Evesham. In his Time there were many Parliaments, but we have only one Summons of Parliament extant of Record in his Reign, *viz.* 49 Henry 3. and we have but few of those many Acts of Parliament that passed in his Time, *viz.* The great Charter, and *Charta de Foresta,* in the Ninth Year of his Reign, which were doubtless pass'd in Parliament; the Statute of Merton, in the 20th Year of his Reign; the Statute of Marlbridge, in the 52d Year; and the *Dictum sive Edictum de Kenelworth,* about the same Time; and some few other old Acts.

In the Time of K. Edw. 1. there are many more Acts of Parliament extant than in the Time of K. Henry 3. Yet doubtless, in this King's Time, there were many more Statutes made than are now extant: Those that are now extant, are commonly bound together in the old Book of *Magna Charta.* By *those Statutes,* great Alterations and Amendments were made in the Common Law; and by those that are now extant, we may reasonably guess, that there were considerable Alterations and Amendments made by those that are not extant, which possibly may be the real, tho' sudden Means of the great Advance and Alteration of the Laws of England in this King's Reign, over what they were in the Time of his Predecessors.

8

The first Summons of Parliament that I remember extant of Record in this King's Time, is 23 Edw. 1. tho' doubtless there were many more before this, the Records whereof are either lost or mislaid: For many Parliaments were held by this King before that Time, and many of the Acts pass'd in those Parliaments are still extant; as, the Statutes of Westminster 1. in the 3d of Edw. 1. The Statutes of Gloucester, 6 Edw. 1. The Statutes of Westminster 2. and of Winton, 13 Edw. 1. The Statutes of Westminster 3. and of *Quo Warranto,* 18 Edw. 1. And divers others in other Years, which I shall have Occasion to mention hereafter.

In the Time of K. Edw. 2. many Parliaments were held, and many Laws were enacted; but we have few Acts of Parliament of his Reign extant, especially of Record.

And now, because I intend to give some short Account of some general Observations touching Parliaments, and of Acts of Parliament pass'd in the Times of those three Princes, *viz.* Henry 3. Edw. 1. and Edw. 2. because they are of greatest Antiquity, and therefore the Circumstances that atended them most liable to be worn out by Process of Time, I will here mention some Particulars relating to them to preserve their Memory, and which may also be useful to be known in relation to other Things.

We are therefore to know, That there are these several Kinds of Records of Things done in Parliament, or especially relating thereto, *viz.* 1. The Summons to Parliament. 2. The Rolls of Parliament. 3. Bundles of Petitions in Parliament. 4. The Statutes, or Acts of Parliament themselves. And, 5. The *Brevia de Parliamento,* which for the most part were such as issued for the Wages of Knights and Burgesses; but with these I shall not meddle.

First, as to the Summons to Parliament. These Summons to Parliament are not all entred of Record in the Times of Henry 3. and Edw. 1. none being extant of Record in the Time of Hen. 3. but that of 49 Hen. 3. and none in the Time of Edw. 1. till the 23 Edw. 1. But after that Year, they are for the most part extant of Record, *viz. In Dorso Claus' Rotulorum,* in the Backside of the Close Rolls.

Secondly, As to the Rolls of Parliament, *viz.* The Entry of the several Petitions, Answers and Transactions in Parliament. Those

9

are generally and successively extant of Record in the *Tower*, from 4 Edw. 3. downward till the End of the Reign of Edw. 4. Excepting only those Parliaments that intervened between the 1st and the 4th, and between the 6th and the 11th, of Edw. 3.

But of those Rolls in the Times of Hen. 3. and Edw. 1. and Edw. 2. many are lost and few extant; also, of the Time of Henry 3. I have not seen any Parliament Roll; and all that I ever saw of the Time of Edw. 1. was one Roll of Parliament in the Receipt of the Exchequer of 18 Edw. 1. and those Proceedings and Remembrances which are in the *Liber placitor' Parliamenti* in the *Tower*, beginning, as I remember, with the 20th Year of Edw. 1. and ending with the Parliament of Carlisle, 35 Edw. 1. and not continued between those Years with any constant Series; but including some Remembrances of some Parliaments in the Time of Edw. 1. and others in the Time of Edw. 2.

In the Time of Edw. 2. besides the *Rotulus Ordinationum*, of the Lords Ordoners, about 7 Edw. 2. we have little more than the Parliament Rolls of 7 & 8 Edw. 2. and what others are interspersed in the Parliament Book of Edw. 1. above mentioned, and, as I remember, some short Remembrances of Things done in Parliament in the 19 Edw. 3.

Thirdly, As to the Bundles of Petitions in Parliament. They were for the most part Petitions of private Persons, and are commonly endorsed with Remissions to the several Courts where they were properly determinable. There are many of those Bundles of Petitions, some in the Times of Edw. 1. and Edw. 2. and more in the Times of Edw. 3. and the Kings that succeeded him.

Fourthly, The Statutes, or Acts of Parliament themselves. These seem, as if in the Time of Edw. 1. they were drawn up into the Form of a Law in the first Instance, and so assented to by both Houses, and the King, as may appear by the very Observation of the Contexture and Fabrick of the Statutes of those Times. But from near the Beginning of the Reign of Edw. 3. till very near the End of Hen. 6. they were not in the first Instance drawn up in the Form of Acts of Parliament; but the Petition and the Answer were entred in the Parliament Rolls, and out of both, by Advice of the Judges, and others of the King's Council, the Act was drawn up conformable to the Petition and Answer, and the Act itself for the most part entred in a Roll, called, *The Statute Roll,* and the Tenor thereof affixed to Proclamation Writs, directed to the several Sheriffs to proclaim it as a Law in their respective Counties.

But because sometimes Difficulties and Troubles arose, by this extracting of the Statute out of the Petition and Answer; about the latter End of Hen. 6. and Beginning of Edward 4. they took a Course to reduce 'em, even in the first Instance, into the full and compleat Form of Acts of Parliament, which was prosecuted (or Entred) commonly in this Form: *Item quædam Petitio exhibita fuit in hoc Parliamento forman actus in se continens, &c.* and abating that Stile, the Method still continues much the same, namely; That the entire Act is drawn up in Form, and so comes to the King for his assent.

The ancient Method of passing Acts of Parliament being thus declared, I shall now give an Account touching those Acts of Parliament that are at this Day extant of the Times of Henry 3. Edw. 1. and Edw. 2. and they are of two Sorts, *viz.* Some of them are extant of Record; others are extant in ancient Books and Memorials, but none of Record. And those which are extant of Record, are either Recorded in the proper and natural Roll, *viz. the Statute Roll;* or they are entred in some other Roll, especially in the *Close Rolls* and *Patent Rolls,* or in both. Those that are extant, but not of Record, are such as tho' they have no Record extant of them, but possibly the same is lost; yet they are preserved in ancient Books and Monuments. and in all Times have had the Reputation and Authority of Acts of Parliament.

For an Act of Parliament made within Time of Memory, loses not its being so, because not extant of Record, especially if it be a general Act of Parliament. For of general Acts of Parliament, the Courts of Common Law are to take Notice without pleading of them; and such acts shall never be put to be tried by the Record, upon an Issue of *Nul tiel Record,* but it shall be tried by the Court, who, if there be any Difficulty or Uncertainty touching it or the right Pleading of it, are to use for their Information ancient Copies, Transcripts, Books, Pleadings and Memorials to inform themselves, but not to admit the same to be put in Issue by a Plea of *Nul tiel Record.*

For, as shall be shewn hereafter, there are very many old

Statutes which are admitted and obtain as such, tho' there be no Record at this Day extant thereof, nor yet any other written Evidence of the same, but what is in a manner only Traditional, as namely, Ancient and Modern Books of Pleadings, and the common receiv'd Opinion and Reputation, and the Approbation of the Judges Learned in the Laws: For the Judges and Courts of Justice are, *ex Officio,* (bound) to take Notice of publick Acts of Parliament, and whether they are truly pleaded or not, and therefore they are the Triers of them. But it is otherwise of private Acts of Parliament, for they may be put in Issue, and tried by the Record upon *Nul tiel Record* pleaded, unless they are produced exemplified, as was done in the Prince's Cafe in my Lord Coke's 8th Rep. and therefore the Averment of *Nul tiel Record* was refused in that Case.

The old Statutes or Acts of Parliament that are of Record, as is before said, are entred either upon the proper Statute Roll, or some other Roll in *Chancery.*

The first Statute Roll which we have, is in the *Tower,* and begins with *Magna Charta,* and ends with Edw. 3. and is called *Magnus Rotulus Statutor'.* There are five other Statute Rolls in that Office, of the Times of Richard 2. Henry 4. Hen. 5. Hen. 6. and Edw. 4.

I shall now give a Scheme of those ancient Statutes of the Times of Henry 3. Edw. 1. and Edw. 2. that are recorded in the first of those Rolls or elsewhere, to the best of my Remembrance, and according to those Memorials I have long had by me, *viz.*

Magna Charta. Magno Rot. Stat. membr. 40. & Rot. Cartar. 28 E. 1 and membr. 16.

Charta de Foresta. Mag. Rot. Stat. membr. 19 & Rot. Cartar. 28 E. 1 membr. 26.

Stat. de Gloucestre. Mag. Rot. Stat. memb. 47.

Westm. 2. Rot. Mag. Stat. membr. 47.

Westm. 3. Rot. Clauso, 18 E. 1. membr. 6. Dorso.

Winton. Rot. Mag. Stat. memb. 41. Rot. Clauso, 8 E. 3. memb. 6. Dorso. Pars. 2. Rot. Clauso, 5 R. 2. membr. 13. Rot. Paten. 25 E. 1. membr. 13.

De Mercatoribus. Mag. Rot. Stat. Membr. 47. In Dorso.

De Religiosis. Mag. Rot. Stat. membr. 47.

Articuli Cleri. Mag. Rot. Stat. membr. 34. Dorso 2 Pars. Pat. E.
1. 2. membr. 34. 2 Pars. Pat. 2 E. 3. membr. 15.
De hiis qui ponendi sunt in Assisis. Mag. Rot. Stat. membr. 41.
De Finibus levatis. Mag. Rot. Stat. membr. 37.
De defensione Juris liberi Parliam. Lib. Parl. E. 1. fo. 32.
Stat. Eborum. Mag. Rot. Stat. membr. 32.
De conjunctis infeofatis. Mag. Rot. Stat. membr. 34.
De Escætoribus. Mag. Rot. Stat. membr. 35. Dorso, & Rot.
Claus. 29 E. 1. membr. 14. Dorso.
Stat. de Lincolne. Mag. Rot. Stat. membr. 32.
Stat. de Priscis. Rot. Mag. Stat. membr. 33. In Schedula de
libertatibus perquirendis, vel Rot. Claus. 27 E. 1. membr. 24.
Stat. de Acton Burnel. Rot. Mag. Stat. membr. 46. Dorso, &
Rot. Claus. 11. E. 1. membr. 2.
Juramentum Vicecomit. Rot. Mag. Stat. membr. 34. Dorso,
& Rot. Claus. 5 E. 2. membr. 23.
Articuli Stat. Gloucestriæ. Rot. Claus. 2 E. 2. Pars. 2. membr. 8.
De Pistoribus & Braciatoribus. 2 Pars, Claus. vel Pat. 2 R 2.
membr. 29.
De asportatis Religiosor. Mag. Rot. Stat. membr. 33.
Westm. 4. De Vicecomitibus & Viridi cæra. Rot. Mag. Stat.
membr. 33. In Dorso.
Confirmationes Chartarum. Mag. Rot. Stat. membr. 28.
De Terris Templariorum. Mag. Rot. Stat. membr. 31. in
Dorso, & Claus. 17 E. 2. membr. 4.
Litera patens super prisis bonorum Cleri. Rot. Mag. Stat.
membr. 33. In Dorso.
De Forma mittendi extractas ad Scaccar. Rot. Mag. Stat.
membr. 36. & membr. 30. In Dorso.
Statutum de Scaccar. Mag. Rot. Stat.
Statutum de Rutland. Rot Claus. 12 E. 1.
Ordinatio Forestæ. Mag. Rot. Stat. membr. 30. & Rot. Claus.
17 E. 2. Pars 2. membr. 3.

According to a strict Inquiry made about 30 Years since, these
were all the old Statutes of the Times of Hen. 3. Edw. 1. and
Edw. 2. that were then to be found of Record; what other Statutes
have been found since, I know not.

The Ordinance called *Butler's,* for the Heir to punish Waste in
the Life of the Ancestor, tho' it be of Record in the Parliament
Book of Edw. 1. yet it never was a Statute, nor never so received,
but only some Constitution of the King's Council or Lords in

Parliament, and which never obtain'd the Strength or Force of an Act of Parliament.

Now those Statutes that ensue, tho' most of 'em are unquestionable Acts of Parliament, yet are not of Record that I know of, but only their Memorials preserved in ancient Printed and Manuscript Books of Statutes; yet they are at this Day for the most part generally accepted and taken as Acts of Parliament, tho' some of 'em are now antiquated and of little Use, *viz.*

The Statutes of Merton, Marlbridge, Westm. 1. Explanatio Statuti Gloucestriæ, De Champertio, De visu Frankplegii, De pane & Cervisia, Articuli Inquisitionis super Stat. de Winton, Circumspecte agatis, De districtione Scaccarii, De Conspirationibus, De vocatis ad Warrant. Statut. de Carliol, De Prerogativa Regis, De modo faciendi Homag. De Wardis & Releivis Dies Communes in Banco. Stat. de Bigamis, Dies Communes in Banco in casu consimili. Stat. Hiberniæ, De quo Warranto, De Essoin calumpniand. Judicium collistrigii, De Frangentibus Prisonar'. De malefactoribus in Parcis, De Consultationibus, De Officio Coronatoris, De Protectionibus, Sententia lata super Chartas, Modus levandi Fines. Statut. de Gavelet, De Militibus, De Vasto, De anno Bissextili, De appellatis, De Extenta Manerii, Compositio Mensearum vel Computatio Mensarum. Stat. de Quo Warranto, Ordinatio de Inquisitionibus, Ordinatio de Foresta, De admensura Terre, De dimissione Denarior. Statut. de Quo Warranto novum, Ne Rector prosternat arbores in Cæmeterio, Consuetudines & Assisa de Foresta, Compositio de Ponderibus, De Tallagio, De visu Terræ & servitio Regis, Compositio ulnarum & particarum, De Terris amortizandis, Dictum de Kenelworth, &c.

From whence we may collect these Two observations, *viz.*

First, That altho' the Record itself be not extant, yet general Statutes made within Time of Memory, namely, since 1 *Richardi Primi,* do not lose their Strength, if any authentical Memorials thereof are in Books, and seconded with a general receiv'd Tradition attesting and approving the same.

Secondly, That many Records, even of Acts of Parliament, have in long Process of Time been lost, and possibly the Things themselves forgotten at this Day, which yet in or near the Times wherein they were made, might cause many of those authoritative Alterations in some Things touching the Proceedings and Decisions in Law: The Original Cause of which Change being otherwise at this Day hid and unknown to us; and indeed, Histories (and Annals) give us an Account of the Suffrages of many Parliaments, whereof we at this Time have none, or few Footsteps extant in Records or Acts of Parliament. The Instance of the great Parliament at Oxford, about 40th of Henry 3. may, among many others of like Nature, be a concurrent Evidence of this: For tho' we have Mention made in our Histories of many Constitutions made in the said Parliament at Oxford, and which occasioned much Trouble in the Kingdom, yet we have no Monuments of Record concerning that Parliament, or what those Constitutions were.

And thus much shall serve touching those Old Statutes or *Leges Scriptæ,* or Acts of Parliament made in the Times of those three Kings, Henry 3. Edw. 1. and Edw. 2. Those that follow in the Times of Edw. 3. and the succeeding Kings, are drawn down in a continued Series of Time, and are extant of Record in the Parliament Rolls, and in the Statute Rolls, without any remarkable Omission, and therefore I shall say nothing of them.

II

Concerning the Lex non Scripta, i. e. The Common or Municipal Laws of this Kingdom

In the former Chapter, I have given you a short Account of that Part of the Laws of England which is called *Lex Scripta,* namely, Statutes or Acts of Parliament, which in their original Formation are reduced into Writing, and are so preserv'd in their Original Form, and in the same Stile and Words wherein they were first made: I now come to that Part of our Laws called, *Lex non Scripta,* under which I include not only General Customs, or the Common Law properly so called, but even those more particular Laws and Customs applicable to certain Courts and Persons, whereof more hereafter.

And when I call those Parts of our Laws *Leges non Scriptæ,* I do not mean as if all those Laws were only Oral, or communicated from the former Ages to the later, merely by Word. For all those Laws have their several Monuments in Writing, whereby they are transferr'd from one Age to another, and without which they would soon lose all kind of Certainty: For as the Civil and Canon Laws have their *Responsa Prudentum Consilia & Decisions, i.e.* their Canons, Decrees, and Decretal Determinations extant in Writing; so those Laws of England which are not comprized under the Title of Acts of Parliament, are for the most part extant in Records of Pleas, Proceedings and Judgments, in Books of Reports, and Judicial Decisions, in Tractates of Learned Men's Arguments and Opinions, preserved from ancient Times, and still extant in Writing.

But I therefore stile those Parts of the Law, *Leges non Scriptæ*, because their Authoritative and Original Institutions are not set down in Writing in that Manner, or with that Authority that Acts of Parliament are, but they are grown into Use, and have acquired their binding Power and the Force of Laws by a long and immemorial Usage, and by the Strength of Custom and Reception in this Kingdom. The Matters indeed, and the Substance of those Laws, are in Writing, but the formal and obliging Force and Power of them grows by long Custom and Use, as will fully appear in the ensuing Discourse.

Fow the Municipal Laws of this Kingdom, which I thus call *Leges non Scriptæ*, are of a vast Extant, and indeed include in their Generality all those several Laws which are allowed, as the Rule and Direction of Justice and Judicial Proceedings, and which are applicable to all those various Subjects, about which Justice is conversant. I shall, for more Order, and the better to guide my Reader, distinguish them into Two Kinds, *viz.*

First, The Common Law, as it is taken in its proper and usual Acceptation.

Secondly, Those particular Laws applicable to particular subjects, Matters or Courts.

1. Touching the former, *viz.* The Common Law in its usual and proper Acceptation. This is that Law by which Proceedings and Determinations in the King's *Ordinary Courts* of Justice are directed and guided. This directs the Course of Discents of Lands, and the Kinds; the Natures, and the Extents and Qualifications of Estates; therein also the Manner, Forms, Ceremonies and Solemnities of transferring Estates from one to another: The Rules of Settling, Acquiring, and Transferring of Properties; The Forms, Solemnities and Obligation of Contracts; The Rules and Directions for the Exposition of Wills, Deeds and Acts of Parliament. The Process, Proceedings, Judgments and Executions of the King's *Ordinary Courts* of Justice; The Limits, Bounds and Extents of Courts, and their Jurisdictions. The several Kinds of *Temporal* Offences, and Punishments at Common Law; and the Manner of the Application of the several

Kinds of Punishments, and infinite more Particulars which extend themselves as large as the many Exigencies in the Distribution of the King's *Ordinary* Justice requires.

And besides these more common and ordinary Matters to which the Common Law extends, it likewise includes the Laws applicable to divers Matters of very great Moment; and tho' by Reason of that Application, the said Common Law assumes divers Denominations, yet they are but Branches and Parts of it; like as the same Ocean, tho' it many times receives a different Name from the Province, Shire, Island or Country to which it is contiguous, yet these are but Parts of the same Ocean.

Thus the Common Law includes, *Lex Prerogativa,* as 'tis applied with certain Rules to that great Business of the King's Prerogative; so 'tis called *Lex Forestæ,* as it is applied under its special and proper Rules to the Business of Forests; so it is called *Lex Mercatoria,* as it is applied under its proper Rules to the Business of Trade and Commerce; and many more instances of like Nature may be given: Nay, the various and particular Customs of Cities, Towns and Manors, are thus far Parts of the Common Law, as they are applicable to those particular Places, which will appear from these Observations, *viz.*

First, The Common Law does determine what of those Customs are good and reasonable, and what are unreasonable and void. *Secondly,* The Common Law gives to those Customs, that it adjudges reasonable, the Force and Efficacy of their Obligation. *Thirdly,* The Common Law determines what is that Continuance of Time that is sufficient to make such a Custom. *Fourthly,* The Common Law does interpose and authoritatively decide the Exposition, Limits and Extension of such Customs.

This Common Law, though the Usage, Practice and Decisions of the King's Courts of Justice may expound and evidence it, and be of great Use to illustrate and explain it; yet it cannot be authoritatively altered or changed but by Act of Parliament. But of this Common Law, and the Reason of its Denomination, more at large hereafter.

Now, *Secondly,* As to those particular Laws I before mentioned, which are applicable to particular Matters, Subjects or Courts: These make up the second Branch of the Laws of England, which I include under the general Term of *Leges non Scriptæ,* and by those particular Laws I mean the Laws Ecclesiastical, and the Civil Law, so far forth as they are admitted in certain Courts, and certain Matters allow'd to the Decision of those Courts, whereof hereafter.

It is true, That those Civil and Ecclesiastical Laws are indeed Written Laws; the Civil Law being contain'd in their Pandects, and the Institutions of Justinian, &c. (their Imperial Constitutions or Codes answering to our *Leges Scriptæ,* or Statutes.) And the Canon or Ecclesiastical Laws contain'd for the most part in the Canons and Constitutions of Councils and Popes, collected in their *Decretum Gratiani,* and the Decretal Epistles of Popes, which make up the Body of their *Corpus Juris Canonici,* together with huge Volumes of Councils and Expositions, Decisions, and Tractates of learned Civilians and Canonists, relating to both Laws; so that it may seem at first View very improper to rank these under the Branch of *Leges non Scriptæ,* or Unwritten Laws.

But I have for the following Reason rang'd these Laws among the Unwritten Laws of England, *viz.* because it is most plain, That neither the Canon Law nor the Civil Law have any Obligation as Laws within this Kingdom, upon any Account that the Popes or Emperors made those Laws, Canons, Rescripts or Determinations, or because Justinian compiled their *Corpus Juris Civilis,* and by his Edicts confirm'd and publish'd the same as authentical, or because this or that Council or Pope made those or these Canons or Degrees, or because Gratian, or Gregory, or Boniface, or Clement, did, as much as in them lie, authenticate this or that Body of Canons or Constitutions; for the King of England does not recognize any Foreign Authority as superior or equal to him in this Kingdom, neither do any Laws of the Pope or Emperor, as they are such, bind here: But all the Strength that either the Papal or Imperial Laws have obtained in this Kingdom, is only because they have been received and admitted either by the Consent of Parliament, and so are Part of the Statute Laws of the Kingdom, or else by immemorial Usage and Custom in some particular Cases and Courts, and no otherwise; and therefore so far as such Laws are received and allowed of here, so far they obtain and no farther; and the Authority and Force they have here is not founded on, or derived from themselves; for so they bind no more with us than our Laws bind in *Rome* or *Italy*. But their Authority is founded merely on their being admitted and received by us, which alone gives 'em their Authoritative Essence, and qualifies their Obligation.

And hence it is, That even in those Courts where the Use of those Laws is indulged according to that Reception which has been allowed 'em: If they exceed the Bounds of that Reception, by extending themselves to other Matters than has been allowed 'em; or if those Courts proceed according to that Law, when it is controuled by the Common Law of the Kingdom: The Common Law does and may prohibit and punish them; and it will not be a sufficient Answer, for them to tell the King's Courts, that *Justinian* or Pope *Gregory* have decreed otherwise. For we are not bound by their Decrees further, or otherwise than as the Kingdom here has, as it were transposed the same into the Common and Municipal Laws of the Realm, either by Admission of, or by Enacting the same, which is that alone which can make 'em of any Force in England. I need not give particular Instances herein; the Truth thereof is plain and evident, and we need go no further than the Statutes of 24 H. 8. *cap.* 12. 25 H. 8. *c.* 19, 20, 21. and the learned Notes of *Selden* upon *Fleta,* and the Records there cited; nor shall I spend much Time touching the Use of those Laws in the several Courts of this Kingdom: But will only briefly mention some few Things concerning them.

There are Three Courts of Note, wherein the Civil, and in one of them the Canon or Ecclesiastical Law, has been with certain Restrictions allow'd in this Kingdom, *viz. 1st.* The Courts Ecclesiastical, of the Bishops and their derivative Officers. *2dly.* The Admiralty Court. *3dly. The Curia Militaris,* or Court of the Constable and Marshal, or Persons commission'd to exercise that Jurisdiction. I shall touch a little upon each of these.

First, The Ecclesiastical Courts, they are of two Kinds, *viz. 1st.* Such as are derived immediately by the King's Commission; such was formerly the Court of High Commission; which tho', without the help of an Act of Parliament, it could not in Matters of Ecclesiastical Cognizance use any Temporal Punishment or Censure, as Fine, Imprisonment, &c. Yet even by the Common Law, the Kings of England, being delivered from Papal Usurpation, might grant a Commission to hear and determine Ec-clesiastical Causes and Offences, according to the King's Ec-clesiastical Laws, as Cawdry's Case, Cook's 5th Report. *2dly.* Such as are not derived by any immediate Commission from the King; but the Laws of England have annexed to certain Offices, Ecclesiastical Jurisdiction, as incident to such Offices: Thus every Bishop by his Election and Confirmation, even before Consecra-tion, had Ecclesiastical Jurisdiction annex'd to his Office, as *Judex Ordinarius* within his Diocese; and diverse Abbots anciently, and most Archdeacons at this Day, by Usage, have had the like Juris-diction within certain Limits and Precincts.

But altho' these are *Judices Ordinarii,* and have Ecclesiastical Jurisdiction annex'd to their Ecclesiastical Offices, yet this Juris-diction Ecclesiastical *in Foro Exteriori* is derived from the Crown of England: For there is no External Jurisdiction, whether Ec-clesiastical or Civil, within this Realm, but what is derived from the Crown: It is true, both anciently, and at this Day, the process of Ecclesiastical Courts runs in the Name, and issues under: the Seal of the Biship; and what Practice stands so at this Day by Virtue of several Acts of Parliament, too long here to recount. But that is no Impediment of their deriving their Jurisdictions from the Crown; for till 27 H. 8. *cap.* 24. The Process in Coun-ties Palatine ran in the Name of the Counts Palatine, yet no Man ever doubted, but that the Palatine Jurisdictions were derived from the Crown.

Touching the Severance of the Bishop's Consistory from the Sheriff's Court: See the Charter of King Will. 1. and Mr. Selden's Notes on Eadmerus.

Now the Matters of Ecclesiastical Jurisdiction are of Two Kinds, Criminal and Civil.

The Criminal Proceedings extend to such Crimes, as by the Laws of this Kingdom are of Ecclesiastical Cognizance; as Heresy, Fornication, Adultery, and some others, wherein their Proceed-ings are, *Pro Reformatione Morum,* & *pro Salute Animæ;* and the Reason why they have Conuzance of those and the like offences, and not of others, as Murther, Theft, Burglary, &c. is not so much from the Nature of the Offence (for surely the one is as much a Sin as the other, and therefore, if their Cognizance were of Offences *quatenus peccata contra Deum,* it would extend to all

Sins whatsoever, it being against God's Law). But the true Reason is, because the Law of the Land has indulged unto that Jurisdiction the Conuzance of some Crimes and not of others.

The Civil Causes committed to their Cognizance, wherein the Proceedings are *ad Instantiam Partis,* ordinarily are Matters of Tythes, Rights of Institution and Induction to Ecclesiastical Benefices, Cases of Matrimony and Divorces, and Testamentary Causes, and the Incidents thereunto, as Insinuation or Probation of Testaments, Controversies touching the same, and of Legacies of Goods and Moneys, &c.

Altho' *de Jure Communi* the Cognizance of Wills and Testaments does not belong to the Ecclesiastical Court, but to the Temporal or Civil Jurisdiction; yet *de Consuetudine Angliæ pertinet ad Judices Ecclesiasticos,* as *Linwood* himself agrees, *Exercit. de Testamentis, cap. 4. in Glossa.* So that it is the Custom or Law of England that gives the Extent and Limits of their external Jurisdiction in *Foro Contentioso.*

The Rule by which they proceed, is the Canon Law, but not in its full Latitude, and only so far as it stands uncorrected, either by contrary Acts of Parliament, or the Common Law and Custom of England; for there are divers Canons made in ancient Times, and Decretals of the Popes that never were admitted here in England, and particularly in relation to Tythes; many things being by our Laws privileg'd from Tythes, which by the Canon Law are chargeable, (as Timber, Oar, Coals, &c.) without a Special Custom subjecting them thereunto.

Where the Canon Law, or the *Stylus Curiæ,* is silent, the Civil Law is taken as a Director, especially in Points of Exposition and Determination, touching Wills and Legacies.

But Things that are of Temporal Cognizance only, cannot by Charter be delivered over to Ecclesiastical Jurisdiction, nor be judged according to the Rules of the Canon or Civil Law, which is *aliud Examen,* and not competent to the Nature of Things of Common Law Cognizance: And therefore, Mich. 8 H. 4. *Rot.* 72. *coram Rege,* when the Chancellor of Oxford proceeded according to the Rule of the Civil Law in a Case of Debt, the Judgment was reversed in B. R. wherein the principal Error assigned was, because they proceeded *per Legem Civilem ubi quilibet ligeus Domini Regis Regni sui Angliæ in quibuscunque placitis*

& *querelis infra hoc Regnum factis & emergentibus de Jure tractari debt per Communem Legem Angliæ;* and altho' King H. 8. 14 *Anno Regni sui,* granted to the University a liberal Charter to proceed according to the Use of the University, *viz.* By a Course much conform'd to the Civil Law; yet that Charter had not been sufficient to have warranted such Proceedings without the Help of an Act of Parliament: And therefore in 13 Eliz. an Act passed, whereby that Charter was in Effect enacted; and 'tis thereby that at this Day they have a kind of Civil Law Proceedure, even in Matters that are of themselves of Common Law Cognizance, where either of the Parties to the Suit are privileged.

The Coertion or Execution of the Sentence in Ecclesiastical Courts, is only by Excommunication of the Person contumacious, and upon Signification thereof into *Chancery,* a Writ *de Excommunicatio capiendo* issues, whereby the Party is imprisoned till Obedience yielded to the Sentence. But besides this Coertion, the Sentences of the Ecclesiastical Courts touching some Matters do introduce a real Effect, without any other Execution; as a Divorce, *a Vinculo Matrimonii* for the Causes of Consanguinity, Precontract, or Frigidity, do induce a legal Dissolution of the Marriage; so a Sentence of Deprivation from an Ecclesiastical Benefice, does by Virtue of the very Sentence, without any other Coertion or Execution, introduce a full Determination of the Interest of the Person deprived.

And thus much concerning the Ecclesiastical Courts, and the Use of the Canon and Civil Law in them, as they are the Rule and Direction of Proceedings therein.

Secondly, The second special Jurisdiction wherein the Civil Law is allow'd, at least as a Director or Rule in some Cases, is the Admiral Court or Jurisdiction. This Jurisdiction is derived also from the Crown of England, either immediately by Commission from the King, or mediately, which is several Ways, either by Commission from the Lord High Admiral, whose Power and Constitution is by the King, or by the Charters granted to particular Corporations bordering upon the Sea, and by Commission from them, or by Prescription, which nevertheless in Presumption of Law is derived at first from the Crown by Charter not now extant.

The Admiral Jurisdiction is of Two Kinds, *viz. Jurisdictio*

Voluntaria, which is no other but the Power of the Lord High Admiral, as the King's General at Sea over his Fleets; or *Jurisdictio Contentiosa,* which is that Power of Jurisdiction which the Judge of the Admiralty has in *Foro Contentioso;* and what I have to say is of this later Jurisdiction.

The Jurisdiction of the Admiral Court, as to the Matter of it, is confined by the Laws of this Realm to Things done upon the High Sea only; as Depredations and Piracies upon the High Sea; Offences of Masters and Mariners upon the High Sea; Maritime Contracts made and to be executed upon the High Sea; Matters of Prize and Reprizal upon the High Sea. But touching Contracts or Things made within the Bodies of English Counties, or upon the Land beyond the Sea, tho' the Execution thereof be in some Measure upon the High Sea, as Charter Parties, or Contracts made even upon the High Sea, touching Things that are not in their own Nature Maritime, as a Bond or Contract for the Payment of Money, so also of Damages in Navigable Rivers, within the Bodies of Counties, Things done upon the Shore at Low-Water, Wreck of the Sea, &c. These Things belong not to the Admiral's Jurisdiction: And thus the Common Law, and the Statutes of 13 Rich. 2. *cap.* 15. 15 Rich. 2. *cap.* 3. confine and limit their Jurisdiction to Matters Maritime, and such only as are done upon the High Sea.

This Court is not bottom'd or founded upon the Authority of the Civil Law, but hath both its Power and Jurisdiction by the Law and Custom of the Realm, in such Matters as are proper for its Cognizance; and this appears by their Process, *viz.* The Arrest of the Persons of the Defendants, as well as by Attachment of their Goods; and likewise by those Customs and Laws Maritime, whereby many of their Proceedings are directed, and which are not in many Things conformable to the Rules of the Civil Law; such are those ancient Laws of Oleron, and other Customs introduced by the Practice of the Sea, and Stile of the Court.

Also, The Civil Law is allowed to be the Rule of their Proceedings, only so far as the same is not contradicted by the Statute of this Kingdom, or by those Maritime Laws and Customs, which in some Points have obtain'd in Derogation of the Civil Law: But by the Statute 28 Hen. 8. *cap.* 15. all Treasons, Murders, Felonies, done on the High Sea, or in any Haven, River, Creek, Port or Place, where the Admirals have to pretend to have Jurisdiction, are to be determined by the King's Commission, as if the Offences were done at Land, according to the Course of the Common Law. And thus much shall serve touching the Court of Admiralty, and the Use of the Civil Law therein.

Thirdly, The Third Court, wherein the Civil Law has its Use in this Kingdom, is the Military Court, held before the Constable and Marshal anciently, as the *Judiciis Ordinarii* in this Case, or otherwise before the King's Commissioners of that Jurisdiction, as *Judices Delegati.*

The Matter of their Jurisdiction is declared and limited by the Statutes of 8 R. 2. *cap.* 5. and 13 R. 2. *cap.* 2. And not only by those Statutes, but more by the very Common Law is their Jurisdiction declared and limited as follows, *viz.*

First, Negatively: They are not to meddle with any Thing determinable by the Common Law: And therefore, inasmuch as Matter of Damages, and the Quantity and Determination thereof, is of that Conuzance; the Court of Constable and Marshal cannot, even in such Suits as are proper for their Conuzance, give Damages against the Party convicted before them, and at most can only order Reparation in Point of Honour, as *Mendacium sibi ipsi imponere:* Neither can they, as to the Point of Reparation, in Honour, hold Plea of any such Words or Things, wherein the Party is relievable by the Courts of the Common Law.

Secondly, Affirmatively: Their Jurisdiction extends to Matters of Arms and Matters of War, *viz.*

First, As to Matters of Arms (or Heraldry), the Constable and Marshal had Conuzance thereof, *viz.* Touching the Rights of Coat-Armour, Bearings, Crests, Supporters, Pennons, &c. And also touching the Rights of Place and Precedence, in Cases where either Acts of Parliament or the King's Patent (he being the Fountain of Honour) have not already determined it, for in such Cases they have no Power to alter it. Those Things were anciently allowed to the Conuzance of the Constable and Marshal, as having some Relation to Military Affairs; but so restrain'd, that they were only to determine the Right, and give Reparation to the Party injured in Point of Honour, but not to repair him in Damages.

But, *Secondly,* As to Matters of War. The Constable and Marshal had a double Power, *viz.*

1. A Ministerial Power, as they were Two great ordinary Officers, anciently, in the King's Army; the Constable being in Effect the King's General, and the Marshal was employed in marshalling the King's Army, and keeping the List of the Officers and Soldiers therein; and his Certificate was the Trial of those whose Attendance was requisite. *Vide* Littleton, §. 102.

Again, 2. The Constable and Marshal had also a Judicial Power, or a Court wherein several Matters were determinable: As *1st,* Appeals of Death or Murder committed beyond the Sea, according to the Course of the Civil Law. *2dly,* The Rights of Prisoners taken in War. *3dly,* The Offences and Miscarriages of Soldiers contrary to the Laws and Rules of the Army: For always preparatory to an actual War, the Kings of this Realm, by Advice of the Constable, (and Marshal) were used to compose a Book of *Rules* and *Orders* for the due Order and Discipline of their Officers and Soldiers, together with certain Penalties on the Offenders; and this was called, *Martial Law.* We have extant in the Black Book of the Admiralty, and elsewhere, several Exemplars of such Military Laws, and especially that of the 9th of Rich. 2. composed by the King, with the Advice of the Duke of Lancaster, and others.

But touching the Business of Martial Law, these Things are to be observed, *viz.*

First, That in Truth and Reality it is not a Law, but something indulged rather than allowed as a Law; the Necessity of Government, Order and Discipline in an Army, is that only which can give those Laws a Countenance, *Quod enim Necessitas cogit desendi.*

Secondly, This indulged Law was only to extend to Members of the Army, or to those of the opposite Army, and never was so much indulged as intended to be (executed or) exercised upon others; for others who were not listed under the Army, had no Colour of Reason to be bound by Military Constitutions, applicable only to the Army, whereof they were not Parts; but they were to be order'd and govern'd according to the Laws to which they were subject, though it were a Time of War.

Thirdly, That the Exercise of Martial Law, whereby any Person should lose his Life or Member, or Liberty, may not be permitted in Time of Peace, when the King's Courts are open for all Persons to receive Justice, according to the Laws of the Land. This is in Substance declared by the Petition of Right, 3 Car. 1. whereby such Commissions and Martial Law were repealed, and declared to be contrary to Law: And accordingly was that famous Case of Edmond Earl of Kent; who being taken at Pomsret, 15 Ed. 2. the King and divers Lords proceeded to give Sentence of Death against him, as in a kind of Military Court by a Summary Proceeding; which Judgment was afterwards in 1 Ed. 3. revers'd in Parliament: And the Reason of that Reversal serving to the Purpose in Hand, I shall here insert it as entered in the Record, *viz.*

> Quod cum quicunq; homo ligeus Domini Regis pro Seditionibus, &c. tempore pacis captus & in quacunque Curia Domini Regis ductus fuerit de ejusmodi Seditionibus & aliis Felonius sibi impositis per Legem & Consuetudine Regni arrectari debet & Responsionem adduci, Et inde per Communem Legem, antequam fuerit Morti adjudicand' (triari) &c. Unde cum notorium sit & manifestum quod totum tempus quo impositum fuit eidem Comiti propter Mala & Facionora fecisse, ad tempus in quo captus fuit & in quo Morti adjudicatus fuit, fuit tempus Pacis maximæ, Cum per totum tempus prædictum & Cancellaria & aliæ plac. Curiæ Domini Regis aperte fuer' in quibus cuilibet Lex fiebatur sicut fieri consuevit, Nec idem Dominus Rex unquam tempore illo cum vexillis explicatis Equitabat, &c.

And accordingly the Judgment was revers'd; for Martial Law, which is rather indulg'd than allow'd, and that only in Cases of Necessity, in Time of open War, is not permitted in Time of Peace, when the ordinary Courts of Justice are open.

In this Military Court, Court of Honour, or Court Martial, the Civil Law has been used and allowed in such Things as belong to their Jurisdiction; as the Rule or Direction of their Proceedings and Decisions, so far forth as the same is not controuled by the Laws of this Kingdom, and those Customs and Usages which have obtain'd in England, which even in Matters of Honour are in some Points derogatory to the Civil Law. But this Court has been long disused upon great Reasons.

And thus I have given a brief Prospect of these Courts and Matters, wherein the Canon and Civil Law has been in some Measure allowed, as the Rule or Direction of Proceedings or Decisions: But although in these Courts and Matters the Laws of England, upon the Reasons and Account before expressed, have admitted the Use and Rule of the Canon and Civil Law; yet even herein also, the Common Law of England has retain'd those *Signa Superioritatis,* and the Preference and Superintendence in relation to those Courts: Namely,

1st. As the Laws and Statutes of the Realm have prescribed to those Courts their Bounds and Limits, so the Courts of Common Law have the Superintendency over those Courts, to keep them within the Limits and Bounds of their several Jurisdictions, and to judge and determine whether they have exceeded those Bounds, or not; and in Case they do exceed their Bounds, the Courts at Common Law issue their Prohibitions to restrain them, directed either to the Judge or Party, or both: And also, in case they exceed their Jurisdiction, the Officer that executes the Sentence, and in some Cases the Judge that gives it, are punishable in the Courts at Common Law; sometimes at the Suit of the King, sometimes at the Suit of the Party, and sometimes at the Suit of both, according to the Variety and Circumstances of the Case.

2dly. The Common Law, and the Judges of the Courts of Common Law, have the Exposition of such Statutes or Acts of Parliament as concern either the Extent of the Jurisdiction of those Courts (whether Ecclesiastical, Maritime or Military) or the Matters depending before them; and therefore, if those Courts either refuse to allow these Acts of Parliament, or expound them in any other Sense than is truly and properly the Exposition of them, the King's Great Courts of the Common Law (who next under the King and his Parliament have the Exposition of those Laws) may prohibit and controul them.

And thus much touching those Courts wherein the Civil and

Canon Laws are allowed as Rules and Directions under the Restrictions above-mentioned: Touching which, the Sum of the Whole is this:

First, That the Jurisdiction exercised in those Courts is derived from the Crown of England, and that the last Devolution is to the King, by Way of Appeal.

Secondly, That although the Canon or Civil Law be respectively allowed as the Direction or Rule of their Proceedings, yet that is not as if either of those Laws had any original Obligation in England, either as they are the Laws of Emperors, Popes, or General Councils, but only by Virtue of their Admission here, which is evident; for that those Canons or Imperial Constitutions which have not been receiv'd here do not bind; and also, for that by several contrary Customs and Stiles used here many of those Civil and Canon Laws are controuled and derogated.

Thirdly, That although those Laws are admitted in some Cases in those Courts, yet they are but *Leges sub graviori Lege;* and the Common Laws of this Kingdom have ever obtain'd and retain'd the Superintendency over them, and those *Signa Superioritatis* before-mentioned, for the Honour of the King and the Common Laws of England.

III

Concerning the Common Law of England, its Use and Excellence, and the Reason of its Denomination

I Come now to that other Branch of our Laws, the Common Municipal Law of this Kingdom, which has the Superintendency of all those other particular Laws used in the before-mentioned Courts, and is the common Rule for the Administration of common Justice in this great Kingdom; of which it has been always tender, and there is great Reason for it; for it is not only a very just and excellent Law in it self, but it is singularly accommodated to the Frame of the English Government, and to the Disposition of the English Nation, and such as by a long Experience and Use is as it were incorporated into their very Temperament, and, in a Manner, become the Complection and Constitution of the English Commonwealth.

Insomuch, that even as in the natural Body the due Temperament and Constitution does by Degrees work out those accidental Diseases which sometimes happen, and do reduce the Body to its just State and Constitution; so when at any Time through the Errors, Distempers or Iniquities of Men or Times, the Peace of the Kingdom, and right Order of Government, have received Interruption, the Common Law has wasted and wrought out those Distempers, and reduced the Kingdom to its just State and Temperament, as our present (and former) Times can easily witness.

This Law is that which asserts, maintains, and, with all imaginable Care, provides for the Safety of the King's Royal Person, his Crown and Dignity, and all his just Rights, Revenues, Powers, Prerogatives and Government, as the great Foundation (under God) of the Peace, Happiness, Honour and Justice, of this Kingdom; and this Law is also, that which declares and asserts the Rights and Liberties, and the Properties of the Subject; and is the just, known, and common Rule of Justice and Right between Man and Man, within this Kingdom.

And from hence it is, that the Wisdom of the Kings of England, and their great Council, the Honourable House of Parliament, have always been jealous and vigilant for the Reformation of what has been at any Time found defective in it, and so to remove all such Obstacles as might obstruct the free Course of it, and to support, countenance and encourage the Use of it, as the best, safest and truest Rule of Justice in all Matters, as well Criminal as Civil.

I should be too Voluminous to give those several Instances that occur frequently in the Statutes, the Parliament Rolls, and Parliamentary Petitions, touching this Matter; and shall therefore only instance in some few Particulars in both Kinds, *viz.* Criminal and Civil: And First, in Matters Civil.

In the Parliament 18 Edw. 1. In a Petition in the Lords House, touching Land between Hugh Lowther and Adam Edingthorp: The Defendant alledges, That if the Title should in this Manner be proceeded in, he should lose the Benefit of his Warranty; and also, that the Plaintiff, if he hath any Right, hath his Remedy at Common Law by Assize of *Mortdancestor,* and therefore demands Judgment, *Si de libero Tenemento debeat hic sine brevi Respondere;* and the Judgment of the Lords in Parliament thereupon is enter'd in these Words, *viz.*

> Et quia actio de predicto Tenemento petendo & etiam suum recuperare, si quid habere debeat vel possit eidem Adæ per Assisam mortis Antecessoris competere debet nec est juri consonum vel hactenus in Curia ista usitat' quod aliquis sine Lege Communi, & Brevi de Cancellaria de libero Tenemento suo respondeat & maxime in Casu ubi Breve de Cancellaria Locum habere potest, dictum est præfato Adæ quod sibi perquirat per Breve de Cancellaria, si sibi viderit Expedire.

Rot. Parl. 13 R. 2. No. 10. Adam Chaucer preferr'd his Petition to the King and Lords in Parliament, against Sir Robert

Knolles, to be relieved touching a Mortgage, which he supported was satisfied, and to have Restitution of his Lands. The Defendant appeared, and upon the several Allegations on both Sides, the Judgment is thus entered, *viz.*

> Et apres les Raisons & les Allegeances de l'un party & de l'autre, y sembles a Seigneurs du Parlement que le dit Petition ne estoit Petition du Parlement, deins que le mattier en icel comprize *dovit estre discuss* per le Commune Ley. St pur ceo agard suit que le dit Robert iroit eut sans jour & que le dit Adam ne prendroit rien per say suit icy, eins que il sueroit per le Commune Ley si il luy sembloit ceo faire.

Where we may note, the Words are *Dovit estre,* and not *Poet estre discusse per le,* &c.

Rot. Parl. 50 Ed. 3. *No.* 43. A Judgment being given against the Bishop of Norwich, for the Archdeaconry of Norwich, in the Common Bench, the Bishop petitioned the Lords in Parliament, that the Record might be brought into that House, and to be reversed for Error.

> Et quoy a luy estoit finalement Respondu per common Assent des ils les Justices que si Error y fust si ascun a fine force per le Ley de Angleterre tiel Error fuit voire en Parlement immediatement per voy de Error ains en Bank le Roy, & en nul part ailhors, Mais si le Case avenoit que Error fust fait en Bank le Roy adonque ceo serra amendes en Parlement.

And let any Man but look over the Rolls of Parliament, and the Bundles of Petitions in Parliament, of the Times of Ed. 1. Ed. 2. Ed. 3. Hen. 4. H. 5. & H. 6. he will find Hundreds of Answers of Petitions in Parliament concerning Matters determinable at Common Law, endorsed with Answers to this, or the like Effect, *viz* "Suez vous a le Commune Ley; sequatur ad Communem Legem; Perquirat Breve in Cancellaria si sibi viderit expedire; ne est Petition du Parlement, Mandetur ista Petitio in Cancellarium, vel Cancellario, vel Justiciariis de Banco, vel Thesaurario & Baronibus de Scaccario," and the like.

And these were not barely upon the *Bene placita* of the Lords, but were *De jure,* as appears by those former Judgments given in the Lords House in Parliament; and the Reason is evident;

First, Because, if such a Course of extraordinary Proceeding should be had before the Lords in the first Instance, the Party should lose the Benefit of his Appeal by Writ of Error, according as the Law allows; and that is the Reason, why even in a Writ of Error, or Petition of Error upon a Judgment in any inferior Court, it cannot go *per Saltum* into Parliament, till it has passed the Court of *King's-Bench;* for that the first appeal is thither. *Secondly,* Because the Subject would by that Means lose his Trial *per Pares,* and consequently his Attaint, in case of a Mistake in Point of Issue or Damages: To both which he is entitled by Law.

And although some Petitions of this Nature have been determined in that Manner, yet it has been (generally) when the Exception has not been started, or at least not insisted upon: And One Judgment in Parliament, that Cases of that Nature ought to be determined according to the Course of the Common Law, is of greater Weight than many Cases to the contrary, wherein the Question was not stirred: Yea, even tho' it should be stirred, and the contrary affirm'd upon a Debate of the Question, because greater Weight is to be laid upon the Judgment of any Court when it is exclusive of its Jurisdiction, than upon a Judgment of the same Court in Affirmance of it.

Now as to Matters Criminal, whether Capital or not, they are determinable by the Common Law, and not otherwise; and in Affirmance of that Law, where the Statutes of *Magna Charta,* cap. 29. 5 Ed. 3. *cap.* 9. 25 Ed. 3. *cap.* 4. 29 Ed. 3. *cap.* 3. 27 Ed. 3. *cap.* 17. 38 Ed. 3. *cap.* 9. & 40 Ed. 3. *cap.* 3. The Effect of which is, That no Man shall be put out of his Lands or Tenements, or be imprisoned by any Suggestion, unless it be by Indictment or Presentment of lawful Men, or by Process at Common Law.

And by the Statute of 1 Hen. 4. *cap.* 14. it is enacted, That no Appeals be sued in Parliament at any Time to come: This extends to all Accusations by particular Persons, and that not only of Treason or Felony, but of other Crimes and Misdemeanors. It is true, the Petition upon which that Act was drawn up, begins with Appeals of Felony and Treason, but the Close thereof, as also the King's Answer, refers as well to Misdemeanors as Matters Capital; and because this Record will give a great Light to this whole Business, I will here set down the Petition and the Answer verbatim. *Vide Rot. Parl.* 1 Hen. 4. *No.* 144.

> *Item,* Supplyont les Commens que desore en avant nul appele de Traison ne de autre Felony quelconq; soit accept ou receive en le Parlement ains en vous autres Courts de dans vostre Realm dementiers que en vous dits Courts purra estre Terminer come ad ote fait & use ancienement en temps de vous noble Progeniteurs; Et que chescun Person qui en temps a venir serra accuse ou impeach en vostre Parlement ou en ascuns des vos dits Courts per les Seigniors & Commens di vostre Realm ou per ascun Person & defence ou Response a son Accusement ou Empeachment & sur son Response reasonable Record Judgment & Tryal come de ancienement temps ad estre fait & use per les bones Leges de vostre Realm, nient obstant que les dits Empeachments ou Accusements soient faits per les Seigneurs ou Commens de vostre Relme come que de novel en temps de Ric. nadgarius Roy ad estre fait & use a contrar, a tres grand Mischief & tres grand Maleveys Exemple de vostre Realm.

> Le Roy voet que de cy en avant touts les Appeles de choses faits deins le Relme soient tryez & terminez per les bones Leys faits en temps de tres noble Progeniteurs de nostre dit Seigneur le Roy, Et que touts les Appeles de choses faits hors du Realm, soient triez & terminez devant le Constable & Marshal de Angleterre, & que nul Appele soit fait en Parlement desore en ascun tempts a venir.

This is the Petition and Answer. The Statute as drawn up hereupon, is *general,* and runs thus:

> *Item,* Pur plusieurs grands Inconveniencies & Mischeifs que plusieurs fait ont advenus per colour des plusieurs Appeles faits deins le Realm avant ces heurs ordain est & establuz, Que desore en avant touts Appeles de choses faits deins le Realm soient tries & termines per les bones Leys de le Realm faits & uses en temps de tres noble Progeniteurs de dit nostre Seigneur le Roy; Et que ils les Appeles de choses faits hors du Realm soient tries & termines devant le Constable & Marshal pur les temps esteant; Et ouster accordes est & assentus que nulls Appeles soient desore faits ou pursues en Parlement en nul temps avenir.

Where we may observe, That though the Petition expresses (only) Treason and Felony, yet the Act is general against all

Appeals in Parliament; and many Times the Purview of an Act is larger than the Preamble, or the Petition, and so 'tis here: For the Body of the Act prohibits all Appeals in Parliament, and there was Reason for it: For the Mischief, *viz.* Appeals in Parliament in the Time of King Richard 2. (as in the Petition is set forth) were not only of Treason and Felony, but of Misdemeanors also, as appears by that great Proceeding, 11 R. 2. against divers, by the Lords Appellants, and consequently it was necessary to have the Remedy as large as the Mischief. And I do not remember that after this Statute there were any Appeals in Parliament, either for Matters Capital or Criminal, at the Suit of any Particular Person or Persons.

It is true, Impeachments by the House of Commons, sent up to the House of Lords, were frequent as well after as before this Statute, and that justly, and with good Reason; for that neither the Act nor the Petition ever intended to restrain them, but only to regulate them, *viz.* That the Parties might be admitted to their Defence to them, and as neither the Words of the Act nor the Practice of After-times extended to restrain such Impeachments as were made by the House of Commons, so neither do those Impeachments and Appeals agree in their Nature or Reason; for Appeals were nothing else but Accusations, either of Capital or Criminal Misdemeanors, made in the Lords House by particular Persons; but an Impeachment is made by the Body of the House of Commons, which is equivalent to an Indictment *pro Corpore Regni,* and therefore is of another Nature than an Accusation or Appeal, only herein they agree, *viz.* Impeachments in Cases Capital against Peers of the Realm, have been ever tried and determined in the Lords House; but Impeachments against a Commoner have not been usual in the House of Lords, unless preparatory to a Bill, or to direct an Indictment in the Courts below: But Impeachments at the Prosecutions of the House of Commons, for Misdemeanors as well against a Commoner as any other, have usually received their Determinations and final Judgments in the House of Lords; whereof there have been numerous Precedents in all Times, both before and since the said Act.

And thus much in general touching the great Regard that Parliaments and the Kingdom have had, and that most justly, to the Common Law, and the great Care they have had to preserve and maintain it, as the Common Interest and Birthright of the King and Kingdom.

I shall now add some few Words touching the Stiles and Appellations of the Common Law, and the Reasons of it: 'Tis called sometimes by Way of Eminence, *Lex Terræ,* as in the Statute of *Magna Charta, cap.* 29. where certainly the Common Law is at least principally intended by those Words, *aut per Legem Terræ,* as appears by the Exposition thereof in several subsequent Statutes, and particularly in the Statute 28 Ed. 3. *cap.* 3 which is but an Exposition and Declaration of that Statute: Sometimes 'tis called, *Lex Angliæ,* as in the Statute of Merton, *cap. . . . Nolumus Leges Angliæ mutare,* &c. Sometimes 'tis called, *Lex & Consuetudo Regni,* as in all Commissions of *Oyer* and *Terminer,* and in the Statutes of 18 Ed. 1. *cap. . . .* and *De quo Warranto,* and divers others; but most commonly 'tis called, *The Common Law,* or, *The Common Law of England,* as in the Statute of *Articuli super Chartas, cap.* 15. in the Statute 25 Ed. 3. *cap.* 5. and infinite more Records and Statutes.

Now the Reason why 'tis call'd *The Common Law,* or what was the Occasion that first gave that Determination to it, is variously assigned, *viz.*

First, Some have thought it to be so called by Way of Contradistinction to those other Laws that have obtain'd within this Kingdom; as, *1st.* By Way of Contradistinction to the Statute Law, thus a Writ of Entry *ad Communem Legem,* is so call'd in Contradistinction to Writs of Entry in *Casu consimili,* and *Casu proviso,* which are given by Act of Parliament. *2dly,* By Way of Contradistinction to particular Customary Laws: Thus Discents at Common Law, Dower at Common Law, are in Contradistinction to such Dowers and Discents as are directed by particular Customs. And *3dly,* In Contradistinction to the Civil, Canon, Martial and Military Laws, which are in some particular Cases and Courts admitted, as the Rule of their Proceedings.

Secondly, Some have conceived, that the Reason of this Appellation was this, *viz.* In the Beginning of the Reign of Edward 3. before the Conquest, commonly called, Edward the Confessor, there were several Laws, and of several Natures, which obtain'd in several Parts of this Kingdom, *viz.* The *Mercian* Laws, in the Counties of Gloucester, Worcester, Hereford, Warwick, Oxon, Chester, Salop and Stafford. The *Danish* Laws, in the Counties of York, Derby, Nottingham, Leicester, Lincoln, Northampton, Bedford, Bucks, Hertford, Essex, Middlesex, Norfolk, Suffolk, Cambridge and Huntington. The *West-Saxon* Laws, in the Counties of Kent, Sussex, Surrey, Berks, Southampton, Wilts, Somerset, Dorset, and Devon.

This King, to reduce the Kingdom as well under one Law, as it then was under one Monarchical Government, extracted out of all those Provincial Laws, one Law to be observed through the whole Kingdom: Thus *Ranulphus Cestrensis,* cited by Sir Henry Spelman in his *Glossary,* under the Title *Lex,* says, "Ex tribus his Legibus Sanctus Edvardus unam Legem——" &c. And the same in *totidem verbis,* is affirmed in his History of the last Year of the same King Edward. (*Vide ibid. plura de hoc.*) But Hoveden carries up the *Common Laws,* or those stiled the *Confessor's Laws,* much further; for he in his History of Henry 2. tell us, "Quod istæ Leges prius inventæ & constitutæ erant Tempore Edgari, Avi sui," &c. (*Vide* Hoveden.) And possibly the Grandfather might be the first Collector of them into a Body, and afterwards Edward might add to the Composition, and give it the Denomination of the Common Law; but the Original of it cannot in Truth be referred to either, but is much more ancient, and is as undiscoverable as the Head of Nile: Of which more at large in the following Chapter.

Thirdly, Others say, and that most truly, That it is called the Common Law, because it is the common Municipal Law or Rule of Justice in this Kingdom: So that *Lex Communis,* or *Jus Communis,* is all one and the same with *Lex Patriæ,* or *Jus Patrium;* for although there are divers particular Laws, some by Custom applied to particular Places, and some to particular Causes; yet that Law which is common to the generality of all Persons, Things and Causes, and has a Superintendency over those particular Laws that are admitted in Relation to particular Places or Matters, is *Lex Communis Angliæ,* as the Municipal Laws of other Countries may be, and are sometimes called, *The Common Law of that Country;* as *Lex Communis Norrica, Lex Communis*

37

Burgundica, Lex Communis Lombardica, &c. So that although
all the former Reasons have their Share in this Appellation, yet
the principal Cause thereof seems to be the latter: And hence
some of the Ancients call'd it *Lex Communis,* others *Lex Patriæ;*
and so they were called in their Confirmation by King William 1.
Whereof hereafter.

IV

Touching the Original of the Common Law of England

The Kingdom of England being a very ancient Kingdom, has had many Vicissitudes and Changes (especially before the coming in of King William 1.) under several either Conquests or Accessions of Foreign Nations. For tho' the Britains were, as is supposed, the most ancient Inhabitants, yet there were mingled with them, or brought in upon them, the Romans, the Picts, the Saxons, the Danes, and lastly, the Normans; and many of those Foreigners were as it were incorporated together, and made one Common People and Nation; and hence arises the Difficulty, and indeed Moral Impossibility, of giving any satisfactory or so much as probable Conjecture, touching the Original of the Laws, for the following Reasons, *viz.*

First, From the Nature of Laws themselves in general, which being to be accommodated to the Conditions, Exigencies and Conveniencies of the People, for or by whom they are appointed, as those Exigencies and Conveniencies do insensibly grow upon the People, so many Times there grows insensibly a Variation of Laws, especially in a long Tract of Time; and hence it is, that tho' for the Purpose in some particular Part of the Common Law of England, we may easily say, That the Common Law, as it is now taken, is otherwise than it was in that particular Part or Point in the Time of Hen. 2. when Glanville wrote, or than it was in the time of Hen. 3. when Bracton wrote, yet it is not possible to assign the certain Time when the Change began; nor have we all the Monuments or Memorials, either of Acts of Parliament, or of Judicial Resolutions, which might induce or occasion such Alterations; for we have no authentick Records of any Acts of Parliament before 9 Hen. 3. and those we have of that King's Time, are but few. Nor have we any Reports of Judicial Decisions in any constant Series of Time before the Reign of Edw. 1. tho' we have the Plea Rolls of the Times of Hen. 3. and King John, in some remarkable Order. So that Use and Custom, and Judicial Decisions and Resolutions, and Acts of Parliament, tho' not now extant, might introduce some *New* Laws, and alter some *Old,* which we now take to be the very Common Law itself, tho' the Times and precise Periods of such Alterations are not explicitely or clearly known: But tho' those particular Variations and Accessions have happened in the Laws, yet they being only partial and successive, we may with just Reason say, They are the same English Laws now, that they were 600 Years since in the general. As the Argonauts Ship was the same when it returned home, as it was when it went out, tho' in that long Voyage it had successive Amendments, and scarce came back with any of its former Materials; and as Titius is the same Man he was 40 Years since, tho' Physicians tells us, That in a Tract of seven Years, the Body has scarce any of the same Material Substance it had before.

Secondly, The 2d Difficulty in the Search of the Antiquity of Laws and their Original, is in Relation to that People unto whom the Laws are applied, which in the Case of England, will render many Observables, to shew it hard to be traced. For,

1st, It is an ancient Kingdom, and in such Cases, tho' the People and Government had continued the same *ab Origine* (as they say the Chinese did, till the late Incursion of the Tartars) without the Mixture of other People, or Laws; yet it were an impossible Thing to give any certain Account of the Original of the Laws of such a People, unless we had as certain Monuments thereof as the Jews had of theirs, by the Hand of Moses, and that upon the following Accounts, *viz.*

First, We have not any clear and certain Monuments of the original Foundation of the English Kingdom or State, when, and by whom, and how it came to be planted. That which we have concerning it, is uncertain and traditional; and since we cannot know the Original of the planting of this Kingdom, we cannot certainly know the Original of the Laws thereof, which may be well presum'd to be very near as ancient as the Kingdom itself. Again, *2dly,* Tho' Tradition might be a competent Discoverer of the Original of a Kingdom or State, I mean Oral Tradition, yet such a Tradition were incompetent without written Monuments to derive to us, at so long a Distance, the original Laws and Constitutions of the Kingdom, because they are of a complex Nature, and therefore not orally traducible to so great a Distance of Ages, unless we had the original or authentick Transcript of those Laws as the People the Jews had of their Law, or as the Romans had of their Laws of the Twelve Tables engraven in Brass. But yet further, *3dly,* It is very evident to every Day's Experience, that Laws, the further they go from their original Institution, grow the larger, and the more numerous: In the first Coalition of a People, their Prospect is not great, they provide Laws for their present Exigence and Convenience: But in Process of Time, possibly their first Laws are changed, altered or antiquated, as some of the Laws of the Twelve Tables among the Romans were: But whatsoever be done touching their *Old* Laws, there must of Necessity be a Provision of *New,* and other Laws successively answering to the Multitude of successive Exigencies and Emergencies, that in a long Tract of Time will offer themselves; so that if a Man could at this Day have the Prospects of all the Laws of the Britains before any Invasion upon them, it would yet be impossible to say, which of them were *New,* and which were *Old,* and the several Seasons and Periods of Time wherein every Law took its Rise and Original, especially since it appears, that in those elder Times, the Britains were not reduced to that civiliz'd Estate, as to keep the Annals and Memorials of their Laws and Government, as the Romans and other civiliz'd Parts of the World have done.

It is true, when the Conquest of a Country appears, we can tell when the Laws of conquering People came to be given to the Conquered. Thus we can tell that in the Time of Hen. 2. when the Conquest of Ireland had obtain'd a good Progress, and in the Time of K. John, when it was compleated, the English Laws were settled in Ireland: But if we were upon this Inquiry, what were the Original of those English Laws that were thus settled there; we are still under the same Quest and Difficulty that we are now, *viz.* What is the Original of the English Laws.

41

For they that begin *New* Colonies, Plantations and Conquests; if they settle *New* Laws, and which the Places had not before, yet for the most Part (I don't say altogether) they are the Old Laws which obtain'd in those Countries from whence the Conquerors or Planters came.

Secondly, the 2d Difficulty of the Discovery of the Original of the English Laws is this, That this Kingdom has had many and great Vicissitudes of People that inhabited it, and that in their several Times prevail'd and obtain'd a great Hand in the Government of this Kingdom, whereby it came to pass, that there arose a great Mixture and Variety of Laws: In some Places the Laws of the Saxons, in some Places the Laws of the Danes, in some Places the Laws of the ancient Britains, in some Places, the Laws of the Mercians, and in some Places, or among some People (perhaps) the Laws of the Normans: For altho', as I shall shew hereafter, the Normans never obtain'd this Kingdom by such a Right of Conquest, as did or might alter the established Laws of the Kingdom; yet considering that K. Will. 1. brought with him a great Multitude of that Nation, and many Persons of great Power and Eminence, which were planted generally over this Kingdom, especially in the Possessions of such as had oppos'd his coming in, it must needs be suppos'd, that those Occurrences might easily have a great Influence upon the Laws of this Kingdom, and secretly and insensibly introduce New Laws, Customs and Usages; so that altho' the Body and Gross of the Law might continue the same, and so continue the ancient Denomination that it first had, yet it must needs receive diverse Accessions from the Laws of those People that were thus intermingled with the ancient Britains or Saxons, as the Rivers of Severn, Thames, Trent, &c. tho' they continue the same Denomination which their first Stream had, yet have the Accession of divers other Streams added to them in the Tracts of their Passage which enlarge and augment them. And hence grew those several Denominations of the Saxon, Merician, and Danish Laws, out of which (as before is shewn) the Confessor extracted his Body of the Common Law, and therefore among all those various Ingredients and Mixtures of Laws, it is almost an impossible Piece of Chymistry to reduce every *Caput Legis* to its true Original, as to say, This is a Piece of the Danish, this of the Norman, or this of the Saxon or British Law: Neither was it, or indeed is it much material, which of these is their Original; for 'tis very plain, the Strength and Obligation, and the formal Nature of a Law, is not upon Account that the Danes, or the Saxons, or the Normans, brought it in with them, but they became Laws, and binding in this Kingdom, by Virtue only of their being received and approved here.

Thirdly, A Third Difficulty arises from those accidental Emergencies that happened, either in the Alteration of Laws, or communicating or conveying of them to this Kingdom: For first, the Subdivision of the Kingdom into small Kingdoms under the Heptarchy, did most necessarily introduce a Variation of Laws, because the several Parts of the Kingdom, were not under one common Standard, and so it will soon be in any Kingdoms that are cantonized, and not under one common Method of Dispensation of Laws, tho' under one and the same King. *Again,* The Intercourse and Traffick with other Nations, as it grew more or greater, did gradually make a Communication and Transmigration of Laws from us to them, and from them to us. *Again,* The Growth of Christianity in this Kingdom, and the Reception of Learned Men from other Parts, especially from Rome, and the Credit that they obtained here, might reasonably introduce some *New* Laws, and antiquate or abrogate some *Old* ones that seem'd less consistent with the Christian Doctrines, and by this Means, not only some of the Judicial Laws of the Jews, but also some Points relating to, or bordering upon, or derived from the Canon or Civil Laws, as may be seen in those Laws of the ancient Kings, Ina, Alphred, Canutus, &c. collected by Mr. Lambard.

Having thus far premised, it seems, upon the whole Matter, an endless and insuperable Business to carry up the English Laws to their several Springs and Heads, and to find out their first Original; neither would it be of any Moment or Use if it were done: For whenever the Laws of England, or the several *Capita* thereof began, or from whence or whomsoever derived, or what Laws of other Countries contributed to the Matter of our Laws; yet most certainly their Obligation arises not from their Matter, but from their Admission and Reception, and Authorization in this Kingdom; and those Laws, if convenient and useful for the Kingdom, were never the worse, tho' they were desumed and taken from the Laws of other Countries, so as they had their Stamp of Obligation and Authority from the Reception and Approbation of this Kingdom by Virtue of the Common Law, of which this Kingdom has been always jealous, especially in relation to the Canon, Civil, and Norman Law, for the Reasons hereafter shewn.

Passing therefore from this unsearchable Inquiry, I shall descend to that which gives the Authority, *viz.* The formal Constituents, as I may call them, of the Common Law, and they seem to be principally, if not only, those three, *viz. 1st.* The Common Usage, or Custom, and Practice of this Kingdom, in such Parts thereof as lie in Usage or Custom. *2dly.* The Authority of Parliament, introducing such Laws; and, *3dly.* The Judicial Decisions of Courts of Justice, consonant to one another in the Series and Successions of Time.

1. As to the first of these, Usage and Custom generally receiv'd, do *Obtinere vim Legis,* and is that which gives Power sometimes to the Canon Law, as in the Ecclesiastical Courts; sometimes to the Civil Law, as in the Admiralty Courts; and again, controuls both, when they cross other Customs that are generally receiv'd in the Kingdom. This is that which directs Discents, has settled some ancient Ceremonies and Solemnities in Conveyances, Wills and Deeds, and in many more Particulars. And if it be enquired, What is the Evidence of this Custom, or wherein it consists, or is to be found? I answer, It is not simply an unwritten Custom, not barely *Orally* deriv'd down from one Age to another; but it is a Custom that is derived down in Writing, and transmitted from Age to Age, especially since the Beginning of Edw. 1. to whose Wisdom the Laws of England owe almost as much as the Laws of Rome to Justinian.

2. Acts of Parliament. And here it must not be wonder'd at, that I make Acts of Parliament one of the Authoritative Constituents of the Common Law, tho' I had before contradistinguished the one from the other; for we are to know, that although the Original or Authentick Transcripts of Acts of Parliament are not before the Time of Hen. 3. and many that were in his Time are perish'd and lost; yet certainly such there were, and many of those Things that we now take for Common Law, were undoubtedly Acts of Parliament, tho' now not to be found of Record. And if in the next Age, the Statutes made in the Time of Hen. 3. and

Edw. 1. were lost, yet even those would pass for Parts of the Common Law, and indeed, by long Usage and the many Resolutions grounded upon them, and by their great Antiquity, they seem even already to be incorporated with the very Common Law; and that this is so, may appear, tho' not by Records, for we have none so ancient, yet by an authentical and unquestionable History, wherein a Man may, without Much Difficulty, find, That many of those *Capitala Legum* that are now used and taken for Common Law, were things enacted in Parliaments or Great Councils under William 1. and his Predecessors, Kings of England, as may be made appear hereafter. But yet, those Constitutions and Laws being made before Time of Memory, do now obtain, and are taken as Part of the Common Law and immemorial Customs of the Kingdom; and so they ought now to be esteem'd tho' in their first Original they were Acts of Parliament.

3. Judicial Decisions. It is true, the Decisions of Courts of Justice, tho' by Virtue of the Laws of this Realm they do bind, as a Law between the Parties thereto, as to the particular Case in Question, 'till revers'd by Error or Attaint, yet they do not make a Law properly so called, (for that only the King and Parliament can do); yet they have a great Weight and Authority in Expounding, Declaring, and Publishing what the Law of this Kingdom is, especially when such Decisions hold a Consonancy and Congruity with Resolutions and Decisions of former Times; and tho' such Decisions are less than a Law, yet they are a greater Evidence thereof than the Opinion of any private Persons, as such, whatsoever.

1st. Because the Persons who pronounce those Decisions, are Men chosen by the King for that Employment, as being of greater Learning, Knowledge, and Experience in the Laws than others. *2dly.* Because they are upon their Oaths to judge according to the Laws of the Kingdom. *3dly.* Because they have the best Helps to inform their Judgments. *4thly.* Because they do *Sedere pro Tribunali,* and their Judgments are strengthen'd and upheld by the Laws of this Kingdom, till they are by the same Law revers'd or avoided.

Now Judicial Decisions, as far as they refer to the Laws of this Kingdom, are for the Matter of them of Three Kinds:

First, They are either such as have their reasons singly in the Laws and Customs of this Kingdom, as, Who shall succeed as Heir to the Ancestor, what is the Ceremony requisite for passing a Freehold, what Estate, and how much shall the Wife have for her Dower? And many such Matters wherein the ancient and express Laws of the Kingdom give an express Decision, and the Judge seems only the instrument to pronounce it; and in these Things, the Law or custom of the Realm is the only Rule and Measure to judge by, and in reference to those Matters, the Decisions of Courts are the Conservatories and Evidences of those Laws.

Secondly, Or they are such Decisions, as by Way of Deduction and Illation upon those Laws are framed or deduced; as for the Purpose, Whether of an Estate thus or thus limited, the Wife shall be endowed? Whether if thus or thus limited, the Heir may be barr'd? And infinite more of the like complicated Questions. And herein the Rule of Decision is, First, the Common Law and Custom of the Realm, which is the great *Substratum* that is to be maintain'd; and then Authorities or Decisions of former Times in the same or the like Cases, and then the Reason of the Thing itself.

Thirdly, Or they are such as seem to have no other Guide but the common Reason of the Thing, unless the same Point has been formally decided, as in the Exposition of the Intention of Clauses in Deeds, Wills, Covenants, &c. where the very Sense of the Words, and their Positions and Relations, give a rational Account of the Meaning of the Parties, and in such Cases the Judge does much better herein, than what a bare grave Grammarian or Logician, or other prudent Men could do; for in many Cases there have been former Resolutions, either in Point or agreeing in Reason or Analogy with the Case in Question; or perhaps also, the Clause to be expounded is mingled with some Terms or Clauses that require the Knowledge of the Law to help out with the Construction or Exposition: Both which do often happen in the same Case, and therefore it requires the Knowledge of the Law to render and expound such Clauses and Sentences; and doubtless a good Common Lawyer is the best Expositor of such Clauses, &c. *Vide* Plowden, 122, to 130, 140, &c.

V

How the Common Law of England stood at and for some Time after the coming in of King William 1.

It is the Honour and Safety, and therefore the just Desire of Kingdoms that recognize no Superior but God, that their Laws have those two Qualifications, *viz. 1st.* That they be not dependent upon any Foreign Power; for a Dependency in Laws derogates from the Honour and Integrity of the Kingdom, and from the Power and Sovereignty of the Prince thereof. *Secondly,* That they taste not of Bondage or Servitude; for that derogates from the Dignity of the Kingdom, and from the Liberties of the People thereof.

In Relation to the former Consideration, the Kings of this Realm, and their great Councils, have always been jealous and careful, that they admitted not any Foreign Power, (especially such as pretended Authority to improve Laws upon other free Kingdoms or States) nor to countenance the Admission of such Laws here as were derived from such a Power.

Rome, as well Ancient as Modern, pretended a kind of universal Power and Interest; the former by their Victories, which were large, and extended even to Britain itself; and the later upon the Pretence of being Universal Bishop or Vicar-General in all Matters Ecclesiastical; so that upon Pretence of the former, the Civil Law, and upon Pretence of the later, the Canon Law was introduc'd, or pretended to some Kind of Right in the Territories of some absolute Princes, and among others here in England: But this kingdom has been always very jealous of giving too much Countenance to either of those Laws, and has always shewn a just

Indignation and Resentment against any Encroachments of this Kind, either by the one Law or the other. It is true, as before is shewn, that in the Admiralty and Military Courts, the Civil Law has been admitted, and in the Ecclesiastical Courts, the Canon Law has been in some Particulars admitted. But still they carry such Marks and Evidences about them, whereby it may be known that they bind not, nor have the Authority of Laws from themselves, but from the authoritative Admission of this Kingdom.

And, as thus the Kingdom, for the Reasons before given, never admitted the Civil or the Canon Law to be the Rule of the Administration of Common Justice in this Kingdom; so neither has it endured any Laws to be imposed upon the People by any Right of Conquest, as being unsuitable to the Honour or Liberty of the English Kingdom, to recognize their Laws as given them at the Will and Pleasure of a Conqueror. And hence it was, that altho' the People unjustly assisted King Hen. 4. in his Usurpation of the Crown, yet he was not admitted thereunto, until he had declared, that he claimed not as a Conqueror, but as a Successor; only he reserved to himself the Liberty of extending a Pretence of Conquest against the Scroops that were slain in Battle against him; which yet he durst not rest upon without a Confirmation in Parliament. *Vide Rot. Parl.* 1 H. 4. *No.* 56. & *Pars* 2. *Ibid.* No 17.

And upon the like Reason it was, That King William 1. tho' he be called the Conqueror, and his attaining the Crown here, is often in History, and in some Records, called *Conquestus Angliæ;* yet in Truth it was not such a Conquest as did, or could alter the Laws of this Kingdom, or impose Laws upon the People *per Modum Conquestus,* or *Jure Belli:* And therefore, to wipe off that false Imputation upon our Laws, as if they were the Fruit or Effect of a Conquest, or carried in them the Badge of Servitude to the Will of the Conqueror, which Notion some ignorant and prejudiced Persons have entertain'd; I shall rip up, and lay open this whole Business from the Bottom, and to that End enquire into the following Particulars, *viz.*

1. Of the Thing called Conquest, what it is, when attained, and the Rights thereof.

2. Of the several Kinds of Conquest, and their Effects, as to the Alteration of Laws by the Victor.

48

3. How the English Laws stood at the Entry of King William the First.

4. By what Title he entred, and whether by such a Right of Conquest as did, or could, alter the English Laws.

5. Whether *De Facto* there was any Alteration of the said Laws, and by what Means after his coming in.

First, Touching the first of these, *viz.* Conquest, what it is, when attain'd, and the Rights thereof. It is true, That it seems to be admitted as a kind of Law among all Nations, That in Case of a Solemn War between Supream Princes, the Conqueror acquires a Right of Dominion, as well as a Property over the Things and Persons that are fully conquered; and the Reasons assign'd are Principally these, *viz.*

1st. Because both Parties have apealed to the highest Tribunal that can be, *viz.* The Trial by War, wherein the great Judge and Sovereign of the World, *The Lord of Hosts,* seems in a more especial Manner than in other Cases to decide the Controversy. *2dly.* Because unless this should be a final Decision, Mankind would be destroy'd by endless Broils, Wars and Contentions; therefore, for the Preservation of Mankind, this great Decision ought to be final, and the conquer'd ought to acquiesce in it. *3dly.* Because if this should not be admitted, and be by, as it were, the tacit Consent of Mankind accounted a lawful Acquisition, there would not be any Security or Peace under any Government: For by the various Revolutions of Dominion acquired by this Means, have been, and are to this Day the Successions of Kingdoms and States preserved. What was once the Romans, was before that the Græcians, and before them the Persians, and before the Persians, the Assyrians; and if this just Victory were not allowed to be a firm Acquest of Dominion, the present Possessors would be still obnoxious to the Claim of the former Proprietors, and so they would be in a restless State of Doubts, Difficulties and Changes upon the Pretention of former Claims: Therefore, to cut off this Instability and Unsettledness in Dominion and Property, it would seem that the common Consent of all Nations has tacitly submitted, that Acquisition by Right of Conquest, in a Solemn War between Persons not Subjects of each other by Bonds of Allegiance or Fidelity, should be allowed as one of the lawful Titles of acquiring Dominion over the Persons, Places and Things so conquer'd.

But whatever be the real Truth or Justice of this Position, yet we are much at a Loss touching the Things in *Hypothesi, viz.* Whether this be the Effect of every Kind of Conquest? Whether the War be Just or Unjust? What are the Requisites to the Constituting of a just War? Who are the Persons that may acquire? And what are the Solemnities requisite for that Acquest? But above all, the greatest Difficulty is, when there shall be said, Such a Victory as acquires this Right? Indeed, if there be a total Deletion of every Person of the Opposing Party or Country, then the Victory is compleat, because none remains to call it in Question. But suppose they are beaten in one Battle, may they not rally again? Or if the greater Part be subdued, may not the lesser keep their Ground? Or if they do not at the present, may they not in the next Age regain their Liberty? Or if they be quiet for a Time, may they not as they have Opportunity, renew their Pretentions? And altho' the Victor, by his Power, be able to quell and suppress them, yet he is beholden to his Sword for it, and the Right that he got by his Victory before, would not be sufficient without a Power and Force to establish and secure him against new Troubles. And on the other Side, if those few subdu'd Persons can by Force regain what they once had a Pretence to, a former Victory will be but a weak Defence; and if it would, they would have the like Pretence to a Claim of Acquest by Victory over him, as he had over them.

It seems therefore a difficult Thing to determine in what indivisible Moment this Victory is so compleat, that *Jure Belli* the Acquest of Dominion is fully gotten, and therefore Victors use to secure themselves against Disputes of that Kind, and as it were to under-pin their Acquest *Jure Belli,* that they might not be lost by the same Means, whereby they were gained by the Continuation of eternal Forces of Standing Armies, Castles, Garrisons, Munitions, and other Acts of Power and Force, so as thereby to over-bear and prevent an ordinary Possibility of the Prevailing of the conquered or subdued People, against the Conqueror or Victor. He that lays the Weight of his Title upon Victory or Conquest, rarely rests in it as a compleat Conquest, till he has added to it somewhat of Consent or Faith of the conquered, submitting voluntarily to him, and then, and not till then, he thinks his Title secure, and his Conquest compleat: And indeed, he has no Reason to think his Title can be otherwise secure; for where the Title is meerly Force or Power, his Title will fail, if the conquered can with like Force or Power over-match his, and to regain their former Interest or Dominion.

Now this Consent is of Two Kinds, either Express'd, or Imply'd. An express Consent is, when after a Victory the Party conquered do expresly submit themselves to the Victors, either simply or absolutely, by Dedition, yielding themselves, giving him their Faith and their Allegiance; or else under certain Pacts, Conventions, Agreements, or Capitulations, as when the subdued Party, either by themselves, or by Substitutes, or Delegates by them chosen, do yield their Faith and their Allegiance to the Victor upon certain Pacts or Agreements between them; as for holding or continuing their Religion, their Laws, their Form of Civil Administration, &c.

And thus, tho' Force were perhaps the Occasion of this Consent, yet in Truth 'tis Consent only that is the true proximate and fix'd Foundation of the Victor's Right; which now no longer rests barely upon external Force, but upon the express Consent and Pact of the subdu'd People, and consequently this Pact or Convention is that which is to be the immediate Foundation of that Dominion; and upon a diligent Observation of Most Acquests gotten by Conquest, or so called, we shall find this to be the Conclusion of almost all Victories, they end in Deditions and Capitulations, and Faith given to the Conqueror, whereby oftentimes the former Laws, Privileges, and Possessions are confirmed to the Subdued, without which the Victors seldom continue long or quiet in their New Acquests, without extream Expence, Force, Severity and Hazard.

An implied Consent is, when the Subdued do continue for a long Time quiet and peaceable under the Government of the Victor, accepting his Government, submitting to his Laws, taking upon them the Offices and Employments under him, and obeying and owning him as their Governor, without opposing him, or claiming their former Right. This seems to be a tacit Acceptance of, and Assent to him; and tho' this is gradual, and possibly no determinate Time is stinted, wherein a Man can say, this Year,

51

or this Month, or this Day, such a tacit Consent was compleated and concluded: For Circumstances may make great Variations in the Sufficiency of the Evidence of such an Assent; yet by a long and quiet Tract of peaceable Submission to the Laws and Government of the Victor, Men may reasonably conjecture, that the conquered have relinquished their Purpose of regaining by Force what by Force they lost.

But still all this is intended of a lawful Conquest by a Foreign Prince or State, and not an Usurpation by a Subject, either upon his Prince or Fellow Subject; for several Ages and Discents do not purge the Unlawfulness of such an Usurpation.

Secondly. Concerning the several Kinds of Conquests, and their Effects, as to the Alteration of Laws by the Victor. There seems to be a double kind of Conquest, which induces a various Consideration touching the Change of Laws, *viz. Victoria in Regem & Populum, & Victoria in Regem tantum.* The Conquest over the People or Country, is when the War is denounced by a Prince or State Foreign, and no Subject, and when the Intention and Denunciation of the War is against the King and People or Country, and the Pretention of Title is by the Sword, or *Jure Belli;* such were most of the Conquests of ancient Monarchs, *viz.* The Assyrian, Persian, Græcian, and Roman Conquests; and in such Cases, the Acquisitions of the Victor were absolute and universal, he gain'd the Interest and Property of the very Soil of the Country subdued; which the Victor might, at his Pleasure, give, fell or arrent: He gain'd a Power of abolishing or changing their Laws and Customs, and of giving New, or of imposing the Law of the Victor's Country. But although this the Conqueror might do, yet a Change of the Laws of the conquered Country was rarely universally made, especially by the Romans: Who, though in their own particular Colonies planted in conquered Countries, they observed the Roman Law, which possibly might by Degrees, without any rigorous Imposition, gain and insinuate themselves into the conquered People, and so gradually obtain, and insensibly conform them, at least so many of them as were conterminous to the Colonies and Garrisons to the Roman Laws; yet they rarely made a rigorous and universal Change of the Laws of the conquered Country, unless they were such as were foreign and barbarous, or altogether inconsistent with the Victor's Government: But in other Things, they commonly indulged unto the conquered, the Laws and Religion of their Country upon a double Account, *viz.*

First. On Account of Humanity, thinking it a hard and over-severe Thing to impose presently upon the conquered a Change of their Customs, which long Use had made dear to them. And, *2dly.* Upon the Account of Prudence; for the Romans being a wise and experienced People, found that those Indulgences made their Conquests the more easy, and their Enjoyments thereof the more firm, when as a rigorous Change of the Laws and Religion of the People would render them in a restless and unquiet Condition, and ready to lay hold of any Opportunity of Defection or Rebellion, to regain their ancient Laws and Religion, which ordinary People count most dear to them; (though at this Day the Indulgence of a Paganish Religion is not used to be allowed by any Christian Victor, as is observed in Calvin's Case in the Seventh Report;) and to give One Instance for all, it was upon this Account, That though the Romans had wholly subdued Syria and Palestina, yet they allow'd to the Inhabitants the Jews, &c. the Use of their Religion and Laws, so far forth as consisted with the Safety and Security of the Victor's Interest: And therefore, though they reserved to themselves the Cognizance of such Causes as concern'd themselves, their Officers or Revenues, and such Cases as might otherwise disturb the Security of their Empire, as Treasons, Insurrections, and the like; yet 'tis evident they indulged the People of the Jews, &c. to judge by their own Law, not only of some Criminal Proceedings, but even of Capital in some Cases, as appears by the History of the Gospels, and Acts of the Apostles.

But still this was but an Indulgence, and therefore was resumable by the Victor, unless there intervened any Capitulation between the Conqueror and the Conquered to the contrary; which was frequent, especially in those Cases, when it was not a compleat Conquest, but rather a Dedition upon Terms and Capitulations, agreed between the Conqueror and the Conquered; wherein usually the yielding Party secured to themselves, by the Articles of their Dedition, the Enjoyment of their Laws and Religion; and then by the Laws of Nature and of Nations, both which oblige in the Observation of Faith and Promises, those Terms and Capitulations, were to be observed. Again, *2dly.* When after a full Conquest, the conquered People resumed so much Courage and Power as began to put them into a Capacity of regaining their former Laws and Liberties. This commonly was the Occasion of Terms and Capitulations between the Conquerors and Conquered. Again, *3dly.* When by long Succession of Time, the Conquered had either been incorporated with the conquering People, whereby they had worn out the very Marks and Discriminations between the Conquerors and Conquered; and if they continued distinct, yet by a long Prescription, Usage and Custom, the Laws and Rights of the conquered People were in a Manner settled, and the long Permission of the Conquerors amounted to a tacite Concession or Capitulation, for the Enjoyment of their Laws and Liberties.

But of this more than enough is said, because it will appear in what follows, That William 1. never made any such Conquest of England.

Secondly, Therefore I come to the Second Kind of Conquest, *viz.* That which is only *Victoria in Regem:* And this is where the Conqueror either has a real Right to the Crown or chief Government of a Kingdom, or at least has, or makes some Pretence of Claim thereunto; and, in Pursuance of such Claim, raises War, and by his Forces obtains what he so pretends a Title to. Now this Kind of Conquest does only instate the Victor in those Rights of Government, which the conquered Prince, or that Prince to whom the Conqueror pretends a Right of Succession, had; whereby he becomes only a Successor *Jure Belli,* but not a Victor or Conqueror upon the People; and therefore has no more Right of altering their Laws, or taking away their Liberties or Possessions, than the conquered Prince, or the Prince to whom he pretends a Right of Succession, had; for the Intention, Scope and Effect of his Victory extends no further than the Succession, and does not at all affect the Rights of the People. The Conqueror is, as it were, the Plaintiff, and the conquered Prince is the Defendant, and the Claim is a Claim of Title to the Crown; and because each of them pretends a Right to the Sovereignty, and there is no other competent Trial of the Title between them, they put themselves upon the great Trial by Battle; wherein there is nothing in Question touching the Rights of the People, but only touching the Right of the Crown, and that being decided by the Victory, the Victor comes in as a Successor, and not *Jure Victoriæ,* as in relation to the Peoples Rights; the most Sacred whereof are their Laws and Religion.

Indeed, those that do voluntarily assist the conquered Prince, commonly undergo the same Hazard with him, and do, as it were, put their Interest upon the Hazard and Issue of the same Trial, and therefore commonly fall under the same Severity with the conquered, at least *de facto;* because, perchance the Victor thinks he cannot be secure without it: But yet Usage, and indeed common Prudence, makes the Conquerors use great Moderation and Discrimination in relation to the Assistants of the conquered Prince; and to extend this Severity only to the eminent and busy Assistants of the Conquered, and not to the Gregarii, or such as either by Constraint or by Necessity were enforced to serve against him; and as to those also, on whom they exercise their Power, it has been rarely done *Jure Belli aut Victoriæ,* but by a judiciary Proceeding, as in Cases of Treason, because now the great Title by Battle has pronounced for the Right of the Conqueror, and at best no Man must dare to say otherwise now, whatsoever Debility was in his Pretension or Claim. We shall see the Instances hereof in what follows.

Thirdly, As to the Third Point, How the Laws of England stood at the entry of King William 1. and it seems plain, that at the Time of his Entry into England, the Laws, commonly call'd, *The Laws of Edward the Confessor,* were then the standing Laws of the Kingdom. Hoveden tells us, in a Digression under his History of King Henry 2. that those Laws were originally put together by King Edgar, who was the Confessor's Grandfather, *viz.*

Verum tamen post mortem ipsius Regis Edgari usq; ad Coronationem Sancti Regis Edvardi quod-Tempus Continet Sexaginta & Septem Annos prece (vel pretio) Leges sopitæ sunt & Jus prætermissæ sed postquam Rex Edvardus in Regno fuit sublimatus Concilio Baronum Angliæ Legem Annos Sexaginta & Septem

Sopitam, excitavit & confirmavit, & ea lex sic confirmata vocata
est Lex Sancti Edvardi, non quod ipse prius invenisset eam sed
cum prætermissa fuisset & oblivioni penitus dedita a morte avi
sui Regis Edgari qui primus inventor ejus fuisse dicitur usque
ad sua Tempora, viz. Sexaginta & Septem Annos.

And the same Passage in *totidem Verbis* is in the History of
Litchfield, cited in Sir Robert Twisden's Prologue to the Laws of
King William 1. But although possibly those Laws were collected
by King Edgar, yet it is evident, by what is before said, they were
augmented by the Confessor, by that Extract of Laws before-
mentioned, which he made out of that Threefold Law, that obtain'd in several Parts of England, *viz.* The Danish, the Mercian,
and the West-Saxon Laws.

This Manual (as I may call it) of Laws, stiled, *The Confessor's
Laws,* was but a finall Volume, and contains but few Heads, being
rather a Scheme or Directory touching some Method to be observed in the Distribution of Justice, and some particular Proceedings relative thereunto, especially in Matters of Crime, as
appears by the Laws themselves, which are now printed in Mr.
Lambart's Saxon Laws, p. 133. and other Places; yet the English
were very zealous for them, no less or otherwise than they are at
this Time for the Great Charter; insomuch, that they were never
satisfied till the said Laws were reinforced and mingled for the
most Part with the Coronation Oath of King William 1. and
some of his Successors.

And this may serve shortly touching this Third Point, whereby
we see that the Laws that obtain'd at the Time of the Entry of
King William 1. were the English Laws, and principally those
of Edward the Confessor.

Fourthly, The Fourth Particular is, The Pretensions of King
William 1. to the Crown of England, and what kind of Conquest he made; and this will be best rendered and understood
by producing the History of that Business, as it is delivered over
to us by the ancient Historians that lived in or near that Time:
The Sum, or *Totum* whereof, is this.

King Edward the Confessor having no Children, nor like to
have any, had Three Persons related to him, whom he princi-

pally favoured, *viz. 1st.* Edgar Ætheling, the Son of Edward, the Son of Edmond Ironside, *Mat. Paris, Anno* 1066. *Edmundus autem latus serreum Rex naturalis de stirpe Regum genuit Edwardum & Edwardus genuit Edgarum cui dejure debebatur Regnum Anglorum. 2dly.* Harold, the Son of Goodwin, Earl of Kent, the Confessor's Father-in-Law, he having married Earl Goodwin's Daughter: And *3dly,* William Duke of Normandy, who was allied to the Confessor thus, *viz.* William was the Son of Robert, the Son of Richard Duke of Normandy, which Richard was Brother unto the Confessor's Mother. *Vide* Hoveden, *sub initio Anni primi Willielmi primi.*

There was likewise a great Familiarity, as well as this Alliance, between the Confessor and Duke William; for the Confessor had often made considerable Residencies in Normandy. And this gave a fair Expectation to Duke William of succeeding him in this Kingdom: And there was also, at least pretended, a Promise made him by the Confessor, That Duke William should succeed him in the Crown of England; and because Harold was in great Favour with the King, and of great Power in England, and therefore the likeliest Man by his Assistance to advance, or by his Opposition to hinder or temperate the Duke's Expectation, there was a Contract made between the Duke and Harold in Normandy in the Confessor's Lifetime, That Harold should, after the Confessor's Death, assist the Duke in obtaining the Crown of England. (*Vide* Brompton, Hoveden, &c.) Shortly after which the Confessor died, and then stepp'd up the Three Competitors to the Crown, *viz.*

1. Edgar Ætheling, who was indeed favoured by the Nobility, but being an Infant, was overborn by the Power of Harold, who thereupon began to set up for himself: Whereupon Edgar, with his Two Sisters, fled into Scotland; where he, and one of his Sisters, dying without Issue, Margaret, his other Sister and Heir, married Malcolm, King of Scots; from whence proceeded the Race of the Scottish Kings.

2. Harold, who having at first raised a Power under Pretence of supporting and preserving Duke William's Title to this Kingdom, and having by Force suppress'd Edgar, he thereupon claimed the Crown to himself; and pretending an Adoption or Bequest of the Kingdom upon him by the Confessor, he forgot

his Promise made to Duke William, and usurped the Crown, which he held but the Space of 9 Months and 4 Days. Hoveden.

3. William, Duke of Normandy, who pretended a Promise of Succession by the Confessor, and a Capitulation or Stipulation by Harold for his Assistance; and had, it seems, so far interested the Pope in Favour of his Pretensions, that he pronounced for William against both the others.

Hereupon the Duke makes his Claim to the Crown of England, gathered a powerful Army, and came over, and upon the 14th of October, *Anno* 1067, gave Harold Battle, and overthrew him at that Place in Sussex, where William afterwards founded Battle-Abby, in Memory of that Victory; and then he took upon him the Government of the Kingdom, as King thereof, and upon Christmas following was solemnly crown'd at Westminster by the Archbishop of York; and he declared at his Coronation, That he claimed the Crown not *Jure Belli,* but *Jure Successionis;* and Brompton gives us this Account thereof, *Cum nomen Tyranni exhorresceret & nomen legitimi principis induere vellet petiit consecrari;* and accordingly, says the same Author, the Archbishop of York, in respect of some present incapacity in the Archbishop of Canterbury, *Munus hoc adimplevit ipsumque Gulielmum Regem ad jura Ecclesiæ Anglicanæ tuenda & conservanda populumque suum recte regendum, & Leges rectas Statuendum, Sacramento Solemniter adstrinxit;* and thereupon he took the Homage of the Nobility.

This being the true, though short Account of the State of that Business, there necessarily follows from thence those plain and unquestionable Consequences,

First, That the Conquest of King William 1. was not a Conquest upon the Country or People, but only upon the King of it, in the Person of Harold, the Usurper; for William 1. came in upon a Pretence of Title of Succession to the Confessor; and the Prosecution and Success of the Battle he gave to Harold was to make good his Claim of Succession, and to remove Harold, as an unlawful Usurper upon his Right; which Right was now decided in his Favour, and determined by that great Trial by Battle.

Secondly, That he acquired in Consequence thereof no greater

Right than what was in the Confessor, to whom he pretended a
Right of Succession; and therefore could no more alter the Laws
of the Kingdom upon the Pretence of Conquest, than the Confessor himself might, or than the Duke himself could have done,
had he been the true and rightful Successor to the Crown, in
Point of Descent from the Confessor; neither is it material,
whether his Pretence were true or false, or whether, if true, it
were available or not, to entitle him to the Crown; for whatsoever it was, it was sufficient to direct his Claim, and to qualify
his Victory so, that the *Jus Belli* thereby acquired could be only
Victoria in Regem, sed non in Populum, and put him only in
the State, Capacity and Qualification of a Successor to the King,
and not as Conqueror of the Kingdom.

Thirdly, And as this his antecedent Claim kept his Acquest
within the Bounds of a Successor, and restrained him from the
unlimited Bounds and Power of a Conqueror; so his subsequent
Coronation, and the Oath by him taken, is a further unquestionable Demonstration, that he was restrain'd within the Bounds of
a Successor, and not enlarged with the Latitude of a Victor; for
at his Coronation he binds himself by a solemn Oath to preserve
the Rights of the Church, and to govern according to the Laws,
and not absolutely and unlimitedly according to the Will of a
Conqueror.

Fourthly, That if there were any Doubt whether there might
be such a Victory as might give a Pretension to him, of altering
Laws, or governing as a Conqueror; yet to secure from that possible Fear, and to avoid it, he ends his Victory in a Capitulation;
namely, he takes the ancient Oath of a King unto the People,
and the People reciprocally giving or returning him that Assurance that Subjects ought to give their Prince, by performing their
Homage to him as their King, declared by the Victory he had
obtain'd over the Usurper, to be the Successor of the Confessor:
And consequently, if there might be any Pretence of Conquest
over the People's Rights, as well as over Harold's, yet the Capitulation or Stipulation removes the Claim or Pretence of a Conqueror, and enstates him in the regulated Capacity and State of a
Successor. And upon all this it is evident, That King William 1.
could not abrogate or alter the ancient Laws of the Kingdom,

any more than if he had succeeded the Confessor as his lawful Heir, and had acquir'd the Crown by the peaceable Course of Descent, without any Sword drawn.

And thus much may suffice, to shew that King William 1. did not enter by such a Right of Conquest, as did or could alter the Laws of this Kingdom.

Therefore I come to the last Question I proposed to be considered, *viz.* Whether *de Facto* there was anything done by King William 1. after his Accession to the Crown, in Reference either to the Alteration or Confirmation of the Laws, and how and in what Manner the same was done: And this being a Narrative of Matters of Fact, I shall divide into those Two Inquiries, *viz.* *1st.* What was done in Relation to the Lands and Possessions of the English: And *2dly,* What was done in Relation to the Laws of the Kingdom in general; for both of these will be necessary to make up a clear Narrative touching the Alteration or Suspension, Confirmation or Execution of the Laws of this Kingdom by him.

First, Therefore touching the former, *viz.* What was done in Relation to the Lands and Possessions of the English. Those Two Things must be premised, *viz.* First, a Matter of Right, or Law; which is this, That in Case this had been a Conquest upon the Kingdom, it had been at the Pleasure of the Conqueror to have taken all the Lands of the Kingdom into his own Possession, to have put a Period to all former Titles, to have cancelled all former Grants, and to have given, as it were, the Date and Original to every Man's Claim, so as to have been no higher nor ancienter than such his Conquest, and to hold the same by a Title derived wholly from and under him. I do not say, that every absolute Conqueror of a Kingdom will do thus, but that he may if he will, and have Power to effect it.

Secondly, The Second Thing to be premised is, a Matter of Fact, which is this; That Duke William brought in with him a great Army of Foreigners, that would have expected a Reward of their Undertaking, and therefore were doubtless very craving and importunate for Gratifications to be made them by the Conqueror. *Again,* it is very probable, that of the English themselves, there were Persons of very various Conditions and Inclinations; some perchance did adhere to the Duke, and were assistant to him openly, or at least under-hand, towards the bringing him in; and those were sure to enjoy their Possessions privately and quietly when the Duke prevailed. *Again,* some did, without all Question, adhere to Harold, and those in all Probability were severely dealt with, and dispossess'd of their Lands, unless they could make their Peace. *Again,* possibly there were others who assisted Harold, partly out of Fear and Compulsion; yet those, possibly, if they were of any Note or Eminence, fared little better than the rest. *Again,* there were some that probably stood Neuters, and medled not; and those, though they could not expect much Favour, yet they might in Justice expect to enjoy their own. *Again,* it must needs be supposed, That the Duke having so great an Army of Foreigners, so many ambitious and covetous Minds to be satisfied, so many to be rewarded in Point of Gratitude; and after so great a Concussion as always happens upon the Event of a Victory, it must needs, upon those and such like Accounts, be evident to any Man that considers Things of this Nature, that there were great Outrages and Oppressions committed by the Victor's Soldiers and their Officers, many false Accusations made against innocent Persons, great Disturbances and Evictions of Possessions, many right Owners being unjustly thrown out, and consequently many Occupations and Usurpations of other Men's Rights and Possessions, and a long while before those Things could be reduced to any quiet and regular Settlement.

These general Observations being premised, we will now see what *de Facto* was done in Relation to Men's Possessions, in Consequence of this Victory of the Duke.

First, It is certain that he took into his Hands all the Demesn Lands of the Crown which were belonging to Edward the Confessor at the Time of his Death, and avoided all the Dispositions and Grants thereof made by Harold, during his short Reign; and this might be one great End of his making that noble Survey in the fourth Year of his Reign, called generally *Doomsday-Read,* in some Records, as *Rot.* Winton, &c. thereby to ascertain what were the Possessions of the Crown in the Time of the Confessor, and those he entirely resumed: And this is the Reason why in some of our old Books it is said, *Ancient Demesn* is that which was held by King William the Conqueror; and in others 'tis said, *Ancient Demesn* is that which was held by King Edward the Confessor, and both true in their Kind; and in this Respect, *viz.* That whatsoever appeared to be the Confessor's at the Time of his Death, was assumed by King William into his own Possession.

Secondly, It is also certain, That no Person simply, and *quatenus* an English Man, was dispossess'd of any of his Possessions, and consequently their Land was not pretended unto as acquired *Jure Belli,* which appears most plainly by the following Evidences, *viz.*

First, That very many of those Persons that were possessed of Lands in the Time of Edward the Confessor, and so returned upon the Book of Doomsday, retain'd the same unto them and their Descendants, and some of their Descendants retain the same Possessions to this Day, which could not have been, if presently *Jure Belli ac Victoriæ universalis,* the Lands of the English had been vested in the Conqueror. And again,

Secondly, We do find, that in all Times, even suddenly after the Conquest, the Charters of the ancient Saxon Kings were pleaded and allowed, and Titles made and created by them to Lands, Liberties, Franchises and Regalities, affirm'd and adjudg'd under William 1. Yea, when that Exception has been offered, That by the Conquest those Charters had lost their Force, yet those Claims were allowed as in 7 E. 3. *Fines,* as mentioned by Mr. Selden, in his Notes upon Eadmerus, which could not be, if there had been such a Conquest as had vested all Mens Rights in the Conqueror.

Thirdly, Many Recoveries were had shortly after this Conquest, as well by Heirs as Successors of the Seisin of their Predecessors before the Conquest. We shall take one or two Instances for all; namely, that famous Record *apud* Pinendon, by the Archbishop of Canterbury, in the Time of King William 1. of the Seisin and Title of his Predecessors before the Conquest: See the whole Process and Proceedings thereupon in the End of Mr. Selden's Notes upon Eadmerus; and see Spelman's *Glossary,* Title *Drenches.* Upon these Instances, and much more that might be added, it is without Contradiction, That the Rights and Inheritances of the English *qua Tales,* were not abrogated or impeach'd by this Conquest, but continued notwithstanding the same; for, as is before observ'd, it was *Jure Belli quoad Regem, sed non quoad Populum.*

But to descend to some Particulars: The English Persons that the Conqueror had to deal with, were of Three Kinds, *viz. First,* Such as adhered to him aginst Harold the Usurper; and, without all Question, those continued the Possession of their Lands, and their Possessions were rather encreased by him, than any Way diminished. *Secondly,* Such as adhered to Harold, and opposed the Duke, and fought against him; and doubtless, as to those, the Duke after his Victory used his Power, and dispossess'd them of their Estates: Which Thing is usual upon all Conclusions and Events of this Kind, upon a double Reason; *1st,* To secure himself against the Power of those that oppos'd him, and to weaken them in their Estates, that they should not afterwards be enabled to make Head against him. And, *2dly,* To gratify those that assisted him, and to reward their Services in that Expedition; and to make them firm to his Interest, which was now twisted with their own: For it can't be imagined, but that the Conqueror was assisted with a great Company of Foreigners, some that he favour'd, some that had highly deserved for their Valour, some that were necessitous Soldiers of Fortune, and others that were either ambitious or covetous: All whose Desires, Deserts, or Expectations, the Conqueror had no other Means to satisfy, but by the Estates of such as had appeared open Enemies to him; and doubtless, many innocent Persons suffered in this Kind, under false Suggestions and Accusations, which occasioned great Exclamations by the Writers of those Times against the Violences and Oppressions which were used after this Victory. And, *Thirdly,* Such as stood Neuters, and meddled not on either Side during the Controversy: And doubtless, for some Time after this great Change, many of those suffered very much, and were hardly used in their Estates, especially such as were of the more eminent Sort.

Gervasius Tilburiensis, who wrote in the Time of Hen. 2. *Libro* 1. *Cap. Quid Murdrum & quare sic dictum,* gives us a large Account of what he had traditionally learned touching this Matter, to this Effect, *viz.* "Post Regni Conquisitionem & Perduellium Subjectionem, &c. Nomine autem Successionis a temporibus subactæ Gentis nihil sibi Vendicarent," &c. *i. e.* After the Conquest of the Kingdom, and Subjection of the Rebels, when the King himself and his great Men had surveyed their new Acquisitions; and strict Inquiry was made, who there were that, fighting against the King, had saved themselves by Flight; From these, and the Heirs of such as were slain in Battle, fighting against him, all Hopes of Succession, or of possessing their Estates, were lost; for the People being subdued, they held their Lives as a Favour, &c.

But Gervase, as he speaks so liberally in Relation to the Conquest, and the *Subacta Gens,* as he terms us; so it should seem, he was in great Measure mistaken in this Relation: For it is most plain, That those that were not engaged visibly in the Assistance of Harold, were not, according to the Rules of those Times, disabled to enjoy their Possessions, or make Title of Succession to their Ancestors, or transmit to their Posterity as formerly, tho' possibly some Oppressions might be used to particular Persons here and there to the contrary. And this appears by that excellent Monument of Antiquity, set down in Sir H. Spelman's *Glossary,* in the Title of *Drenches* or *Drenges,* which I shall here transcribe, *viz.*

> Edwinus de Sharborne, Et quidam alii qui ejecti fuerunt & Terris suis abierunt ad conquestorem & dixerunt ei, quod nunquam ante conquestum, nec in conquestum, nec post, fuerunt contra Regem ipsum in Concilio, aut in auxilio sed tenuerunt se in pace, Et hoc parati sunt probare qualiter Rex vellet Ordinare, Per quod idem Rex facit Inquiri per totam Angliam si ita fuit, quod quidem probatum fuit, propter quod idem Rex præcepit ut omnes illi qui sic tenuerunt se in pace in forma prædicta quod ipsi rehaberent omnes Terras & Dominationes suas adeo integre & in pace ut unquam habuerent vel tenuerunt ante conquestum suum, Et quod ipsi in posterum vocarentur Drenges.

But it seems the Possessions of the Church were not under this Discrimination, for they being held not in Right of the Person, but of the Church, were not subject to any Confiscation by the Adherence of the Possessor to Harold the Usurper: And therefore, tho' it seems Stigand Archbishop of Canterbury, at

64

the coming in of William 1. had been in some Opposition against him, which probably might be the true Cause why he perform'd not the Office of his Coronation, which of Right belonged to him, tho' some other Impediments were pretended, *Vide* Eadmerus *in initio Libri,* and might also possibly be the Reason why a considerable Part of his Possessions were granted to Odo Bishop of Bayonne, but were afterwards recovered by Lanfrank, his Successor, at Pinendon, *in pleno Comitatu, ubi Rex præcepit* totum Comitatum *absque mora considere, & homines Comitatus omnes Francigenos & præcipue Anglos in antiquis Legibus & Consuetudinibus peritos, in unum convenire.*

To this may be added those several Grants and Charters made by King William 1. mentioned in the History of Ely, and in Eadmerus, for restoring to Bishopricks and Abbies such Lands, or Goods, as had been taken away from them, *viz.*

Willielmus Dei gratia Rex Anglorum, Lanfranco Archiepiscopo Cantuar' & Galfrido Episcopo Constantiarum & Roberto Comiti de ou & Richardo filio Comitis Gilberti & Hugoni de Monteforti, suisque aliis proceribus Regni Angliæ salutem. Summonete Vicecomites meos ex meo præcepto, & ex parte mea eis dicite ut reddant Episcopatibus meis & Abbatiis totum Dominium omnesque Dominicas terras quas de Domino Episcopatuum meorum, & Abbatiarum, Episcopi mei & Abbates eis vel lenitate timore vel cupiditate dederunt vel habere consenserunt vel ipsi violentia sua inde abstraxerunt, & quod hacteuus injuste possiderunt de Dominio Ecclesiarum mearum. Et nisi reddiderint sicut eos ex parte mea summonebitis, vos ipsos velint nolint, constringite reddere; Et quod si quilibet alius vel aliquis vestrum quibus hanc Justitiam imposui *ejusdem querelae* fuerit reddat similiter quod de Domino Episcopatuum vel Abbatiarum mearum habuit ne propter illud quod inde aliquis vestrum habebit, minus exerceat super meos Vicecomites vel alios, quicunque teneant Dominium Ecclesiarum mearum, quod Præcipio, &c.

Willielmus Rex Anglor' omnibus suis fidelibus suis & Vicecomitibus in quorum Vicecomitatibus Abbatia de Heli Terras habet salutem. Præcipio ut Abbatia pred. habeat Omnes consuetudines suas scilicet Saccham & Socham Toll & Team & Infanganetheof, Hamsocua, & Grithbrice Fithwite & Ferdwite infra Burgum & extra & omnes alias forisfacturas in terra sua super suos homines sicut habuit Die qua Rex Edwardus fuit vivus &

mortuus, & sicut mea jussione dirationatæ apud Keneteford per plures Scyras ante meos Barones, viz. Galfridum Constantientem Ep. & Baldewine Abbatem, &c. Teste Rogero Bigot. Willielmus Rex Angl. Lanfranco Archiepo', & Rogero Comiti Moritoniæ, & Galfrido Constantien Epo. salutem. Mando vobis & Præcipio ut iterum faciatis congregari omnes Scyras quæ interfuerunt placito habito de Terris Ecclesia de Heli, antequam mea conjux in Normaniam novissime veniret, cum quibus etiam sint de Baronibus meis, qui competenter adesse poterint & prædicto placito interfuerint & qui terras ejusdem Ecclesiæ tenent; Quibus in unum congregatis *eligantur plures de illis Anglis* qui sciunt quomodo Terræ jacebant præfatæ Ecclesiæ Die qua Rex Edwardus Obiit, & quod inde dixerint ididem jure jurando testentur; quo facto restituentur Ecclesiæ terræ quæ in Dominico suo erant die obitus Regis Edwardi; Exceptis his quas homines clamabant me sibi dedisse; illas vero Literis mihi significate quæ sint, & qui eas tenent; Qui autem tenent Theinlandes quæ proculdubio debent teneri de Ecclesia faciant concordiam cum Abbate quam Meliorem poterint, & si nolurunt terræ remaneant ad Ecclesiam, Hoc quoque detinentibus Socham & Saccam fiat, &c. Willielmus Rex Anglorum, Lanfranco Archiepisc', & G. Episc. & R. Comiti M. salutem, &c. Defendite ne *Remigius Episcopus novas consuetudines requirat* infra Insulam de Heli, Nolo enim quod ibi habeat *nisi illud quod Antecessor ejus habebat Tempore Regis Edwardi* Scilicet qua die ipse Rex mortuus est. Et si Remig. Episcopus inde *Placitare voluerit placitet inde sicut fecisset tempore Regis Edw. & placitum istum sit in vestra* præsentia; De custodia de Norguic Abbatem Simeonem quietum esse demittite; Sed ibi municionem suam conduci faciat & custodiri. Facite *remanere placitum de Terris* quas Calumniantur Willielmus de ou, & Radulphus filius Gualeranni, & Robertus Gernon; si inde *placitare noluerint* sicut *inde placitassent tempore Regis Edwardi,* & sicut iu eodem tempore Abbatia *consuetudines suas* habebat, Volo ut eas omnio faciatis *habere* sicut Abbas per *Chartas suas, & per Testes suos* eas *deplacitare* poterit.

I might add many more Charters to the foregoing, and more especially those famous Charters in Spelman's Councils, Vol. 2. Fol. 14. & 165. whereby it appears, That King William 1. *Communi Concilio, & Concilio Archiepiscoporum, Episcoporum & Abbatum, & omnium Principum & Baronum Regni,* instituted the Courts for holding Pleas of Ecclesiastick Causes, to be separate and distinct from those Courts that had Jurisdiction of Civil Causes. *Sed de his plusquam fatis.*

And thus I conclude the Point I first propounded, *viz.* How King William 1. after his Victory, dealt with the Possessions of the English, whereby it appears that there was no Pretence of an Universal Conquest, or that he was a Victor *in Populum;* neither did he claim the Title of English Lands upon that Account, but only made Use of his Victory thus far, to seize the Lands of such as had oppos'd him: Which is universal in all Cases of Victories, tho' without the Pretence of Conquest.

Secondly, Therefore I come to the Second general Question, *viz.* What was done in Relation to the Laws? It is very plain, that the King, after his Victory, did, as all wise Princes would have done, endeavour to make a stricter Union between England and Normandy; and in order thereunto, he endeavoured to bring in the French instead of the Saxon Language, then used in England: "Deliberavit" (says Holcot) "quomodo Linguam Saxonicam possit destruere, & Anglicam & Normanicam idiomate concordare & ideo ordinavit quod nullus in Curia Regis placitaret nisi in Lingua Gallica, &c." From whence arose the Practice of Pleading in our Courts of Law in the Norman or French Tongue, which Custom continued till the Statute of 36 E. 3. c. 15.

And as he thus endeavoured to make a Community in their Language, so possibly he might endeavour to make the like in their Laws, and to introduce the Norman Laws into England, or as many of 'em as he thought convenient; and it is very probable, that after the Victory, the Norman Nobility and Soldiers were scattered through the whole Kingdom, and mingled with the English, which might possibly introduce some of the Norman Laws and Customs insensibly into this Kingdom: And to that End the Conqueror did industriously mingle the English and Normans together, shuffling the Normans into English Possessions here, and putting the English into Possessions in Normandy, and making Marriages among them, especially between the Nobility of both Nations.

This gave the English a Suspicion, that they should suddenly have a Change of their Laws before they were aware of it. But it fell out much better: For first, there arising some Danger of a Defection of the English, countenanced by the Archbishop of

York in the North, and Frederick, Abbot of St. Albans in the South; the King, by the Perswasions of Lanfrank, Archbishop of Canterbury, "Probonopacis apud Berkhamstead juravit super Animas reliquias Sancti Altani tactisque Sacrosanctis Evangelis (ministrante juramento Abbate Frederico) ut bonas & approbatas antiquas Regni Leges quas sancti & pii Angliæ Reges ejus Antecessores, & maxime Rex Edvardus statuit inviolabiliter observaret; Et sic pacificati ad propria læti recesserunt." *Vide Mat. Paris, in Vita Frederici Abbatis Sancti Albani.*

But altho' now, upon this Capitulation, the ancient English Laws were confirm'd, and namely, the Laws of St. Edward the Confessor; yet it appeared not what those Laws were: And therefore, in the Fourth Year of his Reign, we are told by Hoveden, in a Digression he makes in his History under the Reign of King Hen. 2. and also in the Chronicle of Lithfield.

> Willielmus Rex, Anno quarto Regni sui Consilio Baronum suorum fecit Summonari per Universos Consulatos Angliæ, Anglos Nobiles & Sapientes & sua Lege eruditos ut eorum jura & consuetudines ab ipsis audiret, Electis igitur de singulis totius Patriæ Comitatibus viri duodecim, jurejurando confirmaverunt ut quoad possint recto tramite neque ad Dextram neque ad Sinistram partem divertentes Legum suarum consuetudinem & sancitam patefacerent. nihil prætermittentes nihil addentes, nihil prævaricando mutantes, &c.

And then sets down many of those ancient Laws approv'd and confirm'd by the King, and *Commune Concilium;* wherein it appears, that he seems to be most pleased with those Laws that came under the Title of *Lex Danica,* as most consonant to the Norman Customs.

> Quo auditu mox universi compatrioti qui Leges dixerint Tristes effecti, uno ministerio deprecati sunt quatenus permitteret Leges sibi proprias &. consuetudines antiquas habere in quibus vixerunt Patres, & ipsi in iis nati & nutriti sunt, quia *durum Valde sibi foret suscipere Leges ignotas, & judicare de iis quæ nesciebant;* Rege vero ad flectendum ingrato existente, tandem eum persecuti sunt deprecantes quatenus pro Anima Regis Edvardi qui es sub diem suum eis concesserat Barones & Regnum & cujus orant Leges non aliorum extraneorum cogere quam sub Legibus perseverare patriis; Unde Consilio habito Præcatui Baronem tandem acquievit, &c.

Gervasius Tilburiensis, who lived near that Time, speaks shortly, and to the Purpose, thus: "Propositis Legibus Anglicanis secundum triplicitam earum Distinctionem, *i.e.* Merchenlage, Westsaxon-lage, & Dane-lage quasdam autem approbans illis transmarinas Legis Neustriæ quas ad Regni Pacem tuendam efficasissime videbantur adjecit."

So that by this, there appears to have been a double Collection of Laws, *viz.*

First, The Laws of the Confessor, which were granted and confirmed by King William, and are also called the Laws of King William, which are transcribed in Mr. Selden's Notes upon Eadmerus, Page 173. the Title whereof is thus, viz. "Hae sunt Leges & Consuetudines quas Willielmus Rex concessit universo populo Angliæ post subactam Terram eadem sunt quas Edvardus Rex cognatus ejus observavit ante eum": And these seem to be the very same that Ingulfus mentions to have been brought from London, and placed by him in the Abbey of Crowland in the fifteenth Year of the same King William, *attuli eadem Vice mecum Londini in meum Monasterium Legum Volumen, &c.*

Secondly, There were certain additional Laws at that Time establish'd, which Gervasius Tilburiensis calls, *Leges Neustriæ quæ efficacissimæ videbantur ad tuendam Regni pacem;* which seems to be included in those other Laws of King William transcribed in the same Notes upon Eadmerus, Pag. 189, 193, &c. which indeed were principally designed for the Establishment of King William in the Throne, and for the securing of the Peace of the Kingdom, especially between the English and Normans, as appears by these Instances, *viz.*

The Law de Murdro, or the Common Fine for a Norman or Frenchman slain, and the offender not discovered: The Law for the Oath of Allegiance to the King: The Introduction of the Trial by single Combat, which many Learned Men have thought was not in Use here in England before Will. 1. And the Law touching Knights Service, which Bracton, *Lib.* 2 supposes to be introduced by the Conqueror, *viz.*

> Quod omnes Comites Milites & Servientes & universi liberi homines totius Regni habeant & teneant se semper bene in Armis & in Equis ut decet & quod sint semper prompti & bene parati ad Servitium suum integrum nobis explendum & peragendum cum semper Opus affuerit secundum quod nobis de Feodo debent

& Tenementis suis de Jure facere & sicut illis statuimus per Commune Concilium totius Regini prædicti, & illis dedimus & concessimus in Feodo jure hæreditario.

Wherein we may observe, that this Constitution seems to point at Two Things, *viz.* The assizing of Men for Arms, which was frequent under the Title *De assidenda ad Arma,* and is afterwards particularly enforc'd and rectified by the Statute of Winton, 13 Ed. 1. and next of Conventional Services reserved by *Tenures* upon Grants made out of the Crown or Knights Service, called in Latin, *Forinsecum,* or *Regale Servitium.*

And *Note,* That these Laws were not imposed *ad Libitum Regis,* but they were such as were settled *per Commune Concilium Regni,* and possibly at that very Time when Twelve out of every County were return'd to ascertain the Confessor's Laws, as before is mentioned out of Hoveden, which appears to be as sufficient and effectual a Parliament as ever was held in England.

By all which it is apparent, *First,* That William 1. did not pretend, nor indeed could he pretend, notwithstanding this Nominal Conquest, to alter the Laws of this Kingdom without common Consent *in Communi Concilio Regni,* or in Parliament. And, *Secondly,* That if there could be any Pretence of any such Right, or if in that turbulent Time something of that Kind had happened; yet by all those solemn Capitulations, Oaths, and Concessions, that Pretence was wholly avoided, and the ancient Laws of the Kingdom settled, and were not to be altered, or added unto, at the Pleasure of the Conqueror, without Consent in Parliament.

In the Seventeenth Year of his Reign, (or as some say, the Fifteenth) he began that great Survey, recorded in Two Books, called, *The Great Doomsday Book,* and *Little Doomsday Book,* and finished it in the Twentieth Year of his Reign, *Anno Domini* 1086, as appears by the learned Preface of Mr. Selden to Eadmerus, and indeed by the Books themselves. The Original Record of which is still extant, remaining in the Custody of the Vice-Chamberlains of his Majesty's Exchequer. This Record contains a Survey of all the ancient Demesn Lands of the Kingdom, and contains in many Manors, not only the Tenants Names, with the Quantity of Lands and their Values, but likewise the Number and Quality of the Residents or Inhabitants, with divers Rights,

Privileges, and Customs claimed by them; and being made and found by Verdict or Presentment of Juries in every Hundred or Division upon their Oaths, there was no receeding from, or avoiding what was written in this Record: And therefore as Gervasius Tilburiensis says, Page 41. "Ob hoc nos eundem Librum Judiciarium Nominamus; Non quod in eo de propositis aliquibus dubiis seratur sententia, sed quod ab eo sicut ab ultimo Die Judicii non licet ulla ratione descedere."

And thus much shall suffice touching the Fifth General Head; namely, of the Progress made after the Coming-in of King William, relating to the Laws of England, their Establishment, Settlement, and Alteration. If any one be minded to see what this Prince did in reference to Ecclesiasticks, let him consult Eadmerus, and the learned Notes of Mr. Selden upon it, especially Page 167, 168, &c. where he shall find how this King divided the Episcopal Consistory from the County Court, and how he restrain'd the Clergy and their Courts from exercising ecclesiastical Jurisdiction upon Tenants *in Capite*.

VI

Concerning the Parity or Similitude of the Laws of England and Normandy, and the Reasons thereof

The great Similitude that in many Things appears between the Laws of England, and those of Normandy, has given some Occasion to such as consider not well of Things, to suppose that this happened by the Power of the Conqueror, in conforming the Laws of this Kingdom to those of Normandy; and therefore will needs have it, that our English Laws still retain the Mark of that Conquest, and that we received our Laws from him as from a Conqueror; than which Assertion, (as it appears even by what has before been said) nothing can be more untrue. Besides, if there were any Laws derived from the Normans to us, as perhaps there might be some, yea, possibly many; yet it no more concludes the Position to be true, that we received such Laws *per Modum Conquestus,* than if the Kingdom of England should at this Day take some of the Laws of *Persia, Spain, Egypt,* or *Assyria,* and by Authority of Parliament settle them here. Which tho' they were for their Matter Foreign, yet their obligatory Power, and their formal Nature or Reason of becoming Laws here, were not at all due to those Countries, whose Laws they were, but to the proper and intrinsical Authority of this Kingdom by which they were received as, or enacted into, Laws: And therefore, as no Law that is Foreign, binds here in England, till it be received and authoritatively engrafted into the Law of England; so there is no Reason in common Prudence and Understanding for any Man to conclude, that no Rule or Method of Justice is to be admitted in a Kingdom, tho' never so useful or beneficial, barely upon this Account, That another People entertain'd it, and made it a Part of their Laws before us.

But as to the Matter itself, I shall consider, and enquire of the following Particulars, *viz.*

1. How long the Kingdom of England and Dutchy of Normandy stood in Conjunction under one Governor.
2. What Evidence we have touching the Laws of Normandy, and of their Agreement with ours.
3. Wherein consists that Parity or Disparity of the English and Norman Laws.
4. What might be reasonably judged to be the Reason and Foundation of that Likeness, which is to be found between the Laws of both Countries.

First, Touching the Conjunction under one Governor of England and Normandy, we are to know, That the Kingdom of England and Dutchy of Normandy were *de facto* in Conjunction under these Kings, viz. William 1. William 2. Henry 1. King Stephen, Henry 2. and Richard 1. who, dying without Issue, left behind him Arthur Earl of Britain, his Nephew, only Son of Geoffry Earl of Britain, second Brother of Richard 1. and John the youngest Brother to Richard 1. who afterward became King of England by usurping the Crown from his Nephew Arthur. But the Princes of Normandy still adhered to Arthur, "sicut Domino Ligeo suo dicentes Judicium & Consuetudinem esse illarum Regionum ut Arthurus Filius, Fratris Senioris in Patrimonio sido debito & hæreditate Avunculo suo succedat eodem jure quod Gaulfridus Pater ejus esset habiturus si Regi Richardo defuncto supervixisset."

And therein they said true, and the Laws of England were the same, Witness the Succession of Richard 2. to Edward 3. also the Laws of Germany, and the ancient Saxons were accordant hereunto; and it was accordingly decided in a Trial by Battle, under Otho the Emperor, as we are told by Radulphus, *de Diceto sub Anno* 945. And such are the Laws of France to this Day, *Vide Chopimus de Domanio Franciæ, Lib.* 2. *Tit.* 12. and such were the ancient Customs of the Normans, as we are told by the *Grand Contumier, cap.* 99. And such is the Law of Normandy, and of the Isles of Jersey and Guernsey (which some Time were Parcel thereof) at this Day, as is agreed by Terrier, the best Expositor of their Customs, *Lib.* 2. *cap.* 2. And so it was adjudg'd within my Remembrance in the Isle of Jersey, in a Controversy there, between John Perchard and John Rowland, for the Goods and Estate of Peter Perchard.

But nevertheless, John the Uncle of Arthur came by Force and Power, *Et Rotomagum Gladio Ducatus Normanniæ accinctus est per Ministerium Rotomagensis Archiepiscopi,* as Mat. Paris says; and shortly after also usurped the Crown of England, and imprisoned his Nephew Arthur, who died in the Year 1202, being as was supposed murthered by his said Uncle, *Vide* Mat. Paris, *in fine Regni Regis Rici' Primi,* and Walsingham in his *Ypodigma Neustriæ sub eodem Anno 1202.*

And to countenance his Usurpation in Normandy, and to give himself the better Pretence of Title, he by his Power so far prevailed there, that he obtained a Change of the Law there, purely to serve his Turn, by transferring the Right of Inheritance from the Son of the elder Brother to the younger Brother, as appears by the *Grand Contumier, cap.* 99. But withal, the *Gloss* takes Notice of it as an Innovation, and brought in by Men of Power, tho' it mentions not the particular Reason, which was aforesaid.

The King of France (of whom the Dutchy of Normandy was holden) highly resented the Injury done by King John to his Nephew Arthur, who, as was strongly suspected, came not fairly to his End. He summoned King John as Duke of Normandy into France, to give an Account of his Actions, and upon his Default of appearing, he was by King Philip of France forejudged of the Said Dutchy, *Vide* Mat. Paris, *in initio Regni Johannis;* and this Sentence was so effectually put in Execution, that in the Year 1204, Mat Paris tells us, "Tota Normannia, Turania Andegavia, & Pictavia cum Civitatibus & Castellis & Rebus aliis præter Rupellam, Toar, & Mar Castellam sunt in Regis Francorum Dominium devoluta."

But yet he retained, tho' with much Difficulty, the Islands of Jersey and Guernsey, and the uninterrupted Possession of some Parts of Normandy for some Time after, and both he and and his Son King Hen. 3. kept the Stile and Title of Dukes of Normandy, &c. 'till the 43d Year of King Hen. 3. at which Time for 3000 *Livres Tournois,* and upon some other Agreements, he resigned Normandy and Anjou to the King of France, and never afterwards used that Title, as appears by the Continuation of Mat. Paris, *sub Anno* 1260, only the four Islands, some Time Parcel of Normandy, were still, and to this Day, are enjoyed by the Crown of England, *viz.* Jersey, Guernsey, Sarke, and Aldernay, tho' they are still governed under their ancient Norman Laws.

Secondly, As to the Second Enquiry, What Evidence we have touching the Laws of Normandy: The best, and indeed only common Evidence of the ancient Customs and Laws of Normandy, is that Book which is called, *The Grand Contumier of Normandy,* which in later Years has been illustrated, not only with a Latin and French Gloss, but also with the Commentaries of Terrier, a French Author.

This Book does not only contain many of the ancienter Laws of Normandy, but most plainly it contains those Laws and Customs which were in Use here in the Time of King Hen. 2. King Rich. 1. and King John, yea, and such also as were in Use and Practice in that Country after the Separation of Normandy from the Crown of England; for we shall find therein, in their Writs and Processes, frequent Mention of King Rich. 1. and the entire Text of the 110th Chapter thereof is an Edict of Philip King of France, after the Severance of Normandy from the Crown of England. (I speak not of those additional Edicts which are annex'd to that Book of a far later Date.) So that we are not to take that Book as a Collection of the Laws of Normandy, as they stood before the Accession or Union thereof to the Crown of England; but as they stood long after, under the Time of those Dukes of Normandy that succeeded William 1. and it seems to be a Collection made after the Time of K. Hen. 3. or at least after the Time of K. John, and consequently it states their Laws and Customs as they stood in Use and Practice about the Time of that Collection made, which observation will be of Use in the ensuing Discourse.

Thirdly, Touching the Third Particular, *viz.* The Agreement and Disparity of the Laws of England and Normandy. It is very true, we shall find a great Suitableness in their Laws, in many Things agreeing with the Laws of England, especially as they stood in the Time of King Hen. 2. the best Indication whereof we have in the Collection of Glanville; the Rules of Discents, of Writs, of Process, of Trials, and some other Particulars, holding a great Analogy in both Dominions, yet not without their Differences and Disparities in many Particulars, *viz.*

First, Some of those Laws are such as were never used in England; for Instance, There was in Normandy a certain Tribute paid to the Duke, called Monya, *i. e.* a certain Sum yielded to him (in Consideration that he should not alter their Coin) payable every three Years, *Vide Contumier, cap.* 15. But this Payment was never admitted in England; indeed it was taken for a Time, but was ousted by the first Law of King Hen. 1. as an Usurpation. Again, by the Custom of Normandy, the Lands descended to the Bastard Eigne, born before Marriage of the same Woman, by whom the same Man had other Children after Marriage, *Contumier, cap.* 27. But the Laws of England were always contrary, as appears by Glanville, *Lib.* 7. *cap.* 13. And the Statute of Merton, which says, *Nolumus Leges Anglicans Mutare,* &c. Again, by the Laws of Normandy, if a Man died without Issue, or Brother, or Sister, the Lands did descend to the Father, *Contumier, cap.* 15. Terrier, *cap.* 2. But in England, this Law seems never to have been used.

2dly, Again, Some Laws were used in Normandy, which were in Use in England long before the supposed Norman Conquest, and therefore could in no Possibility have their original Force, or any binding Power here upon that Pretence: For Instance, it appears by the Custumier of Normandy, that the Sheriff of the County was an Annual Officer, and so 'tis evident he was likewise in England before the Conquest: And among the Laws of Edward the Confessor, it is provided, "Quod Aldermanni in Civitatibus eandem habeant Dignitatem qualem habent Ballivi hundredorum in Ballivis suis sub Vicecomitem": Again, Wreck of the Sea, and Treasure Trove was a Prerogative belonging to the Dukes of Normandy, as appears by the Contumier, cap. 17, & 18. and so it was belonging to the Crown of England before the Conquest, as appears by the Charter of Edward the Confessor to the Abby or Ramsey of the Manor of Ringstede, *cum toto ejectu Maris quod* Wreccum *dicitur,* and the like, *vide ibid.* of Treasure Trove, & *vide* the Laws of Edward the Confessor, *cap.*

14. So Fealty, Homage, and Relief, were incident to Tenures by the Laws of Normandy, *Vide Contumier, cap.* 29. And so they were in England before the Conquest, as appears by the Laws of Edward the Confessor, *cap.* 35. and the Laws of Canutus, mentioned by Brompton *cap.* 8. So the Trial by Jury of Twelve Men was the usual Trial among the Normans in most Suits, especially in Assizes, & *Juris Utrums,* as appears by the *Contumier, cap.* 92, 93, & 94. and that Trial was in Use here in England before the Conquest, as appears in Brompton among the Laws of King Elthred, *cap.* 3. which gives some Specimen of it, *viz.* "Habeant placita in singulis Wapentachiis & exeant Seniores duodecim Thani vel Præpositus cum iis & jurent quod neminem innocentem accusare nec Noxium concelare."

3dly, Again, In some Things, tho' both the Law of Normandy and the Law of England agreed in the Fact, and in the Manner of Proceeding, yet there was an apparent Discrimination in their Law from ours: As for Instance, The Husband seized in Right of the Wife, having Issue by her, and she dying, by the Custom of Normandy he held but only during his Widowhood, *Contumier, cap.* 119. But in England, he held during his Life by the Curtesy of England.

4thly, But in some Things, the Laws of Normandy agreed with the Laws of England, especially as they stood in the Times of Hen. 2. and Rich. 1. so that they seem to be as it were Copies or Counterparts one of another; tho' in many Things, the Laws of England are since changed in a great Measure from what they then were? For Instance, at this Day in England, and for very many Ages past, all Lands of Inheritance, as well Socage Tenures, as of Knights Service, descend to the eldest Son, unless in Kent and some other Places where the Custom directs the Descent to all the Males, and in some places to the youngest; but the ancient Law used in England, though it directed Knights Services and Serjeanties to descend to the eldest Son, yet it directed Vassalagies and Soccage Lands to descend to all the Sons, Glanvil. *Lib.* 7. *cap.* 3. and so does the Laws of Normandy to this Day. *Vide Contumier, cap.* 26. & *post hic, cap.* 11.

Again, Leprosy at this Day does not impede the Descent; but by the Laws in Use in England, in the elder Times, unto the Time of King John, and for some Time afterwards, Leprosy did impede the Descent, as *Placito Quarto Johannis,* in the Case of W. Fulch, a Judge of that Time, and accordingly were the Laws of Normandy. *Vide Le Contumier, cap.* 27.

Again, At this Day, by the Law of England, in Cases of Trials by Twelve Men, all ought to agree, and any one dissenting, no Verdict can be given; but by the Laws of Normandy, tho' a Verdict ought to be by the concurring Consent of Twelve Men, yet in Case of Dissent or Disagreement of the Jury, they used to put off the lesser Number that were Dissenters, and added a kind of Tales equal to the greater Number so agreeing, until they had got a Verdict of Twelve Men that concurred, *Contumier, c.* 95. And we may find some ancient Footsteps of the like Use here in England, tho' long since antiquated, *Vide* Bracton, *Lib.* 4. *cap.* 19. where he speaks thus,

> Contingit etiam multotiens quod Juratores in veritate dicenda sunt sibi contrarii ita quod in unam concordare non possunt sententiam, Quo casu de Consilio Curiæ affortietur Assisa, ita quod apponantur alii juxta numerum majoris partis quæ dissenserit, vel saltem quatuor vel sex & adjungantur aliis, vel etiam per seipsos sine aliis, de veritate discutiant & judicent, & per se respondeant & eorum veredictum allocabitur & tenebitur cum quibus ipsi convenirent.

Again, At this Day, by the Laws of England, a Man may give his Lands in Fee-simple, which he has by Descent, to any one of his Children, and disinherit the rest: But by the ancient Laws used here, it seems to be otherwise; as Mich. 10. Johannis Glanv. *Lib.* 7. *cap.* 2. the Case of William de Causeia. And accordingly were the Laws of Normandy, as we find in the *Grand Contumier, cap.* 36. "Quand le Pere avoit plusieurs fills, ils ne peut fairde de son Heritage le un Meilleur que le auter"; and yet it seems to this Day, in England, it holds some Resemblance in Cases of Frank-Marriage, *viz.* That the Doness, in Case she will have any Part of her Father's other Lands, ought to put her Lands in Hochpot.

Again, By the Law of England, the younger Brother shall not exclude the Son of the elder, who died in the Life-time of the Father: And this was the ancient Law of Normandy, but received some Interruption in Favour of King John's Claim, *Vide Contumier, cap.* 25. & *hic ante;* and indeed, generally the Rule of

Descents in Normandy was the same in most Cases with that of Descents with us at this Day; as for Instance, That the Descent of the Line of the Father shall not resort to that of the Mother, *Et e converso;* and that the Course was otherwise in Cases of Purchases. But in most Things the Law of Normandy was consonant to the Law with us, as it was in the Time of King Richard 1. and King John; except in Cases of Descents to *Bastard* eigne, excluding *Mulier puisne,* as aforesaid.

Again, at this Day there are many Writs now in Use which were anciently also in Use here, as well as in Normandy: As Writs of Rights, Writs of Dower, Writs *De novel Desseisin, de Mortdancestor, Juris utrum, Darrein presentment,* &c. And some that are now out of Use, though anciently in Use here in England; as Writs *De Feodo vel Vado, De Feodo vel Warda,* &c. All which are taken notice of by Glanville, *Lib.* 13. *cap.* 28, 29. And the very same Forms of Writs in Effect were in Use in Normandy, as appears by the *Contumier per Totum,* and the Writ *De Feodo vel Vado,* (*ibid. cap.* 11.) according to Glanville, *Lib.* 13. *cap.* 27. runs thus, *viz.*

> Rex Vicecomiti salutem: Summone per bonos summonitores duodenim liberos & legales homines de vicineto quod sint coram me vel Justiciis meis eo die parati Sacramento Recognoscere utrum N. teneat unam Carucatem Terræ in illa villa quæ R. clamat versus eum per Breve meum in Feodo an in vadio, invadiatem ei ab ipso R. vel ab H. antecessore ejus, (vel aliter si sit Feodam vel hæreditas ipsius N. an in vadio invadiata ei ab ipso R. vel ab H. &c. Et interim terram illam videant, &c. (Vide ibid.)

And according to the *Grand Contumier,* that Writ runs thus, *viz.*

> Si Rex fecerit te securum de clamore suo prosequend' summoneas Recognitores de Viceneto quod sint ad primas Assisas Ballivæ, ad cognoscendum utrum Carucata Terræ in B. quod. G. deforceat R. sit Feodum tenentis vel vadium novum dictum per manus G. post Coronationem Regis Richardi & pro quanta, & utrum sit propinquior Hæres ad redimendum vadium, & videatur interum Terræ, &c.

So that there seems little Variance, either in the Nature or in the Form of those Writs used here in the Time of Henry 2. And those used in Normandy when the Contumier was made.

Again, The Use was in England, to limit certain notable Times, within the Compass of which those Titles which Men design'd to be relieved upon, must accrue: Thus it was done in the Time of Henry 3. by the Statute of Merton, *cap.* 8. at which Time the Limitation in a Writ of Right was from the Time of King Henry 1. and by that Statute it is reduced to the Time of King Henry 2. and for Assizes of Mortdancestor they were thereby reduced from the last Return of King John out of Ireland, which was 12 Johannis, and for Assizes of *Novel Disseisin, a prima Transfretatione Regis in Normanniam,* which was 5 Hen. 3. and which before that had been *post ultimum redditum* Henricus 3. de Britannia, as appears by Bracton. And this Time of Limitation was also afterwards, by the Statutes of Westm. I. *Cap.* 39. and *West.* 2. *cap.* 2. 46. reduced unto a narrow Scantlet, the Writ of Right being limited to the First Coronation of King Richard 1.

But before the Limitation set by that Statute of Merton, there were several Limitations set for severals Writs; for we find among the Pleas of King John's Time, the Limitation of Writs, *De Tempore quo Rex Henricus avus noster fuit vivus & Mortuus;* and in a Writ of Aile, *Die quo Rex Henricus obiit* in the Time of Henry 2. as appears by Glanville, *Lib.* 13. *cap.* 3. there were then divers Limitations in Use, as in *Mortdancestors, post prima Coronationem nostram, viz. Henrici secundi,* Glanvil. *Lib.* 1. *cap.* 1. and touching Assizes of *Novel Disseisin, Vide ibid. cap.* 32. where he tells us, *Cum quis intra Assisam,* &c. And the Time of Limitation in an Assize, was then *post ultimam meam Transfretationem,* (*viz. Henrici primi*) *in Normanniam, Lib.* 13. *cap.* 33. But in a Writ of Right, as also in a Writ of Customs and Services, it was *de Tempore Regis Henrici avi mei, viz.* Hen. 1. *vid. ib. Lib.* 12. *cap.* 10, 16. and it seems very apparent, that the Limitations anciently in Normandy, for all Actions Ancestral was *post primam Coronationem Regis Henrici fecundi,* as appears expresly in the *Contumier, cap.* 111. *De Feofe & Gage.*

So that anciently the Time of Limitation in Normandy was the same as in England, and indeed borrowed from England, *viz.* In all Actions Ancestrel from the Coronation of Henry 2. And thus in those Actions wherein the Limitation was anciently from the Coronation of King Richard 1. was substituted as in the Writ *De Feofe & Gage,* in the *Contumier, cap.* 111. *De Feofe &*

Forme, cap. 112. In the Writ *De Ley Apparisan, ib. cap.* 24. &
cap. 22. "Ascun Gage ne peut estre requise en Normandy, si il ne
suit engage post le Coronement de Roy Richard ou deins quar-
ante annus": So that the old Limitation, as well for the Redemption of Mortgages, as for bringing those Writs above-mentioned, was *post Coronationem Regis Henrici Secundi;* but
altered, as it seems, by King Philip, the Son of Lewis King of
France, after King John's Ejectment out of Normandy, and since
the Time from the Coronation of King Richard 1. is estimated
to bear Proportion to 40 Years. It is probable this Change of
the Limitation by King Philip of France, was about the Beginning of the Reign of King Henry 3. or about 30 or 40 Years
after the Coronation of Richard 1. from whose Coronation about
30 Years were elapsed, 5 *aut.* 6 *Henrici* 3. for anciently the Limitation in this Case was 30 Years.

Fourthly, I now come to the Fourth Inquiry, *viz.* How this
great Parity between the Laws of England and Normandy came
to be effected; and before I come to it, I shall premise Two Observables, which I would have the Reader to carry along with
him through the whole Discourse, *viz. First,* That this Parity of
Laws does not at all infer a Necessity, that they should be imposed by the Conqueror, which is sufficiently shewn in the foregoing Chapters; and in this it will appear that there were divers
other Means that caused a Similitude of both Laws, without any
Supposition of imposing them by the Conqueror. *Secondly,* That
the Laws of Normandy were in the greater Part thereof borrowed
from ours, rather than ours from them, and the Similitude of the
Laws of both Countries did in greater Measure arise from their
Imitation of our Laws, rather than from our Imitation of theirs,
though there can't be denied a Reciprocal Imitation of each others
Laws was, in some Measure at least, had in both Dominions: And
these Two Things being premised, I descend to the Means whereby this Parity or Similitude of the Laws of both Countries did
arise, as follow, *viz.*

First, Mr. Camden and some others have thought, there was
ever some Congruity between the ancient Customs of this Island
and those of the Country of France, both in Matters Religious
and Civil; and tells us of the ancient Druids, who were the

common Instructors of both Countries. *Gallia Causidicos docuit facunda Britannos:* And some have thought, that anciently both Countries were conjoined by a small Neck of Land, which might make an easier Transition of the Customs of either Country to the other; but those Things are too remote Conjectures, and we need them not to solve the Congruity of Laws between England and Normandy. Therefore,

Secondly, It seems plain, that before the Normans coming in Way of Hostility, there was a great Intercourse of Commerce and Trade, and a mutual Communication, between those Two Countries; and the Consanguinity between the Two Princes gave Opportunities of several Interviews between them and their Courts in each others Countries: And it is evident by History, that the Confessor, before his Accession to the Crown, made a long Stay in Normandy, and was there often, which of Consequence must draw many of the English thither, and of the Normans hither; all which might be a Means of their mutual Understanding of the Customs and Laws of each others Country, and gave Opportunities of Incorporating and ingrafting divers of them into each other, as they were found useful or convenient; and therefore the Author of the Prologue to the *Grand Custumier* thinks it more probable, That the Laws of Normandy were derived from England, than that ours were derived from thence.

Thirdly, 'Tis evident, that when the Duke of Normandy came in, he brought over a great Multitude, not only of ordinary Soldiers, but of the best of the Nobility and Gentry of Normandy; hither they brought their Families, Language and Customs, and the Victor used all Art and Industry to incorporate them into this Kingdom: And the more effectually to make both People become one Nation, he made Marriages between the English and Normans, transplanting many Norman Families hither, and many English Families thither; he kept his Court sometimes here, and sometimes there; and by those Means insensibly derived many Norman Customs hither, and English Customs thither, without any severe Imposition of Laws on the English as Conqueror: And by this Method he might easily prevail to bring in, even without the Peoples Consent, some Customs and Laws that perhaps were of Foreign Growth; which might the more easily be done, considering how in a short Time the People of both Nations were intermingled; they were mingled in Marriages, in Families, in the Church, in the State, in the Court, and in Councils; yea, and in Parliaments in both Dominions, though Normandy became, as it were, an Appendix to England, which was the nobler Dominion, and received a greater Conformity of their Laws to the English, than they gave to it.

Fourthly, But the greatest Means of the Assimilation of the Laws of both Kingdoms was this: The Kings of England continued Dukes of Normandy till King John's Time, and he kept some Footing there notwithstanding the Confiscation thereof by the King of France, as aforesaid; and during all this Time, England, which was an absolute Monarch, had the Prelation or Preference before Normandy, which was but a Feudal Dutchy, and a small Thing in respect of England; and by this Means Normandy became, as it were, an Appendant to England, and successively received its Laws and Government from England; which had a greater Influence on Normandy than that could have on England; insomuch that oftentimes there issued Precepts into Normandy to summon Persons there to answer in Civil Causes here; yea, even for Lands and Possessions in Normandy; as *Placito* 1 *Johannis,* a Precept issued to the Seneschal of Normandy, to summon Robert Jeronymus, to answer to John Marshal, in a Plea of Land, giving him 40 Days Warning; to which the Tenant appeared, and pleaded a Recovery in Normandy: And the like Precept issued for William de Bosco, against Jeoffry Rusham, for Lands in Corbespine in Normandy.

And on the other Side, *Trin.* 14 *Johannis,* in a Suit between Francis Borne and Thomas Adorne, for certain Lands in Ford. The Defendant pleaded a Concord made in Normandy in the Time of King Richard 1. upon a Suit there before the King, for the Honour of Bonn in Normandy, and for certain Lands in England, whereof the Lands in Question were Parcel, before the Seneschal of Normandy, *Anno* 1099. But it was excepted against, as an insufficient Fine, and varying in Form from other Fines; and therefore the Defendant relied upon it as a Release.

By these, and many the like Instances, it appears as follows, *viz.*

First, That there was a great Intercourse between England and

Normandy before and after the Conqueror, which might give a great Opportunity of an Assimilation and Conformity of the Laws in both Countries. *Secondly,* That a much greater Conformation of Laws arose after the Conqueror, during the Time that Normandy was enjoyed by the Crown of England, than before. And *Thirdly,* That this Similitude of the Laws of England and Normandy was not by Conformation of the Laws of England to those of Normandy, but by Conformation of the Laws of Normandy to those of England, which now grew to a great Height, Perfection and Glory; so that Normandy became but a Perquisite or Appendant of it.

And as the Reason of the Thing speaks it, so the very Fact itself attests it. For

First, It is apparent, That in Point of Limitation in Actions Ancestral, from the Time of the Coronation of King Henry 2. it was anciently so here in England in Glanville's Time, and was transmitted from hence into Normandy; for it is no way reasonable to suppose the contrary, since Glanville mentions it to be enacted here, *Concilio procerum;* and though this be but a single Point, or Instance, yet the Evidence thereof makes out a Criterion, or probable Indication, that many other Laws were in like Manner so sent hence into Normandy.

Secondly, It appears, That in the Succession of the Kings of England, from King William 1. to King Henry 2. the Laws of England received a great Improvement and Perfection, as will plainly appear from Glanville's Book, written in the Time of King Henry 2. especially if compared with those Sums or Collections of Laws, either of Edward the Confessor, William 1. or Henry 1. whereof hereafter.

So that it seems, by Use, Practice, Commerce, Study and Improvement of the English People, they arrived in Henry 2d's Time to a greater Improvement of the Laws; and that in the Time of King Richard 1. and King John, they were more perfected, as may be seen in the Pleadings, especially of King John's Time: And tho' far inferior to those of the Times of Succeeding Kings, yet they are far more regular and perfect than those that went before them. And now if any do but compare the *Contumier* of Normandy, with the Tract of Glanville, he will plainly find that the Norman Tract of Laws followed the Pattern of Glanville, and was writ long after it, when possibly the English Laws were yet more refined and more perfect; for it is plain beyond Contradiction, that the Collection of the Customs and Laws of Normandy was made after the Time of King Henry 2. for it mentions his Coronation, and appoints it for the Limitation of Actions Ancestrel, which must at least be 30 Years after; nay, the *Contumier* appears to have been made after the Act of Settlement of Normandy in the Crown of France; for therein is specified the Institution of Philip King of France, for appointing the Coronation of King Richard 1. for the Limitation of Actions which was after the said Philip's full Possession of Normandy.

Indeed, if those Laws and Customs of Normandy had been a Collection of the Laws they had had there before the coming in of King William 1. it might have been a Probability that their Laws, being so near like ours, might have been transplanted from thence hither; but the Case is visibly otherwise, for the *Contumier* is a Collection after the Time of King Richard 1. yea, after the Time of King John, and possibly after Henry 3d's Time, when it had received several Repairings, Amendments and Polishings, under the several Kings of England, William 1. William 2. Henry 1. King Steven, Henry 2. Richard 1. and King John; who were either knowing themselves in the Laws of England, or were assisted with a Council that were knowing therein.

And as in this Tract of Time the Laws of England received a great Advance and Perfection, as appears by that excellent Collection of Glanville, written even in Henry 2's Time, when yet there were near 30 Years to acquire unto a further Improvement before Normandy was lost; so from the Laws of England thus modelled, polished and perfected, the same Draughts were drawn upon the Laws of Normandy, which received the fairest Lines from the Laws of England, as they stood at least in the Beginning of King John's Time, and were in Effect in a great Measure the Defloration of the English Laws, and a Transcript of them, though mingled and interlarded with many particular Laws and Customs of their own, which altered the Features of the Original in many Points.

VII

Concerning the Progress of the Laws of England after the Time of King William 1. until the Time of King Edward 2.

That which precedes in the Two foregoing Chapters, gives us some Account of the Laws of England, as they stood in and after the great Change which happened under King William 1. commonly called The Conqueror. I shall now proceed to the History thereof in the ensuing Times, until the Reign of King Edward 2.

William 1. having Three Sons; Robert the eldest, William the next, and Henry the youngest, disposed of the Crown of England to William his second Son, and the Dutchy of Normandy to Robert his eldest Son; and accordingly William 2. commonly called, William Rufus, succeeded his Father in this Kingdom. We have little memorable of him in relation to the Laws, only that he severely press'd and extended the Forest Laws.

Henry 1. Son of William 1. and Brother of William 2. succeeded his said Brother in the Kingdom of England, and afterwards expelled his eldest Brother Robert out of the Dutchy of Normandy also. He proceeded much in the Benefit of the Laws, *viz.*

First, He restored the Free-Election of Bishops and Abbots, which before that Time he and his Predecessors invested, *per Annulum & Bacculum;* yet reserving those Three Ensigns of the Patronage thereof, *viz. Conge d' Eslire,* Custody of the Temporalties, and Homage upon their Restitution. *Vide* Hoveden, *in Vita sua.*

But *Secondly,* The great Essay he made, was the composing an Abstract or Manual of Laws, wherein he confirm'd the Laws

86

of Edward the Confessor, *Cum illis Emendationibus quibus eam Pater meus emendavit Baronum suorum Concilio;* and then adds his own Laws, some whereof seem to taste of the Canon Law. The whole Collection is transcribed in the Red Book of the Exchequer; from whence it is now printed in the End of Lambard's Saxon Laws; and therefore not needfull to be here repeated.

They, for the most Part, contain a Model of Proceedings in the County Courts, the Hundred Courts, and the Courts Leet; the former to be held Twelve Times in the Year, the latter twice; and also of the Courts Baron. These were the ordinary usual Courts, wherein Justice was then, and for a long Time after, most commonly administred; also they concern Criminal Proceedings, and the Punishment of Crimes, and some few Things touching Civil Actions and Interests, as in Chapter 70, directing Descents, *viz.*

> Si quis sine Liberis decesserit Pater aut Mater ejus in Hereditatem succedant, vel Frater vel Soror, si Pater & Mater desint; si nec hos habeat, Frater vel Soror Patris vel Matris, & deinceps in quintum Genetalium, qui cum propiores in parentela sint hereditario Jure succedant; Et dum virilis sexus extiterit & hæreditas ab inde sit Femina non hæreditetur; primum Patris Feodum primogenitus Filius habeat. Emptiones vero & deinceps Acquisitiones det cui magis velit, sed si Bockland habeat quam ei Parentes dederint, Mittat eam extra cognationem suam.

I have observ'd and inserted this Law, for Two Reasons, *viz. First,* To justify what I before said, That the Laws of Normandy took the English Laws for their Pattern in many Things; *Vide le Contumier, cap.* 25, 26, 36, &c. And *Secondly,* To see how much the Laws of England grew and increased in their Particularity and Application between this Time and the Laws of William 1. which in Chapter 36, has no more touching Descents but this, *viz. Si quis intestatus obierit, liberi ejus hæreditatem equaliter dividant.* But Process of Time grafted thereupon, and made particular Provisions for particular Cases, and added Distributions and Subdivisions to those General Rules.

These Laws of King Henry 1. are a kind of Miscellany, made up of those ancient Laws, called, The Laws of the Confessor, and King William 1. and of certain Parts of the Canon and Civil

Law, and of other Provisions, that Custom and the Prudence of the King and Council had thought upon, chosen, and put together.

King Stephen succeeded, by Way of Usurpation, upon Maud the sole Daughter and Heir of King Hen. 1. The Laws of Hen. 1. grew tedious and ungrateful to the People, partly because new, and so not so well known, and partly because more difficult and severe than those ancient Laws, called, The Confessor's; for Walsingham, in his *Ypodigma Neustriæ,* tells us, That the Londoners petitioned Queen Maud, *ut liceret eis uti Legibus sancti Edvardi & non legibus Patris sui Henrici, quia graves erant;* and that her Refusal gave Occasion to their Defection from her, and strengthened Stephen in his Usurpation; who according to the Method of Usurpers, to secure himself in the Throne, was willing and ready to gratify the Desires of the People herein; and furthermore, took his Oath, *1st,* That he would not retain in his Hands the Temporalties of the Bishops: *2dly,* That he would remit the Severity of the Forest Laws; and *3dly,* That he would also remit the Tribute of Danegelt: But he performed nothing.

His Times were troublesome, he did little in relation to the Laws; nor have we any Memorial of any Record touching his Proceedings therein, only there are some few Pipe Rolls of his Time, relating to the Revenue of the Crown.

Henry 2. the Son of Maud, succeeded Stephen, he reigned long, *viz.* about Thirty Five Years; and tho' he was not without great Troubles and Difficulties, yet he built up the Laws and the Dignity of the Kingdom to a great Height and Perfection. For,

First, In the Entrance of his Government he settled the Peace of the Kingdom; he also reformed the Coin, which was much adulterated and debased in the Times and Troubles of King Stephen, *Et Leges Henrici avi sui præcepit per totum Regnum inviolabiliter observari.* Hoveden.

Secondly, Against the Insolencies and Usurpations of the Clergy; he by the Advice of his Council or Parliament at Clarendon, enacted those Sixteen Articles mentioned by Mat. Paris, *sub Anno* 1164. They are long, and therefore I remit you thither for the Particulars of them.

'Tis true, Thomas Becket, Archbishop of Canterbury, boldly

and insolently took upon him to declare many of those Articles void, especially those Five mentioned in his Epistle to Suffragans, recorded by Hoveden, *viz. 1st,* That there should be no Appeal to the Bishop without the King's Licence. *2dly,* That no Archbishop or Bishop should go over the Seas at the Pope's Command without the King's Licence. *3dly,* That the Bishop should not excommunicate the King's Tenants *in Capite* without the King's Licence. *4thly,* That the Bishop should not have the Conuzance of Perjury, or *Fidei Læsionis.* And, *5thly,* That the Clergy should be convened before Lay Judges, and that the King's Courts should have Conuzance of Churches and of Tythes.

Thirdly, He raised up the Municipal Laws of the Kingdom to a greater Perfection, and a more orderly and regular Administration than before; 'tis true, we have no Record of judicial Proceedings so ancient as that Time, except the Pipe Rolls in the Exchequer, which are only Accounts of his Revenue: But we need no other Evidence hereof than the Tractate of Glanville, which tho' perhaps it was not written by that Ranulphus de Glanvilla, who was *Justitiarius Angliæ* under Hen. 2. yet it seems to be wholly written at that Time; and by that Book, tho' many Parts thereof are at this Day antiquated and altered, and in that long Course of Time, which has elapsed since that King's Reign, much enlarged, reformed, and amended; yet by comparing it with those Laws of the Confessor and Conqueror, yea, and the Laws of his Grandfather King Hen. 1. which he confirmed; it will easily appear, that the Rule and Order, as well as the Administration of the Law, was greatly improved beyond what it was formerly, and we have more Footsteps of their Agreement and Concord herein with the Laws, as they were used from the Time of Edw. 1. and downwards, than can be found in all those obsolete Laws of Hen. 1. which indeed were but disorderly, confused and general Things, rather the Cases and Shells of directing the Way of Administration than Institutions of Law, if compared with Glanville's Tractate of our Laws.

Fourthly, The Administration of the Common Justice of the Kingdom, seems to be wholly dispensed in the County Courts, Hundred Courts, and Courts Baron, except some of the greater Crimes reformed by the Laws of King Hen. 1. and that Part thereof which was sometimes taken up by the *Justitiarius An-*

glicæ: This doubtless bred great Inconvenience, Uncertainty, and Variety in the Laws, *viz.*

First, by the Ignorance of the Judges, which were the Freeholders of the County: For altho' the Alderman or Chief Constable of every Hundred was always to be a Man learned in the Laws; and altho' not only the Freeholders, but the Bishops, Barons, and great Men, were by the Laws of King Hen. 1. appointed to attend the County Court; yet they seldom attend there, or if they did, in Process of Time they neglected the Study of the English Laws, as great Men usually do.

Secondly, Another Inconvenience was, That this also bred great Variety of Laws, especially in the several Counties: For the Decisions or Judgments being made by divers Courts, and several Independent Judges and Judicatories, who had no common Interest among them in their several Judicatories, thereby in Process of Time every several County would have several Laws, Customs, Rules, and Forms of Proceeding, which is always the Effect of several Independent Judicatories administred by several Judges.

Thirdly, A Third Inconvenience was, That all the Business of any Moment was carried by Parties and Factions: For the Freeholders being generally the Judges, and Conversing one among another, and being as it were the Chief Judges, not only of the Fact, but of the Law; every Man that had a Suit there, sped according as he could make Parties; and Men of great Power and Interest in the County did easily overbear others in their own Causes, or in such wherein they were interested, either by Relation of Kindred, Tenure, Service, Dependance, or Application.

And altho' in Cases of false Judgment, the Law, even as then used, proved a Remedy by Writ of false Judgment before the King or his Chief Justice; and in Case the Judgment was found to be such in the County Court, all the Suiters were considerably amerced, (which also continued long after in Use with some Severity) yet this proved but an ineffectual Remedy for those Mischiefs.

Therefore the King took another and a more effectual Course; for in the 22d Year of his Reign, by Advice of his Parliament held at Northampton, he instituted Justices *itinerant,* dividing the Kingdom into Six Circuits, and to every Circuit allotting

Three Judges, Knowing or Experienced in the Laws of the Realm: These Justices with their several Circuits are declared by Hoveden, *sub eodem Anno, i. e.* 22 H. 2. *viz.*

1. Hugo Cressy, Walterus filius Roberti, & Robertus Maunsel, for Norfolk, Suffolk, Cambridge, Huntingdon, Bedford, Buckingham, Essex, and Hartford Counties.
2. Hugo de Gundevilla, W. filius Radulphi, & W. Basset, for Lincoln, Nottingham, Derby, Stafford, Warwick, Northampton, and Leicester Counties.
3. Robertus filius Bernardi, Richardus Giffard, & Rogerus filius Ramfrey, for Kent, Surrey, Sussex, Hampshire, Berks, and Oxon Counties.
4. W. filius Stephani, Bertein de Verdun, & Turstavi filius Simonis, for Hereford, Gloucester, Worcester, and Salop Countries.
5. Radulphus filius Stephani, W. Ruffus, & Gilbertus Pipard, for the Counties of Wilts, Dorset, Somerset, Devon, and Cornwall.
6. Robertus deWatts, Radulphus de Glanvilla, & Robertus Picknot, for the Counties of York, Richmond, Lancaster Copland, Westmorland, Northumberland, and Cumberland.

Hi, (Consilio Archiepiscoporum, Episcoporum, Comitum & Baronum Regni, &c. apud Nottingham existentium) missi sunt per singulos Angliæ Comitatus & juraverunt quod cuilibet jus suum conservarent illæ sum. Hoveden fo. 313. & Mat. Paris, in Anno 1176.

And that these Men were well known in the Law, appears by their Companion Radulphus de Glanvilla, who seems to be the Author of the Treatise *De Legibus Angliæ,* and was afterwards made *Justitiarius Angliæ.*

To those Justices, was afterwards committed the Conuzance of all Civil and Criminal Pleas happening within their Divisions, and likewise Pleas of the Crown, Pleas touching Liberties, and the King's Rights; and the better to acquaint them with their Business, there were certain Assises which were first enacted at Clarendon, and afterwards confirmed at Northampton; they were not much unlike the *Capitula Itineris* mentioned in our old *Magna Charta,* but not so perfect, and are set down by Hoveden *ubi supra,* and are too long to be here inserted: I shall only take

Notice of this one, *viz*. Establishing Descents, because I shall hereafter have Occasion to use it, *Si quis obierit Francus Tenens hæredes ipsius remaneant in talem Seisina qualem Pater suus,* &c. But besides those Courts in Eyre, there were two great standing Courts, *viz*. The Exchequer, and the Court of Kings-Bench, *Vel Curiam coram ipso Rege, vel ejus Justiciario;* and it was provided by the above-mentioned *Assisæ,* "Quod Justiciæ faciant omnes Justicias & Rectitudines Spectantes ad Dominium Regis, & ad Coronam suam, per breve Domini Regis vel illorum qui in ejus Loco erunt de Feodo dimidii Militis & infra, Nisi tam grandis sit quærela quod non possit deduci sine Domino Rege vel talis quam Justiciæ ei reponunt pro dubitatione sua, vel ad illos qui in Loco ejus erunt," &c.

Neither do I find any distinct Mention of the Court of Common Bench in the Time of this King, tho' in the Time of King John there is often mention made thereof, and the Rolls of that Court of King John's Time are yet extant upon Record, & *vide post. sub Richardi Primi.*

The Limitation of the Assise of *Novel Disseisin,* is by those Assises appointed to be, *a tempore quo Dominus Rex venit in Angliam proximam post Pacis factam inter ipsum, & Regem filium suum.*

The same King afterwards, in the Twenty fifth Year of his Reign, divided the Limits of his Itinerant Justices into Four Circuits or Divisions, and to each Circuit assigned a greater Number of Justices, *viz*. Five at least, which are thus set down in Hoveden, Folio 337. *viz.*

Anno 1179, 25 H. 2. Magno Concilio celebrato apud Windeshores, Communi Consilio Archiepiscoporum Comitum & Baronum & coram Rege Filio Suo, Rex divisit Angliam in quatuor Partes, & unicuique partium præfecit viros sapientes ad faciendum Justitiam in Terra sua in hunc Modum.

1. Ricardus-Episcopus Winton, Ricardus Thesaurarius Regis, Nicholaus filius Turoldi, Thomas Basset & Robertus de White-field, for the Counties of Southampton, Wilts, Gloucester, Somerset, Devon, Cornwall, Berks and Oxon.

2. Galfridus Eliensis Episcopus, Nicholaus Capellanus Regis, Gilbertus Pipard, Reginald de Wisebeck Capellanus Reges & Gaulfridus Hosce, for the Counties of Cambridge, Huntingdon,

Northampton, Leicester, Warwick, Winchester, Hereford, Stafford and Salop.

3. Johannes Episcopas Norwicensis, Hugo Murdac Clericus Regis, Michael Bellet, Richardus de le Pec, & Radulphus Brito, for Norfolk, Suffolk, Essex, Hartford, Middlesex, Kent, Surrey, Sussex, Bucks and Bedford.

4. Galfredus de Luci, Johannes Comyn, Hugo de Gaerst, Radulphus de Glanvilla, W. de Bendings, Alanus de Furnellis, for the Counties of Nottingham, Derby, York, Northumberland, Westmorland, Cumberland, and Lancaster.

Isti sunt Justiciæ in Curia Regis constituti ad audiendum clamores Populi.

This Prince did these Three notable Things, *viz.*

First, By this Means, he improved and perfected the Laws of England, and doubtless transferred over many of the English Laws into Normandy, which, as before is observed, caused that great Suitableness between their Laws and ours; so that the Similitude did arise much more by a Conformation of their Laws to those of England, than by any Conformation of the English Laws to theirs, especially in the Reigns of King Hen. 2. and his Two Sons, King Richard, and King John, both of whom were also Dukes of Normandy.

Secondly, He check'd the Pride and Insolence of the Pope and the Clergy, by those Constitutions made in a Parliament at Clarendon, whereby he restrained the Exorbitant Power of the Ecclesiasticks, and the Exemption they claimed from Secular Jurisdiction. And,

Thirdly, He subdued and conquered Ireland, and added it to the Crown of England, which Conquest was begun by Richard Earl of Stigule or Strongbow, 14 H. 2. But was perfected by the King himself in the Seventeenth Year of his Reign, and for the greater Solemnity of the Business, was ratified by the Fealties of the Bishops and Nobles of Ireland, and by a Bull of Confirmation from Pope Alexander, who was willing to interest himself in that Business, to ingratiate himself with the King, and to gain a Pretence for that arrogant Usurpation of disposing of Temporal Dominions, *Vide* Hoveden, *Anno* 14 H. 2.

Richard 1. eldest Son of King Henry 2. succeeded his Father.

93

I have seen little of Record touching the Juridicial Proceedings, either of him, or his said Father, other than what occurs in the Pipe-Rolls in the Exchequer, which both in the Time of Hen. 2. Rich. 1. and King John, and all the succeeding Kings, are fairly preserved; and the best Remembrances that we have of this King's Reign in relation to the Law, are what Roger Hoveden's *Annals* have delivered down to us, *viz.*

First, He instituted a Body of Naval Laws in his Return from the Holy Land, in the Island of Oleron, which are yet extant with some Additions; *De quibus, Vide* Mr. Selden's *Mare Clausum, Lib.* 2. *cap.* 24. and I suppose they are the same which are attributed to him by Mat. Paris, *Anno* 1196. and he constituted Justices to put them in Execution.

Secondly, He observed the same Method of distributing Justice as his Father had begun, by Justices *Itinerant per singulos Angliæ Comitatus,* to whom he deliver two Kinds of Extracts or Articles of Inquiry, *viz. Capitula Coronæ,* much reformed and augmented from what they were before, and *Capitula de Judæis;* the whole may be read in Hoveden, *fo.* 423. *sub Anno* 5 R. 1. and by those Articles it appears, That at that Time there was a settled Court for the Common-Pleas, as well as for the King's Bench, tho' it seems that Pleas of Land were then indifferently held in either, as appears by the first and second Articles thereof, where we have, *Placita per breve Domini Regis, vel per breve Capitalis Justiciæ, vel a Capitali Curia Regis coram eis (Justiciis) missa:* The former whereof seems to be the Common-Pleas, which held Pleas by Original Writ, which Writ was under the King's Teste when he was in England; but when he was beyond the Seas, it was under the Teste of the *Justiciarius Angliæ,* as the *Custos Regni* in the King's Absence.

The Power which the Justices Itinerant had to hold Pleas in Writs of Right, or the Grand Assize, was sometimes limited, as here by the *Articuli Coronæ* under Hen. 2. to half a Knight's Fee, or under: For here in these Articles it is, *De Magnis Assisis quæ sunt de centum Solidis & infra.* But in the next Commissions, or *Capitula Coronæ,* it is, *De Magnis Assisis usque ad decem Libratas Terre & infra.*

In his eighth Year, he established a Common Rule for Weights and Measures throughout England, called *Assisa de Mensuris,* wherein we find the Measure of Woollen Cloths was then the same with that of *Magna Charta,* 9 H. 3. *viz. De duobus ulnis infra Lisuras.*

In the Year before his Death, the like Justices Errant went through many Counties of England, to whom Articles, or *Capitula placitorum Coronæ,* not much unlike the former were delivered. *Vide* Hoveden, *sub Anno* 1198. *fo.* 445.

And in the same Year, he issued Commissions in the Trent, Hugh de Neville being Chief Justice; and to those were also delivered Articles of Inquiry, commonly called *Assisæ de Foresta,* which may be read at large in Hoveden, *sub eodem Anno.* These gave great Discontent to the Kingdom, for both the Laws of the Forest, and their Execution were rigorous and grievous.

King John succeeded his said Brother, both in the Kingdom of England, and Dutchy of Normandy; the Evidence that we have, touching the Progress of the Laws of his Time, are principally Three, *viz. First,* His Charters of Liberties. *2dly,* The Records of Pleadings and Proceedings in his Courts; And *3dly,* The Course he took for settling the English Laws in Ireland.

1. Touching the first of these, his Charters of the Liberties of England, and of the Forest, were hardly, and with Difficulty, gained by his Baronage at Stanes, *Anno Dom.* 1215. The Collection of the former was, as Mat. Paris tells us, upon the View of the Charter or Law of King Hen. 1. which says, he contained "quasdam Libertates & Leges a Rege Edvardo Sancto, Ecclesiæ & Magnatibus concessas, exceptis quibusdam Libertatibus quas idem Rex de suo adjecit"; and that thereupon the Baronage fell into a Resolution to have those Laws granted by King John. But as it is certain, that the Laws added by King Hen. 1. to those of the Confessor were many more, and much differing from his; so the Laws contained in the Great Charter of King John, differed much from those of King Hen. 1. Neither are we to think, that the Charter of King John contained all the Laws of England, but only or principally such as were of a more comprehensive Nature, and concerned the Common Rights and Liberties of the Church, Baronage and Commonalty which were of the greatest Moment, and had been most invaded by King John's Father and Brother.

The lesser Charter, or De Foresta, was to reform the Excesses and Encroachments which were made, especially in the Time of

Rich. 1. and Hen. 2. who had made New Afforestations, and much extended the Rigour of the Forest Laws: And both these Charters do in Substance agree with that *Magna Charta,* & *de Foresta,* granted and confirm'd 9 Hen. 3. I shall not need to recite them, or to make any Collections or Inferences from them; they are both extant in the Red Book of the Exchequer, and in Mat. Paris, *sub Anno* 1215, and the Record and the Historian do *Verbatim* agree.

As to the Second Evidence we have of the Progress of the Laws in King John's Time, they are the Records of Pleadings and Proceedings which are still extant: But altho' this King endeavoured to bring the Law, and the Pleadings and Proceedings thereof, to some better Order than he found it; for saving his Profits whereof he was very studious, and for the better Reduction of it into Order and Method, we find frequently in the Records of his Time, Fines imposed, *pro Stultiloquio,* which were no other than Mulcts imposed by the Court for barbarous and disorderly Pleading: From whence afterwards that Common Fine arose, *Pro pulchre placitando,* which was indeed no other than a Fine for want of it; and yet for all this, the Proceeding in his Courts were rude, imperfect, and defective, to what they were in the ensuing Times of Edw. 1. &c. But some few Observables I shall take Notice of upon the Perusal of the Judicial Records of the Time of King John, *viz.*

1st. That the Courts of King's-Bench and Common-Pleas were then distinct Courts, and distinctly held from the Beginning to the End of King John's Reign.

2dly, That as yet, neither one nor both of those Courts dispatch'd the Business of the Kingdom, but a great Part thereof was dispatch'd by the *Justices Itinerant,* which were sometimes in Use, but not without their Intermissions, and much of the Publick Business was dispatch'd in the County Courts, and in other inferior Courts; and so it continued, tho' with a gradual Decrease till the End of King Edw. 1. and for some Time after: And hence it was, That in those elder Times, the Profits of those County Courts for which the Sheriff answered in his Farm, *de Proficuis Comitatus;* also Fines were levied there, and *post Fines,* and Fines *pro licentia concordandi,* and great Fines there answered; Fines *pro Inquisitionibus habendi,* Fines for Misdemeanors, tho' called Amerciaments, arose to great Sums, as will appear to any who shall peruse the ancient *Viscontiels.*

But, as I said before, the Business of Inferior Courts grew gradually less and less, and consequently their Profits and Business of any Moment came to the Great Courts, where they were dispatch'd with greater Justice and Equality. Besides, the greater Courts observing what Partiality and Brocage was used in the inferior Courts, gave a pretty quick Ear to Writs of false Judgment, which was the Appeal the Law allowed from erroneous Judgments in the County Courts; and this, by Degrees, wasted the Credit and Business of those inferior Courts.

3dly, That the Distinction between the King's-Bench and Common-Bench, as to the Point of *Communia placita,* was not yet, nor for some Time after, settled; and hence it is, that frequently in the Time of King John, we shall find that Common Pleas were held in B. R. yea, in Mich. & Hill. 13 *Johannis,* a Fine is levied *coram ipso Rege,* between Gilbert Fitz Roger and Helwise his Wife, Plaintiffs, and Robert Barpyard Tenant of certain Lands in Kirby, &c.

And again, whereas there was frequently a Liberty granted anciently by the Kings of England, and allowed, *Quod non implacitetur nisi coram Rege,* I find *inter Placita de diversis Terminis secundo Johannis,* That upon a Suit between Henry de Rochala, and the Abbot of Leicester before the Justices de Banco, the Abbot pleaded the Charter of King Richard 1. *Quod idem Abbas pro nullo respondeat nisi coram ipso Rege vel Capitali Justitiario suo;* and it is ruled against the Abbot, *Quia omnia Placita quæ coram Justic. de Banco tenentur, coram Domino Regi vel ejus Capitali Justitiario teneri intelliguntur.* But this Point was afterwards settled by the Statute of *Magna Charta, Quod Communia placita non sequantur Curiam nostram.*

4thly. That the four Terms were then held according as was used in After-times with little Variance, and had the same Denominations they still retain.

5thly. That there were oftentimes considerable Sums of Money, or Horses, or other Things given to obtain Justice; sometimes 'tis said to be, *pro habenda Inquisitione ut supra,* and *inter placita incertitemporis Regis Johannis.* The Men of Yarmouth against the Men of Hastings and Winchelsea, *Afferunt Domino Regi tres Palsridos, & sex Asturias Narenses ad Inquisitionem habendam per Legales,* &c. and frequently the same was done, and often accounted for in the Pipe-Rolls, under the Name of *Oblata;* and to remedy this Abuse, was the Provision made in King John's and King Hen. 3d's Charters, *Nulli Vendemus Justitiam vel Rectum.* But yet Fines upon Originals being certain, having continued to this Day, notwithstanding that Provision; but those enormous *Oblata* before mentioned, are thereby remedied and taken away.

6thly, That in all the Time of King John, the Purgation *per Ignem & Aquam,* or the Trial by Ordeal, continued as appears by frequent Entries upon the Rolls; but it seems to have ended with this King, for I do not find it in Use in any Time after: Perchance the Barbarousness of the Trial, and Persuasions of the Clergy, prevailed at length to antiquate it, for many Canons had been made against it.

7thly, In this King's Time, the Descent of Socage as well as Knight's Service Lands to the eldest Son prevailed in all Places, unless there was a special Custom, that the Lands were partible *inter Masculos;* and therefore, Mich. *secundo Johannis,* in *a rationabili parte Bonorum,* by Gilbert Beville against William Beville his elder Brother for Lands in Gunthorpe, the Defendant pleaded, *Quod Nunquam parita vel partibilia fuere;* and because the Defendant could not prove it, Judgment was given for the Demandant: And by Degrees it prevail'd so, that whereas at this Time the Averment came on the Part of the Heir at Law, that the Land *nunquam parita vel partibilis extetit*; in a little Time after the Averment was turn'd on the other Hand, *viz.* That tho' the Land was Socage, yet unless he did aver and prove that it was *partita & partibilis,* he failed in his Demand.

Thirdly, The third Instance of the *Progress* of King John's Reign, in Relation to the Common Law, was his settling the same in *Ireland,* which he made his more immediate and particular Business: But hereof we shall add a particular Chapter by itself, when we have shewn you what Proceedings and Progress was made therein in the Time of Edw. 1. The many and great Troubles that fell upon King John and the whole Kingdom, especially towards the latter End of his Reign, did much hinder the good Effect of settling the Laws of England, and consequently the Peace thereof, which might have been bottom'd, especially upon the Great Charter. But this Unfortunate Prince and Kingdom were so entangled with intestine Wars, and with the Invasion of the French, who assisted the English Barons against their King, and by the Advantages and Usurpations that the Pope and Clergy made by those Distempers, that all ended in a Confusion with the King's Death.

I come therefore to the long and troublesome Reign of Hen. 3. who was about nine Years old at his Father's Death; he being born *in Festo sancti, Remigii* 1207, and King John died *in Festo sancti Lucæ,* 1216, and the young King was crown'd the 28th of October, being then in the tenth Year of his Age, and was under the Tutelage of William Earl-Marshal.

The Nobility were quick and earnest, notwithstanding his Minority, to have the Liberties and Laws of the Kingdom confirm'd; and Preparatory thereto, in the Year 1223, Writs issued to the several Counties to enquire, by twelve good and lawful Knights, *Que fuerunt Libertates in Anglia tempore Regni Henrici avi sui,* returnable *quindena Paschæ.* What Success those Inquisitions had, or what Returns were made thereof, appears not: But in the next Year following, the young King standing in Need of a Supply of Money from the Clergy and Laity, none would be granted, unless the Liberties of the Kingdom were confirm'd, as they were express'd and contain'd in the two Charters of King John; which the King accordingly granted in his Parliament at Westminster, and they were accordingly proclaim'd, *Ita quod Chartæ utrorumque Regum in nulla inveniatur dissimiles,* Mat. Paris. *Anno* 1224.

In the Year 1227, The King holding his Parliament at Oxford, and being now of full Age; by ill Advice, causes the two Charters he had formerly granted to be cancell'd, "Hanc occasionem prætendens, quod Chartæ illæ concessæ fuerunt & Libertates scriptæ & signatæ dum ipse erat sub Custodia, nec sui Corporis aut sigilli aliquam potestatem habuit, unde viribus carere debuit," &c. Which Fact occasion'd a great disturbance in the Kingdom:

And this Inconstancy in the King, was in Truth the Foundation of all his future Troubles, and yet was ineffectual to his End and Purpose; for those Charters were not avoidable for the King's Nonage, and if there could have been any such Pretence, that alone would not avoid them, for they were Laws confirm'd in Parliament.

But the Great Charter, and the Charter of the Forest, did not expire so; for in 1253, they were again, seal'd and publish'd: And because after the Battle of Evesham, the King had wholly subdued the Barons, and thereby a Jealousy might grow, that he again meant to infringe it; in the Parliament at Marlbridge, *cap.* 5. they are again confirm'd. And thus we have the great Settlement of the Laws and Liberties of the Kingdom establish'd in this King's Time: The Charters themselves are not every Word the same with those of King John, but they differ very little in Substance.

This Great Charter, and *Charta de Foresta,* was the great Basis upon which this Settlement of the English Laws stood in the Time of this King and his Son; there were also some additional Laws of this King yet extant, which much polish'd the Common Law, *viz.* The Statutes of Merton and Marlbridge, and some others.

We have likewise two other principal Monuments of the great Advance and Perfection that the English Laws attain'd to under this King, *viz.* The Tractate of Bracton, and those Records of Plea, as well in both Benches, as before the Justices Itinerant, the Records whereof are still extant.

Touching the former, *viz.* Bracton's Tractate, it yields us a great Evidence of the Growth of the Laws between the Times of Henry 2. and Hen. 3. If we do but compare Glanville's Book with that of Bracton, we shall see a very great Advance of the Law in Writings of the latter, over what they are in Glanville. It will be needless to instance Particulars; some of the Writs and Process do indeed in Substance agree, but the Proceedings are much more regular and settled, as they are in Bracton, above what they are in Glanville. The Book itself in the Beginning seems to borrow its Method from the Civil Law; but the greatest Part of the Substance is either of the Course of Proceedings in the Law known to the Author, or of Resolutions and Decisions in the

Courts of King's-Bench and Common-Bench, and before Justices Itinerant, for now the inferior Courts began to be of little Use or Esteem.

As to the Judicial Records of the Time of this King, they were grown to a much greater Degree of Perfection, and the Pleadings more orderly, many of which are extant: But the great Troubles, and the Civil Wars, that happen'd in his Time, gave a great Interruption to the legal Proceedings of Courts; they had a particular Commission and Judicatory for Matters happening in Time of War, stiled, *Placita de Tempore Turbationis,* wherein are many excellent Things: They were made principally about the Battle of Evesham, and after it; and for settling of the Differences of this Kingdom, was the *Dictum,* or *Edictum de Kenelworth* made, which is printed in the old *Magna Charta.*

We have little extant of Resolutions in this King's Time, but what are either remember'd by Bracton, or some few broken and scatter'd Reports collected by Fitzherbet in his Abridgment. There are also some few Sums or Constitutions relative to the Law, which tho' possibly not Acts of Parliament, yet have obtain'd in Use as such; as *De districtione Scaccarii, Statutum Panis & Cervisiæ Dies Communes in Banco Statutum Hiberniæ, Stat. de Scaccario, Judicium Collistrigii,* and others.

We come now to the Time of Edw. 1. who is well stiled our English Justinian; for in his Time the Law, *quasi per Saltum,* obtained a very great Perfection. The Pleadings are short indeed, but excellently good and perspicuous: And altho' for some Time some of those Imperfections and ancient inconvenient Rules obtain'd; as for Instance, in Point of Descents, where the middle Brother held of the eldest, and dying without Issue, the Lands descended to the youngest, upon that old Rule in the Time of Hen. 2. *Nemo Potest esse Dominus & Hæres,* mention'd in Glanville, at least if he had once receiv'd Homage, 13 E. 1. Fitz Avowry 235. Yet the Laws did never in any one Age receive so great and sudden an Advancement, nay, I think I may safely say, all the Ages since his Time have not done so much in Reference to the orderly settling and establishing of the distributive Justice of this Kingdom, as he did within a short Compass of the thirty-five Years of his Reign, especially about the first thirteen Years thereof.

Indeed many Penal Statutes and Provisions, in Relation to the Peace and good Government of the Kingdom, have been since made. But as touching the Common Administration of Justice between Party and Party, and accommodating of the Rules, and of the Methods and Orders of Proceding, he did the most, at least of any King since William 1. and left the same as a fix'd and stable Rule and Order of Proceeding, very little differing from that which we now hold and practice, especially as to the Substance and principal Contexture thereof.

It would be the Business of a Volume to set down all the Particulars, and therefore I shall only give some short Observations touching the same.

First, He perfectly settled the Great Charter, and *Charta de Foresta,* not only by a Practice consonant to them in the Distribution of Law and Right, but also by that solemn Act passed 25 E. 1. and stiled *Confirmationes Cartarum.*

Secondly, He established and distributed the several Jurisdictions of Courts within their proper Bounds. And because this Head has several Branches, I shall subdivide the same, *viz.*

1. He check'd the Incroachments and insolencies of the Pope and the Clergy, by the Statute of Carlisle.

2. He declared the Limits and Bounds of the Ecclesiastical Jurisdiction, by the Statute of *Circumspecte Agatis* & *Articuli Cleri.* For *note,* Tho' this later Statute was not published till Edw. 2. yet was compiled in the Beginning of Edw. 1.

3. He established the Limits of the Court of *Common Pleas,* perfectly performing the Direction of *Magna Charta, Quod Communia placita non sequantur Curia nostra,* in relation to B. R. and in express Terms extending it to the Court of Exchequer by the Statute of *Articuli super Chartas, cap. 4.* It is true, upon my First reading of the *Placita de Banco* of Edw. 1. I found very many Appeals of Death, of Rape, and of Robbery therein; and therefore I doubted, whether the same were not held at least by Writ in the Common Pleas Court: But upon better Inquiry, I found many of the Records before Justices Itinerant were enter'd or fill'd up among the Records of the Common Pleas, which might occasion that Mistake.

4. He establish'd the Extent of the Jurisdiction of the Steward and Marshal. *Vide Articuli super Chartas, cap.* 3. And,

5. He also settled the Bounds of Inferior Courts, not only of Counties, Hundreds, and Courts Baron, which he kept within their proper and narrow Bounds, for the Reasons given before; and so gradually the Common Justice of the Kingdom came to be administred by Men knowing in the Laws, and conversant in the great Courts of B. R. and C. B. and before Justices Itinerant; and also by that excellent Statute of Westminster 1. *cap.* 35. he kept the Courts of Great Men within their Limits, under several Penalties, wherein ordinarily very great Incroachments and Oppressions were exercised.

The *Third* general Observation I make is, He did not only explain, but excellently enforc'd, *Magna Charta,* by the Statute *De Tallagio non concedendo,* 34 E. 1.

Fourthly, He provided against the Interruption of the Common Justice of the Kingdom, by Mandates under the Great Seal, or Privy Seal, by the Statute of *Articuli super Chartas, cap* 6. which, notwithstanding *Magna Charta,* had formerly been frequent in Use.

Fifthly, He settled the Forms, Solemnities, and Efficacies of Fines, confining them to the Common-Pleas, and to Justices Itinerant, and appointed the Place where they brought the Records after their Circuits, whereby one common Repository might be kept of Assurances of Lands; which he did by the Statute *De modo levandi Fines,* 18 E. 1.

Sixthly, He settled that great and orderly Method for the Safety and Preservation of the Peace of the Kingdom, and suppressing of Robberies, by the Statute of Winton.

Seventhly, He settled the Method of Tenures, to prevent Multiplicity of Penalties, which grew to a great Inconvenience, and remedied it by the Statute of *Quia Emptores Terrarum,* 18 E. 1.

Eighthly, He settled a speedier Way for Recovery of Debts, not only for Merchants and Tradesmen, by the Statutes of Acton, Burnel, & *de Mercatoribus,* but also for other Persons, by granting an Execution for a Moiety of the Lands by *Elegit.*

Ninthly, He made effectual Provision for Recovery of Advowsons and Presentations to Churches, which was before infinitely lame and defective, by Statute Westminster 2. *cap.* 1.

Tenthly, He made that great Alteration in Estates from what they were formerly, by Statute Westminster 2. *cap.* 1. whereby Estates of Fee-Simple, conditional at Common Law, were turn'd into Estates-Tail, not removable from the Issue by the ordinary Methods of Alienation; and upon this Statute, and for the Qualifications hereof, are the Superstructures built of 4 H. 7. *cap.* 32. 32 H. 8. and 33 H. 8.

Eleventhly, He introduced quite a new Method, both in the Laws of Wales, and in the Method of their Dispensation, by the Statute of Rutland.

Twelfthly, In brief, partly by the Learning and Experience of his Judges, and partly by his own wise Interposition, he silently and without Noise abrogated many ill and inconvenient Usages, both in his Courts of Justice, and in the Country. He rectified and set in Order the Method of collecting his Revenue in the Exchequer, and removed obsolete and illeviable Parts thereof out of Charge; and by the Statutes of Westminster 1. and Westminster 2. Gloucester and Westminster 3. and of *Articuli super Chartas,* he did remove almost all that was either grievous or impractical out of the Law, and the Course of its Administration, and substituted such apt, short, pithy, and effectual Remedies and Provisions, as by the Length of Time, and Experience had of their Convenience, have stood ever since without any great Alteration, and are now as it were incorporated into, and become a Part of the Common Law itself.

Upon the whole Matter, it appears, That the very Scheme, Mold and Model of the Common Law, especially in relation to the Administration of the Common Justice between Party and Party, as it was highly rectified and set in a much better Light and Order by this King than his Predecessors left it to him, so in a very great Measure it has continued the same in all succeeding Ages to this Day; so that the Mark or *Epocha* we are to take for the true Stating of the Law of England, what it is, is to be considered, stated and estimated from what it was when this King left it. Before his Time it was in a great Measure rude and unpolish'd, in comparison of what it was after his Reduction there-

AFTER WILLIAM I.

of; and on the other Side, as it was thus polished and ordered by
him, so has it stood hitherto without any great or considerable
Alteration, abating some few Additions and Alterations which
succeeding Times have made, which for the most part are in the
subject Matter of the Laws themselves, and not so much in the
Rules, Methods, or ways of its Administration.

As I before observed some of those many great Accessions to
the Perfection of the Law under this King, so I shall now observe
some of those Boxes or Repositories where they may be found,
which are of the following Kinds, *viz.*

First, The Acts of Parliament in the Time of this King are
full of excellent Wisdom and Perspicuity, yet Brevity; but of this,
enough before is said.

Secondly, The Judicial Records in the Time of this King. I
shall not mention those of the Chancery, the Close-Patent and
Charter Rolls, which yet will very much evidence the Learning
and Judgment of that Time; but I shall mention the Rolls of
Judicial Proceedings, especially those in the King's-Bench and
Common-Pleas, and in the Eyres. I have read over many of them,
and do generally observe,

1. That they are written in an excellent Hand.

2. That the Pleading is very short, but very clear and perspicuous, and neither loose or uncertain, nor perplexing the Matter
either with Impropriety, Obscurity, or Multiplicity of Words:
They are clearly and orderly digested, effectually representing
the Business that they intend.

3. That the Title and the Reason of the Law upon which they
proceed (which many times is expresly delivered upon the Record itself) is perspicuous, clear and rational; so that their short
and pithy Pleadings and judgments do far better render the Sense
of the Business, and the Reasons thereof, than those long, intricate, perplexed, and formal Pleadings, that oftentimes of late
are unnecessarily used.

Thirdly, The Reports of the Terms and Years of this King's
Time, a few broken cases whereof are in Fitzherbert's Abridgment; but we have no successive Terms or Years thereof, but only
ancient Manuscripts perchance, not running through the whole
Time of this King, yet they are very good, but very brief: Either

the Judges then spoke less, or the Reporters were not so ready handed as to take all they said. And hence this Brevity makes them the more obscure. But yet in those brief Interlocutions between the Judge and the Pleaders, and in their Definitions, there appears a great deal of Learning and Judgment. Some of those Reports, tho' broken, yet the best of their Kind, are in Lincolns-Inn Library.

Fourthly, The Tracts written or collected in the Time of this wise and excellent Prince, which seem to be of Two Kinds, *viz.* Such as were only the Tractates of private Men, and therefore had no greater Authority than private Collections, yet contain much of the Law then in Use, as Fleta the Mirror, Britton and Thornton; or else, *2dly,* They were Sums or Abstracts of some particular Parts of the Law, as *Novæ Narrationes, Hengam Magna & Parva, Cadit assisa Summa, De Bastardia Summa;* by all which, compared even with Bracton, there appears a Growth and a Perfecting of the Law into a greater Regularity and Order.

And thus much shall serve for the several Periods or Growth of the Common Law until the Time of Edw. 1. inclusively, wherein having been somewhat prolix, I shall be the briefer in what follows, especially feeling that from this Time downwards, the Books and Reports printed give a full Account of the ensuing Progress of the Law.

VIII

A Brief Continuation of the Progress of the Laws, from the Time of King Edward 2. inclusive, down to these Times

Having in the former Chapter been somewhat large in Discoursing of the Progress of the Laws, and the incidental Additions they received in the several Reigns of King William 2. King Hen. 1. King Stephen, King Hen. 2. King Richard 1. King John, King Hen. 3. and King Edw. 1. I shall now proceed to give a brief Account of the Progress thereof in the Time of Edw. 2. and the succeeding Reigns, down to these Times.

Edward 2. succeeding his Father, tho' he was an unfortunate Prince, and by reason of the Troubles and Unevenness of his Reign, the very Law itself had many Interruptions, yet it held its Current in a great Measure according to that Frame and State that his Father had left it in.

Besides the Records of Judicial Proceedings in his Time, many whereof are still extant, there were some other Things that occur'd in his Reign which gave us some kind of Indication of the State and Condition of the Law during that Reign: As,

First, The Statutes made in his Time and especially that of 17 E. 2. stiled *De Prerogativa Regis,* which tho' it be called a Statute, yet for the most part is but a Sum or Collection of certain of the King's Prerogatives that were known Law long before; as for Instance, The King's Wardship of Lands *in Capite* attracting the Wardship of Lands held of others; The King's Grant of a Manor not carrying an Advowson Appendant unless named; The King's Title to the Escheat of the Lands of the Normans, which was in Use from the first Defection of Normandy under King John;

The King's Title to Wreck, Royal Fish, Treasure Trove and many others, which were ancient Prerogatives to the Crown.

Secondly, The Reports of the Years and Terms of this King's Reign; these are not printed in any one entire Volume, or in any Series or Order of Time, only some broken Cases thereof in Fitzherbert's Abridgment, and in some other Books dispersedly; yet there are many entire Copies thereof abroad very excellently reported, wherein are many Resolutions agreeing with those of Edw. 1st's Time. The best Copy of these Reports that I know now extant, is that in Lincoln's-Inn Library, which gives a fair Specimen of the Learning of the Pleaders and Judges of that Time.

King Edw. 3. succeeded his Father; his Reign was long, and under it the Law was improved to the greatest Height. The Judges and Pleaders were very learned: The Pleadings are somewhat more polished than those in the Time of Edw. 1. yet they have neither Uncertainty, Prolixity, nor Obscurity. They were plain and skilful, and in the Rules of Law, especially in relation to Real Actions, and Titles of Inheritance, very learned and excellently polished, and exceeded those of the Time of Edw. 1. So that at the latter End of this King's Reign the Law seemed to be near its Meridian.

The Reports of this King's Time run from the Beginning to the End of his Reign, excepting some few Years between the 10th and 17th, and 30th and 33d Years of his Reign; but those Omitted Years are extant in many Hands in old Manuscripts.

The Book of Assizes is a Collection of the Assizes that happened in the Time of Edw. 3. being from the Beginning to the End extracted out of the Books and Assizes of those that attended the Assizes in the Country.

The Justices Itinerant continued by intermitting Vicissitudes till about the 4th of Edw. 3. and some till the 10th of Edw. 3. Their Jurisdiction extended to pleas of the Crown or Criminal Causes, Civil Suits and Pleas of Liberties, and *Quo Warranto's;* the Reports thereof are not printed, but are in many Hands in Manuscript, both of the Times of Edw. 1. Edw. 2. and Edw. 3. full of excellent Learning. Some few broken Reports of those Eyres, especially of Cornwal, Nottingham, Northampton, and Derby, are collected by Fitzherbert in his Abridgment.

After the 10th of Edw. 3. I do not find any Justices Errant *ad*

Communia Placita, but only *ad Placita Forestæ;* other Things that concerned those Justices Itinerant were supplied and transacted in the Common Bench for *Communia Placita,* in the King's-Bench and Exchequer for *Placita de Libertatibus,* and before Justices of Assize, *Nisi Prius, Oyer* and *Terminer,* and Gaol Delivery for Assizes and pleas of the Crown.

And thus much for the Law in the Time of Edw. 3.

Richard 2. succeeding his Grandfather, the Dignity of the Law, together with the Honour of the Kingdom, by reason of the Weakness of this Prince, and the Difficulties occurring in his Government, seem'd somewhat to decline, as may appear by comparing the Twelve last Years of Edw. 3. commonly called *Quadragesms,* with the Reports of King Richard 2. wherein appears a visible Declination of the Learning and Depth of the Judges and Pleaders.

It is true, we have no printed continued Report of this King's Reign; but I have seen the entire Years and Terms thereof in a Manuscript, out of which, or some other Copy thereof, I suppose Fitzherbert abstracted those broken Cases of this Reign in his Abridgment.

In all those former Times, especially from the End of Edw. 3. back to the Beginning of Edw. 1. the Learning of the Common Law consisted principally in Assizes and Real Actions; and rarely was any Title determined in any Personal Action, unless in Cases of Titles to Rents, or Services by Replevin; and the Reasons thereof were principally these, *viz.*

First, Because these ancient Times were great Favourers of the Possessor, and therefore if about the Time of Edw. 2. a Disseisor had been in Possession by a Year and a Day, he was not to be put out without a Recovery by Assize. Again, if the Disseisor had made a Feoffment, they did not countenance an Entry upon the Feoffee, because thereby he might lose his Warranty, which he might save if he were Impleaded in an Assize or Writ of Entry; and by this Means Real Actions were frequent, and also assizes.

Secondly, They were willing to quiet Men's Possessions, and therefore after a Recovery or Bar in an Assize or Real Action, the Party was driven to an Action of a higher Nature.

Thirdly, Because there was then no known Action wherein a Person could recover his Possession, other than by an Assize or a Real Action; for till the End of Edw. 4. the Possession was not recovered in an *Ejectione firmæ,* but only Damages.

Fourthly, Because an Assize was a speedy and effectual Remedy to recover a Possession, the Jury being ready Impannell'd and at the Bar the first Day of the Return. And altho' by Disusage, the Practisers of Law are not so ready in it, yet the Course thereof in those Times was as ready and as well known to all Professors of the Law as the Course of *Ejectione firmæ* is now.

Touching the Reports of the Years and Terms of Hen. 4. and Hen. 5. I can only say, They do not arrive either in the Nature of the Learning contained in them, or in the Judiciousness and Knowledge of the Judges and Pleaders, nor in any other Respect arise to the Perfection of the last Twelve Years of Edw. 3.

But the Times of Hen. 6. as also of Edw. 4. Edw. 5. and Hen. 7. were Times that abounded with Learning and excellent Men. There is little Odds in the Usefulness or Learning of these Books, only the first Part of Hen. 6. is more barren, spending itself much in Learning of little Moment, and now out of Use; but the second Part is full of excellent Learning.

In the Times of those Three Kings, Hen. 6. Edw. 4. and Hen. 7. the Learning seems to be much alike. But these Two Things are observable in them, and indeed generally in all Reports after the Time of Edw. 3. *viz.*

First, That Real Actions and Assizes were not so frequent as formerly, but many Titles of Land were determined in Personal Actions; and the Reasons hereof seem to be,

1st. Because the Learning of them began by little and little to be less known or understood.

2dly, The ancient Strictness of preserving Possession to Possessors till Eviction by Action, began not to be so much in Use, unless in Cases of Descents and Discontinuances, the latter necessarily drove the Demandant to his *Formedon,* or his *Cui in Vita,* &c. But the Descents that told Entry were rare, because Men preserved their Rights to enter, &c. by continual Claims.

3dly, Because the Statute of 8 H. 6. had helped Men to an

Action to recover their Possessions by a Writ of Forcible Entry, even while the Method of Recovery of Possessions by Ejectments was not known or used.

The *Second* Thing observable is, That tho' Pleadings in the Times of those Kings were far shorter than afterwards, especially after Hen. 8. yet they were much longer than in the Time of King Edw. 3. and the Pleaders, yea and the Judges too, became somewhat too curious therein, so that that Art or Dexterity of Pleading, which in its Use, Nature and Design, was only to render the Fact plain and intelligible, and to bring the Matter to Judgment with a convenient Certainty, began to degenerate from its primitive Simplicity, and the true Use and End thereof, and to become a Piece of Nicety and Curiosity; which how these later Times have improved, the Length of the Pleadings, the many and unnecessary Repetitions, the many Miscarriages of Causes upon small and trivial Niceties in Pleading, have too much witnessed.

I should now say something touching the Times since Hen. 7. to this Day, and therefore shall conclude this Chapter with some general observations touching the Proceedings of Law in these later Times.

And first, I shall begin where I left before, touching the Length and Nicety of Pleadings, which at this Day far exceeds not only that short yet perspicuous Course of Pleading which was in the Time of Hen. 6. Edw. 4. and Hen. 7. but those of all Times whatsoever, as our vast Presses of Parchment for any one Plea do abundantly witness.

And the Reasons thereof seem to be these, *viz.*

First, Because in ancient Times the Pleadings were drawn at the Bar, and the Exceptions (also) taken at the Bar, which were rarely taken for the Pleasure or Curiosity of the Pleader, but only when it was apparent that the Omission or the Matter excepted to was for the most part the very Merit and Life of the Cause, and purposely omitted or mispleaded because his Matter or Cause would bear no better: But now the Pleadings being first drawn in Writing, are drawn to an excessive Length, and with very much Labouriousness and Care enlarged, lest it might afford an Exception not intended by the Pleader, and which could be easily supplied from the Truth of the Case; lest the other Party should catch that Advantage which commonly the adverse Party studies, not in Contemplation of the Merits or Justice of the Cause, but to find a slip to fasten upon, tho' in Truth, either not material to the Merits of the Plea, or at least not to the Merits of the Cause, if the Plea were in all Things conform to it.

Secondly, Because those Parts of Pleading which in ancient Times might perhaps be material, but at this Time are become only mere Styles and Forms, are still continued with much Religion, and so all those ancient Forms at first introduced for Convenience, but now not necessary, or it may be antiquated as to their Use, are yet continued as Things wonderfully material, tho' they only swell the Bulk, but contribute nothing to the Weight of the Plea.

Thirdly, These Pleas being mostly drawn by Clerks, who are paid for Entries and Copies thereof, the larger the Pleadings are, the more Profits come to them, and the dearer the Clerk's Place is, the dearer he makes the Client pay.

Fourthly, An Overforwardness in Courts to give Countenance to frivolous Exceptions, tho' they make nothing to the true Merits of the Cause; whereby it often happens that Causes are not determined according to their Merits, but do often miscarry for inconsiderable Omissions in Pleading.

But, *Secondly,* I shall consider what is the Reason that in the Time of Edw. 1. one Term contained not above two or three Hundred Rolls, but at this Day one Term contains two Thousand Rolls or more.

The Reasons whereof may be these, *viz.*

1st. Many petty Businesses, as Trespasses and Debts under 40 *s.* are now brought to Westminster, which used to be dispatched in the County or Hundred Courts; and yet the Plaintiffs are not to be blamed, because at this Day those inferior Courts are so ill served, and Justice there so ill administred, that they were better seek it (where it may be had) at Westminster, tho' at somewhat more Expence.

2dly, Multitudes of Attorneys practising in the Great Courts at Westminster, who are ready at every Market to gratify the Spleen, Spite or Pride, of every Plaintiff.

3dly, A great Increase of People in this Kingdom above what they were anciently, which must needs multiply Suits.

4thly, A great Increase of Trade and Trading Persons, above what there were in ancient Times, which must have the like Effect.

5thly, Multitudes of new Laws, both Penal and others, all which breed new Questions, and new Suits at Law, and in particular, the Statute touching the devising of Lands, *cum multis aliis.*

6thly, Multiplication of Actions upon the Case, which were rare formerly, and thereby Wager of Law ousted, which discouraged many Suits: For when Men were sure, that in case they rested upon a bare Contract without Specialty, the other Party might wage his Law, they would not rest upon such Contracts without reducing the Debt into a Specialty, if it were of any Value, which created much Certainty, and accorded many Suits.

And herewith I shall conclude this Chapter, shewing what Progress the Law has made, from the Reign of King Edw. 1. down to these Times.

IX

Concerning the settling of the Common Law of England in Ireland and Wales: And some Observations touching the Isles of Man, Jersey and Guernsey, &c.

The Kingdom of Ireland being conquered by Hen. 2. about the Year 1171. He in his Great Council at Oxon, constituted his younger Son, John, King thereof, who prosecuted that Conquest so fully, that he introduced the English Laws into that Kingdom, and swore all the great Men there to the Observation of the same, which Laws were, after the Decease of King John, again reinforc'd by the Writ of King Hen. 3. reciting that of King John, *Rot. Claus.* 10 H. 3. *Memb.* 8. & 10. *Vide infra,* & *Pryn.* 252, 253, &c.

And because the Laws of England were not so suddenly known there, Writs from Time to Time issued from hence, containing divers *Capitula Legum Angliæ,* and commanding their Observation in Ireland, as *Rot. Parl.* 11 H. 3. the Law concerning Tenancy by Curtesy, *Rot. Claus.* 20 H. 3. *Memb.* 3. *Dorso.* The Law concerning the Preference of the Son born after Marriage, to the Son born of the same Woman before Marriage, or *Bastard eigne* & *Mulier puisne, Rot. Clauf.* 20 H. 3. *Memb.* 4. *in Dorso:* So the Law concerning all the Parceners inheriting without doing Homage, and several Transmissions of the like Nature.

For tho' King Hen. 2. had done as much to introduce the English Laws there, as the Nature of the Inhabitants or the Circumstances of the Times would permit; yet partly for want of Sheriffs, that Kingdom being then not divided into Counties, and partly by reason of the Instability of the Irish, he could not fully effect his Design: And therefore, King John, to supply those

Defects as far as he was able, divided Leinster and Munster into the several Counties of Dublin, Kildare, Meath, Uriel, Catherlogh, Kilkenny, Wexford, Waterford, Cork, Limerick, Tiperary, and Kerry; and appointed Sheriffs and other Officers to govern 'em after the Manner of England; and likewise caused an Abstract of the English Laws under his Great Seal to be transmitted thither, and deposited in the Exchequer at Dublin: And soon after, in an Irish Parliament, by a general Consent, and at the Instance of the Irish, he ordain'd, That the English Laws and Customs should thenceforth be observ'd in Ireland; and in order to it, he sent his Judges thither, and erected Courts of Judicature at Dublin.

But notwithstanding these Precautions of King John, yet for that the Brehon Law, and other Irish Customs, gave more of Power to the great Men, and yet did not restrain the Common People to so strict and regular a Discipline as the Laws of England did. Therefore the very English themselves became corrupted by them, and the English Laws soon became of little Use or Esteem, and were look'd upon by the Irish and the degenerate English as a Yoke of Bondage; so that King Hen. 3. was oftentimes necessitated to revive 'em, and by several successive Writs to join the Observation of them. And in the Eleventh Year of his Reign, he sent the following Writ, *viz.*

> Henrici Rex, &c. Baronibus Militibus & aliis liberi Tenentibus Lageniæ, salutem, &c. Satis ut credimus vestra audivit discretio, quod cum bonæ memoriæ Johannes, quondam Rex Angliæ Pater noster venit in Hiberniam, ipse duxit secum viros discretos & Legis peritos, quorum Communi Consilio, & ad instantiam Hiberniensium Statuit & præcepit Leges Anglicanas teneri in Hibernia, ita quod Leges easdem in scriptis readactas reliquit sub sigillo suo ad Scaccar. Dublin. Cum igitur Consuetudo & Lex Angliæ fuerit, quod si aliquis desponsaverit aliquam Mulierem, sive Viduam sive aliam hæreditatem habentem, & ipse postmodum ex ea prolem suscitaverit cujus clamor auditus fuerit infra quatuor parietes idem Vir si supervixerit ipsam uxorem suam, habebit tota vita sua Custodiam Hæreditatis uxoris suæ, licet ea forte habuerit Hæredem de primo viro suo qui fuerit Plenæ ætatis vobis Mandamus injungentes quatenus in loquela quæ est in Curia Willi. Com. Maresc. inter Mauritium Fitz Gerald Petent. & Galfridum de Marisco Justiciarium nostrum Hiberniæ tenen-

tem, vel in Alia Loquela quæ fuerit in Casu prædicto nullo modo Justitiam in contrar' facere præsumatis.

Teste Rege apud Westm.
10 Decemb. Anno 11° Regni Nostri.

And *Note,* In the same Year another Writ was sent to the Lord Justice, commanding him to aid the Episcopal Excommunications in Ireland with the Secular Arm, as in England was used. And about this Time, Hubert de Burgo, the Chief Justice of England, and Earl of Kent, was made Earl of Connaught, and Lord Justice of Ireland during Life; and because he could not personally attend, he on March the 10th, 1227, appointed Richard de Burgo, to be his Deputy, or Lord Justice, to whom the King sent the following Writ:

> Rex dilecto & fideli suo Richardo de Burgo Justiciario suo Hiberniæ salutem. Mandamus vobis firmiter præcipientes, quatenus certo die & loco faciatis venire coram vobis, Archiepiscopos, Episcopos, Abbates, Priores, Comites & Barones, Milites & libere Tenentes & Ballivos singulorum Comitatuum, & coram eis publice legi faciatis Chartam Domini Johannis Regis Patris nostri, cui sigillum suum appensum est, quam fieri fecit, & jurari a Magnatibus Hiberniæ de Legibus & consuetudinibus Anglorum observandis in Hibernia, & Præcipiatis eis ex parte nostra, quod Leges illas & consuetudines in Charta prædicta contentas de cetero firmiter teneant & observent. Et hoc idem per singulos Comitatus Hiberniæ clamari faciatis, & teneri prohibentes firmiter ex parte nostra & forisfacturam nostram, ne quis contra hoc Mandatum nostrum, venire præsumat. Eo excepto quod nec de morte nec de catallis Hibernensium occisorum nihil statuatur ex parte nostra citra quindecim dies a Sancti Michaelis, Anno Regni Nostri 12°. Super quo respectum dedimus Magnat. nostri de Hib. usque ad Terminum prædict' Teste Meipso apud Westm. 8° die Maii, Anno Regni Nostri 12°.

And about the 20th Year of Hen. 3. several Writs were sent into Ireland, especially directing several Statutes which had been made in England to be put in Use, and to be observed in Ireland; as the Statute of Merton in the Case of Bastardy, &c.

But yet it seems by the frequent Grants that were made afterwards to particular Native Irish Men, *quod legibus utantur Anglicanis,* That the Native Irish had not the full Privilege of the

116

English Laws, in Relation at least to the Liberties of English Men, till about the Third of Edw. 3. *Vide Rot. Claus.* 2 E. 3. *Memb.* 17.

As the Common Law of England was thus by King John and Hen. 3. introduced into Ireland, so in the Tenth of Hen. 7. all the precedent Statutes of England were there settled by the Parliament of Ireland. 'Tis true, many ancient Irish Customs continued in Ireland, and do continue there even unto this Day; but such as are contrary to the Laws of England are disallow'd *Vide* Davis's Reports, the Case of Tanistry.

As touching Wales, That was not always the Feudal Territory of the Kingdom of England; but having been long governed by a Prince of their own, there were very many Laws and Customs used in Wales, utterly strange to the Laws of England, the Principal whereof they attribute to their King Howell Dha.

After King Edw. 1. had subdued Wales, and brought it immediately under his Dominion; He first made a strict Inquisition touching the Welsh Laws within their several Commotes and Seigniores, which Inquisitions are yet of Record: After which, in the 12th of Edw. 1. the Statute of Rutland was made, whereby the Administration of Justice in Wales was settled in a Method very near to the Rule of the Law of England. The Preamble of the said Statute is notable, *viz.*

> Edvardus Dei gratia Rex Angliæ Dominus Hiberniæ & Dux Acquitaniæ omnibus Fidelibas suis de Terra sua de Snodon & de aliis terris suis in Wallia Salutem in Domino. Divina Providentia quæ in sua Dispositione non fallitur, inter alia suae Dispensationis Munera, quibus nos & Regnum nostrum Angliæ decorari dignata est, Terram Walliæ cum incolis suis prius nobis juri Feodali subjectam, tam sui gratia in proprietatis nostræ Dominium, obstaculis quibuscunque cessantibus, totaliter & cum integritate convertit, & Coroniæ Regni prædicti tantum partem corporis ejusdem annexuit & univit. Nos, &c.

According to the Method in that Statute prescribed, has the Method of Justice been hitherto administred in Wales, with such Alterations and additions therein as have been made by the several subsequent Statutes of 27 and 34 H. 8. &c.

Touching the Isle of Man. This was sometimes Parcel of the

Kingdom of Norway, and governed by Particular Laws and Customs of their own, tho' many of them hold Proportion, or bear some Analogy, to the Laws of England, and probably were at first and originally derived from hence; seeing the Kingdom of Norway as well as the Isle of Man have anciently been in Subjection to the Crown of England. *Vide Legis Willi. Primi,* in Lambard's *Saxon Laws.*

Berwick was sometimes Parcel of Scotland, but was won by Conquest by King Edw. 1. and after that lost by King Edw. 2. and afterwards regained by Edw. 3. It was governed by the Laws of Scotland, and their own particular Customs, and not according to the Rules of the Common Law of England, further than as by Custom it is there admitted, as in *Liber Parliamenti,* 21 E. 1. in the Case of Moyne and Bartlemew, *pro Dote* in Berwick; yet now by Charter, they send Burgesses to the Parliament of England.

Touching the Islands of Jersey, Guernsey, Sark, and Alderney; They were anciently a Part of the Dutchy of Normandy, and in that Right, the Kings of England held them till the Time of King John; but although King John, as is before shewn, was unjustly deprived of that Dutchy, yet he kept the Islands; and when after that, they were by Force taken from him, he by the like Force regained them, and they have ever since continued in the Possession of the Crown of England.

As to their Laws, they are not governed by the Laws of England, but by the Laws and Customs of Normandy. But not as they are at this Day; for since the actual Division and Separation of those Islands from that Dutchy, there have been several New Edicts and Laws made by the Kings of France which have much altered the old Law of Normandy, which Edicts and Laws bind not in those Islands, they having been ever since King John's Time at least under the actual Allegiance of England.

And hence it is, that tho' there be late Collections of the Laws and Customs of Normandy, as Terrier and some others, yet they are not of any Authority it those Islands; for the Decision of Controversies, as the Grand Contumier of Normandy is, which is (at least in the greatest Part thereof) a Collection of the Laws of Normandy as they stood before the Disjoining of those Islands from the Dutchy, *viz.* before the Time of King Hen. 3. tho' there be in that Collection some Edicts of the Kings of France which were made after that Disjunction; and those Laws, as I have shewn before, tho' in some Things they agree with the Laws of England, yet in many Things they differ, and in some are absolutely repugnant.

And hence it is, that regularly Suits arising in those Islands are not to be tried or determined in the King's Courts in England, but are to be heard, tried, and determined in those Islands, either before the ordinary Courts of Jurats there, or by the Justices Itinerant there, commissioned under the Great Seal of England, to determine Matters there arising; and the Reason is, because their Course of Proceedings, and their Laws, differ from the Course of Proceedings and the Laws of England.

And altho' it be true, that in ancient Times, since the Loss of Normandy, some scattering Instances are of Pleas moved here touching Things done in those Islands, yet the general settled Rule has been to remit them to those Islands, to be tried and determined there by their Law; tho' at this Day the Courts at Westminster hold Plea of all transitory Actions wheresoever they arise, for it cannot appear upon the Record where they did arise. *Mic.* 42 E. 2. *Rot.* 45. *coram Rege.* A great Complaint was made by Petition, against the Deputy Governor of those Islands, for divers Oppressions and Wrongs done there: This Petition was by the Chancellor delivered into the Court of B. R. to proceed upon it, whereupon there were Pleadings on both Sides; but because it appeared to be for Things done and transacted in the said Islands, Judgment was thus given:

> Et quia Negotiam prædict' in Curia hic terminari non potest, eo quod Juratores Insulæ prædict' coram Justitiariis hic venire non possunt, nec de Jure debent, nec aliqua Negotia infra Insula prædicta emergentia terminari non debent, nisi secundum Consuet. Insulæ Prædictæ. Ideo Recordum retro traditur Cancellario ut inde fiat Commissio Domini Regis ad Negotia prædicta in Insula prædicta audienda & Terminanda secundum Consuet' Insulæ prædictæ.

And accordingly 14 *Junii,* 1565, upon a Report from the Attorney General, and Advice with the two Chief Justices, a general Direction was given by the Queen and her Council, That all Suits between the Islanders, or wherein one Party was an Islander, for Matters arising within the Islands, should be there heard and determined.

But still this is to be taken with this Distinction and Limitation, *viz.* That where the Suit is immediately for the King, there the King may make his Suit in any of the Courts here, especially in the Court of King's-Bench: For Instance, in a *Quare Impedit* brought by the King in B. R. here for a Church in those Islands; so in a *Quo Warranto* for Liberties there; so a Demand of Redemption of Lands sold by the King's Tenant within a Year and a Day according to the Custom of Normandy; so in an Information for a Riot, or grand Contempt against a Governor deputed by the King. These and the like Suits have been maintained by the King in his Court of King's-Bench here, tho' for Matters arising within those Islands: This appears, *Paschæ* 16 E. 2. *coram Rege, Rot.* 82. Mich. 18 E. 2. *Rot.* 123, 124, 125. & *Pas.* 1 E. 3. *Rot.* 59.

And for the same Reason it is, that a Writ of *Habeas Corpus* lies into those Islands for one imprisoned there, for the King may demand, and must have an Account of the Cause of any of his Subjects Loss of Liberty; and therefore a Return must be made of this Writ, to give the Court an Account of the Cause of Imprisonment; for no Liberty, whether of a County Palatine, or other, holds Place against those *Brevia Mandatoria,* as that great Instance of punishing the Bishop of Durham for refusing to execute a Writ of *Habeas Corpus* out of the King's Bench, 33 E. 1. makes evident.

And as Pleas arising in the Islands regularly, ought not in the first Instance to be deduced into the Courts here, (except in the King's Case;) so neither ought they to be deduced into the King's Courts here in the second Instance; and therefore if a Sentence or Judgment be given in the Islands, the Party grieved thereby, may have his Appeal to the King and his Council to reverse the same if there be Cause. And this was the Course of Relief in the Dutchy of Normandy, *viz.* by Appeal to the Duke and his Council; and in the same Manner, it is still observed in the Case of erroneous Decrees or Sentences in those Islands, *viz.* To appeal to the King and his Council.

But the Errors in such Decrees or Sentences are not examined by Writ of Error in the King's-Bench, for these Reasons, *viz.*

1st. Because the Courts there, and those here, go not by the same Rule, Method, or Order of Law.

And *2dly,* Because those Islands, though they are Parcel of the Dominion of the Crown of England, yet they are not Parcel of the Realm of England, nor indeed ever were; but were anciently Parcel of the Dutchy of Normandy, and are those Remains thereof which the Power of the Crown and Kingdom of France have not been able to wrest from the Kings of England.

X

Concerning the Communication of the Laws of England unto the Kingdom of Scotland

Because this Inquiry will be of Use, not only in itself, but also as a Parallel Discovery of the Transmission of the English Laws into Scotland, as before is shewn they were into Normandy; I shall in this Chapter pursue and solve their several Queries, *viz.*

1st, What Laws of Scotland hold a Congruity and Suitableness with those of England.

2dly, Whether these be a sufficient Ground for us to suppose, that that Similitude or Congruity began with a Conformation of their Laws to those of England. And,

3dly, What might be reasonably judged to be the Means or Reason of the Conformation of their Laws unto the Laws of England.

As to the First of these Inquiries; It is plain, beyond all Contradiction, that many of the Laws of Scotland hold a Congruity and Similitude, and many of them a perfect Identity with the Laws of England, at least as the English Laws stood in the Times of Hen. 2. Richard 1. King John, Henry 3. and Edw. 1. And altho' in Scotland, Use hath always been made of the Civil Law, in point of Direction or Guidance, where their Municipal Laws, either Customary or Parliamentary failed; yet as to their particular Municipal Laws, we shall find a Resemblance, Parity and Identity, in their Laws with the Laws of England, anciently in Use; and we need go no further for Evidence hereof, than the *Regiam Majestatem,* a Book published by Mr. Skeen in Scotland.

It would be too long to Instance in all the Points that might be produced; and therefore I shall single out some few, remitting the Reader for his further Satisfaction to the Book itself.

Dower of the Wife to be the Third Part of her Husband's Lands of Inheritance; the Writ to recover the same; the Means of forfeiting thereof by Treason or Felony of the Husband or Adultery of the Wife; are in great Measure conformable to the Laws of England. *Vide Regiam Majestatem, Lib.* 2. *cap.* 16, 17. and *Quoniam Attachiamento, cap.* 85.

The Exclusion of the Descent to the elder Brother by his receiving Homage, which tho' now antiquated in England, was anciently received here for Law, as appears by Glanville, *Lib.* 7. *cap.* 1. and *Vide Regiam Majestatem, Lib.* 2. *cap.* 22.

The Exclusion of Daughters from Inheritances by a Son: The Descent to all the Daughters in Coparcenary for want of Sons; the chief House allotted to the eldest Daughter upon this Partition; the Descent to the Collateral Heirs, for want of Lineal, &c. *Ibid. cap.* 24, 25, 26, 27, 28, 33, 34. But this is now altered in some Things *per Stat. Rob. cap.* 3.

The full Ages of Males 21, of Females 14, to be out of Ward in Socage 16. *Ibid. cap.* 42.

That the Custody of Idiots belonged to the King, *Ibid. cap.* 46.

The Custody of Heirs in Socage belong to the next of Kin, to whom the Inheritance can't descend. *Vide Regiam Majest. cap.* 47.

The Son born before Marriage, or *Bastard eigne,* not to be legitimate by the Marriage after, nor was he hereditable by the ancient Laws of Scotland, though afterward altered in Use, as it seems, *Regiam Majest. cap.* 51.

The Confiscation of *Bona Usurariorum,* after their Death, conform to the old Law here used. *Ibid. cap.* 54. tho' now antiquated.

The Laws of Escheats, for want of Heirs, or upon Attainder. *Ibid. cap.* 55.

The Acquittal of Lands given in Frank-Marriage, till the fourth Degree be past, *Ibid. cap.* 57.

Homage, the Manner of making it with the Persons, by, or to whom, as in England, *Ibid. cap.* 61, 62, 63, &c.

The Relief of an Heir in Knights Service, of full Age, *Regiam Majestatem, cap.* 17.

The Preference of the Sister of the whole Blood, before the Sister of the half Blood. *Quoniam Attachiamento, cap.* 89.

The single Value of the Marriage, and Forfeiture of the double Value, precisely agree with the Statute of Marlbridge. *Ibid. cap.* 91.

The Forfeiture of the Lord's disparaging his Ward in Marriage, agrees with *Magna Charta,* and the Statute of Marlbridge. *Quoniam Attachiamento, cap.* 92.

The Preference of the Lord by Priority to the Custody of the Ward. *Ibid. cap.* 95.

The Punishment of the Ravisher of a Ward, by two Years Imprisonment, &c. as here. *Ibid. cap.* 90.

The Jurisdiction of the Lord in Infangtheof. *Ibid. cap.* 100.

Goods confiscate, and Deodands, as here, *Liber De Modo tenendi Cur. Baron. cap.* 62, 63, 64.

And the like of Waifs. *Ibid. cap.* 65.

Widows, not to marry without Consent of the Lord, Statute *Mesei.* 2. *cap.* 23.

Wreck of the Sea, defined precisely as in the Statute Westm. 2. *Vide Ibid. cap.* 25.

The Division of the Deceased's Goods, one Third to the Wife, another Third to the Children, and another to the Executor, &c. conformable to the ancient Law of England, and the Custom of the North to this Day. *Lib.* 2. *cap.* 37.

Also the Proceedings to recover Possessions, by *Mortdancester, Juris Utrum, Assise de Novel disseisin,* &c. The Writs and Process are much the same with those in England, and are directed according to Glanville, and the old Statutes in the Time of Edw. 1. and Hen. 3. *Vide Regiam Majestat. Lib.* 3. *cap.* 27 to 36.

Many more Instances might be given of many of the Municipal Laws of Scotland, either precisely the same with those in England, or very near, and like to them: Tho' it is true, they have some particular Laws that hold not that Conformity to ours, which were introduced either by particular or common Customs, or by Acts of their Parliaments. But, by what has been said and instanced in, it appears, That like as between the Laws of England and Normandy, so also between the Laws of England and Scotland, there was anciently a great Similitude and Likeness.

I come therefore to the Second Thing I proposed to enquire into, *viz.* what Evidence there is, That those Laws of Scotland were either desumed from the English Laws, or from England, transmitted thither in such a Manner, as that the Laws here in England were as it were the Original or prime Exemplar, out of which those parallel or similar Laws of Scotland were copied or transcribed into the Body of their Laws: And this appears evident on the following Reasons, *viz.*

First, For that Glanville (which, as has been observed, is the ancientest Collection we have of English Laws) seem to be even transcribed in many entire *Capita* of the Laws above-mentioned, and in some others where Glanville doubts, that Book doubts; and where Glanville follows the Practice of the Laws then in Use, tho' altered in succeeding Times, at least after the Reign of Edw. 1. there the *Regiam Majestatem* does accordingly; for Instance, *viz.*

Glanville, *Lib.* 7. *cap.* 1. determines, That a Man can't give away part of the Lands which he held by Hereditary Descent unto his Bastard, without the Consent of his Heir, and that he may not give all his Purchases from his eldest Son; and this is also declared to be the Law of Scotland accordingly, *Regiam Majestatem, Lib.* 2. *cap.* 19, 20. Tho' since Glanville's Time, the Law has been altered in England.

Also Glanville, *Lib.* 7. *cap.* 1. makes a great Doubt, Whether the second Son, being enfeoffed by the Father, and dies without Issue; whether the Land shall return to the Father, or descend to his eldest, or to his youngest Brother; and at last gives such a Decision as we find almost in the same Terms and Words recited in the Question and Decisions laid down in *Regiam. Majest. Lib.* 2. *cap.* 22.

Again, Glanville, *Lib.* 7. *cap.* 1. makes it a difficult Question in his Time, Whether the eldest Son dying in the Life-time of his Father, having Issue, the Nephew or the youngest Son shall inherit; and gives the Arguments *pro & contra:* And *Regiam Majestatem, cap.* 33. seems to be even a Transcript thereof out of Glanville.

And further, the Tract concerning Assizes, and the Time of Limitation, the very Form of the Writs, and the Method of the

Process, and the Directions touching their Proceedings are but Transcripts of Glanville, as appears by comparing *Regiam Majestatem, Lib.* 3. *cap.* 36. with Glanville, *Lib.* 13. *cap.* 32. and the Collector of those Laws of Scotland in all the before-mentioned Places, and divers others, quotes Glanville as the Pattern at least of those Laws.

But *Secondly,* A second Evidence is, because many of the Laws which are mentioned in the *Regiam Majestatem quoniam Archiamento,* and other Collections of the Scotish Laws, are in Truth very Translations of several Statutes made in England in the Times of King Hen. 3. and King Edw. 1. For Instance; the Statute of their King Robert 2. *cap.* 1. touching Alienations to Religious Men, is nothing else but an Enacting of the Statute of *Mortmain,* 13 E. 1. *cap.* 13. The Law above-mentioned, touching the Disparagement of Wards, is desumed out of *Magna Charta, cap.* 6. and the Statute of Merton, *cap.* 6. So the Law abovesaid, against Ravishers of Wards, is taken out of Westm. 2. *cap.* 35. So the said Law of the double Value of Marriage, is taken out of Westm. 1. *cap.* 22. The Law concerning Wreck of the Sea, is but a Transcript out of Westm. 1. *cap.* 4. and divers other Instances of like Nature might be given, whereby it may appear, that very many of those Laws in Scotland which are a part of their *Corpus Juris,* bear a Similitude to the Laws of England, and were taken as it were out of those Common or Statute Laws here, that obtain'd in the Time of Edw. 1. and before, but especially such as were in Use or Enacted in the Time of Edw. 1. and the Laws of England, relative to those Matters, were as it were the Original and Exemplar from whence those Similar or Parallel Laws of Scotland were derived or borrowed.

Thirdly, I come now to consider the Third Particular, *viz.* By what Means, or by what Reason this Similitude of Laws in England and Scotland happened, or upon what Account, or how the Laws of England at least in many Particulars, or *Capita Legum,* came to be communicated into Scotland, and they seem to be principally these two, *viz. First,* The Vicinity of that Kingdom to this. And *Secondly,* The Subjection of that Kingdom unto the Kings of England, at least for some considerable Time.

Touching the former of these; *First,* It is very well known, that England and Scotland made but one Island, divided not by the Sea or any considerable Arm thereof, but only by the Inter-jacency of the River Tweed, and some Desart Ground, which did not hinder any easy common Access of the People of the one Kingdom to the other: And by this Means, *First*, The Intercourse of Commerce between that Kingdom and this was very frequent and usual, especially in the Northern Counties, and this Inter-course of Commerce brought unto those of Scotland an Acquaint-ance and Familiarity with our English Laws and Customs, which in Process of Time were adopted and received gradually into Scotland.

Again, *Secondly*, This Vicinity gave often Opportunities of transplanting of Persons of either Nation into the other, espe-cially in those Northern Parts, and thereby the English trans-planted and carried with them the Use of their Native Customs of England, and the Scots transplanted hither, became acquainted with our Customs, which by occasional Remigrations were gradu-ally translated and became diffus'd and planted in Scotland; and it is well known, that upon this Account some of the Nobility and great Men of Scotland had Possessions here as well as there: The Earls of Angus were not only Noblemen of Scotland, but were also Barons of Parliament here, and sate in our English Parliaments, as appears by the Summons to Parliament, *Tempore Edvardi Tertii.*

Again, *Thirdly*, The Kings of Scotland had Feodal Possessions here; for Instance, The Counties of Cumberland, Northumber-land and Westmoreland, were anciently held of the Crown of England by the Kings of Scotland, attended with several Vicissi-tudes and Changes until the Feast of St. Michael, 1237, at which Time Alexander King of Scotland finally released his Preten-sions thereunto, as appears by the Deed thereof enter'd into the Red-Book of the Exchequer, and the Parliament Book of 20 E. 1. and in Consideration thereof, Hen. 3. gave him the Lands of Penreth and Sourby, *Habend' sibi Heredibus suis Regibus Scotiæ*, and by Virtue of that Special Limitation, they came to John the eldest Son of the eldest Daughter of Alexander King of Scot-land, together with that Kingdom; but the Land of Tindale, and the Manor of Huntingdon, which were likewise given to him and his Heirs, but without that Special Limitation, *Regibus Scotiæ*, fell in Coparcenry, one Moiety thereof to the said John

King of Scotland, as the Issue of the eldest Daughter, and the other Moiety to Hastings, who was descended from the younger Daughter of the said Alexander: But those Possessions came again to the Crown of England by the Forfeiture of King John of Scotland, who through the Favour of the King of England he had Restitution of the Kingdom of Scotland, yet never had Restitution of those Possessions he had in England, and forfeited and lost by his levying War against the Kingdom of England, as aforesaid.

And thus I have shewn, that the Vicinity of the Kingdoms of England and Scotland, and the Consequence thereof, *viz.* Translations of Persons and Families, Intercourse of Trade and Commerce, and Possessions obtained by the Natives of each Kingdom in the other, might be one Means for communicating our Laws to them.

But *Secondly,* There was another Means far more effectual for that End, *viz.* The Superiority and Interest that the Kings of England obtain'd over the Crown and Kingdom of Scotland, whereby it is no Wonder that many of our English Laws were transplanted thither by the Power of the English Kings. This Interest, Dominion, or Superiority of the Kings of England in the Realm of Scotland may be considered these Two Ways, *viz.* *1st,* How it stood antecedently to the Reign of King Edw. 1. And *2dly,* How it stood in his Time.

Touching the former of those, I shall not trouble myself with collecting Arguments or Authorities relating thereto; he that desires to see the whole Story thereof, let him consult Walsingham, *sub Anno* 18 Edw. 1. as also *Rot. Parl.* 12 R. 2. *Pars secunda,* No. 3. *Rot. Claus.* 29 E. 1. M. 10. *Dorso,* and the Letter of the Nobility to the Pope asserting it. *Ibid.*

And this might be one Means, whereby the Laws of England in elder Times might in some Measure be introduced into Scotland.

But I rather come to the Times of King Edw. 1. who was certainly the greatest Refiner of the English Laws, and studiously endeavoured to enlarge the Dominions of the Crown of England, so to extend and propagate the Laws of England into all Parts subject to his Dominion. This Prince, besides the ancient Claim he made to the Superiority of the Crown of England over that of Scotland, did for many Years actually enjoy that Superiority in its full Extent, and the Occasion and Progress thereof was thus, as it is related by Walsingham, and consonantly to him appears by the Records of those Times, *viz.* King Edw. 1. having formerly received the Homage and Fealty of Alexander King of Scots, as appears *Rot. Claus.* 5 E. 1. M. 5. *Dorso,* was taken to be *Superior Dominus Scotiæ Regni.*

Alexander dying, left Margaret his only Daughter, and she dying without Issue, about 18 E. 1. there fell a Controversy touching the Succession of the Crown of Scotland, between the King of Norway claiming as Tenant by the Curtesy, Robert de Bruce descended from the younger Daughter of David King of Scots, and John de Baliol descended from the elder Daughter, with divers other Competitors.

All the Competitors submit their Claim to the Decision of Edw. 1. King of England as *Superior Dominus Regni Scotiæ,* who thereupon pronounced his Sentence for John de Baliol, and accordingly put him in Possession of the Kingdom, and required and received his Homage.

The King of England, notwithstanding this, kept still the Possession, & *Insignia* of his Superiority; his Court of King's-Bench sate actually at Roxborough in Scotland, Mich. 20, 21 Ed. 1. *coram Rege,* and upon Complaint of Injuries done by the said John King of Scots, now restor'd to his Kingdom, he summoned him often to answer in his Courts, Mich. 21, 22 Edw. 1. Northumb. Scot. He was summoned by the Sheriff of Northumberland to answer to Walbesi in the King's Court, *Pas.* 21. E. 1. *coram Rege. Rot.* 34. He was in like manner summoned to answer John Mazune in the King's-Bench for an Injury done to him, and Judgment given against the King of Scots, and that Judgment executed.

John King of Scots, being not contented with this Subjection, did in the 24th Year of King Edw. 1. resign back his Homage to King Edward, and bid Defiance to him; wherefore King Edw. 1. the same Year with a powerful Army entered Scotland, took the King of Scots Prisoner, and the greatest part of that Kingdom into his Possession, and appointed the Earl Warren to be *Custos Regni,* Cressingham to be his Treasurer, and Ormsby his Justice, and commanded his Judges of his Courts of England to issue the King of England's Writs into Scotland.

And when in the 27th Year of his Reign, the Pope, instigated by the French King, interpos'd in the Behalf of the King of Scotland, he and his Nobility resolutely denied the Pope's Intercession and Mediation.

Thus the Kingdom of Scotland continued in an actual Subjection to the Crown of England for many Years; for *Rot. Claus.* 33 E. 1. *Membr.* 13. *Dorso,* and *Rot. Claus.* 34 E. 1. *Memb.* 3. *Dorso;* several Provisions are made for the better ordering of the Government of Scotland.

What Proceedings there were herein in the Time of Edw. 2. and what Capitulations and Stipulations were afterwards made by King Edw. 3. upon the Marriage of his Sister by Robert de Bruce touching the Relaxation of the *Superius Dominium* of Scotland, is not pertinent to what I aim at, which is, to shew how the English Laws that were in Use and Force in the Time of Edw. 1. obtained to be of Force in Scotland, which is but this, *viz.*

King Edward 1. having thus obtained the actual Superiority of the Crown of Scotland, from the Beginning of the Reign until his 20th Year, and then placing John de Baliol in that Kingdom, and yet continuing his Superiority thereof, and keeping his Courts of Justice, and exercising Dominion and Jurisdiction by his Officers and Ministers in the very Bowels of that Kingdom, and afterwards upon the Defection of this King John, in the 24th of Edw. 1. taking the whole Kingdom into his actual Administration, and placing his own Judges and great Officers there, and commanding his Courts of King's-Bench (&c.) here, to Issue their Process thither, and continuing in the actual Administration of the Government of that Kingdom during Life: It is no Wonder that those Laws, which obtained and were in Use in England, in and before the Time of this King, were in a great Measure translated thither; and possibly either by being enacted in that Kingdom, or at least for so long Time, put in Use and Practice there, many of the Laws in Use and Practice here in England were in his Time so rivetted and settled in that Kingdom, that 'tis no Wonder to find they were not shaken or altered by the liberal Concessions made afterwards by King Edw. 3. upon the Marriage of his Sister; but that they remain Part of the Municipal Laws of that Kingdom to this Day.

And that which renders it more evident, That this was one of the greatest Means of fixing and continuing the Laws of England in Scotland, is this, *viz.* This very King Edw. 1. was not only a Martial and Victorious, but also a very Wise and Prudent Prince, and one that very well knew how to use a Victory, as well as obtain it: And therefore knew it was the best Means of keeping those Dominions he had powerfully obtain'd, by substituting and translating his own Laws into the Kingdom which he had thus subdued. Thus he did upon his Conquest of Wales; and doubtless thus he did upon his Conquest of Scotland, and those Laws which we find there so nearly agreeing with the Laws of England used in his Time, especially the Statutes of Westm. 1. and Westm. 2. are the Monuments and Footsteps of his Wisdom and Prudence.

And, as thus he was a most Wise Prince, and to secure his Acquests, introduced many other Laws of his Native Kingdom into Scotland; so he very well knew the Laws of England were excellent Laws fitted for the due Administration of Justice to the Constitution of the Governed, and fitted for the Preservation of the Peace of a Kingdom, and for the Security of a Government: And therefore he was very solicitous, by all prudent and careful Means imaginable, to graft and plant the Laws of England in all Places where he might, having before-hand used all possible Care and Industry for Rectifying and Refining the English Laws to their greatest Perfection.

Again, It seems very evident, that the Design of King Edw. 1. was by all Means possible to unite the Kingdom of Scotland (as he had done the Principality of Wales) to the Crown of England, so that thereby Britain might have been one entire Monarchy, including Scotland as well as Wales and England under the same Sceptre; and in order to the accomplishing thereof, there could not have been a better Means than to make the Interest of Scotland one with England, and to knit 'em as it were together in one Communion, which could never have been better done than by establishing one Common Law and Rule of Justice and Commerce among them; and therefore he did, as Opportunity and Convenience served, translate over to that Kingdom as many of our English Customs and Laws as within that Compass of Time he conveniently could.

And thus I have given an Essay of the Reasons and Means, how and why we find so many Laws in Scotland parallel to those in England, and holding so much of Congruity and Likeness to them.

And the Reason why we have but few of their Laws that correspond with ours of a later Date than Edw. 1. or at least Edw. 2. is because since the Beginning of Edw. 3. that Kingdom has been distinct, and held little Communion with us till the Union of the two Crowns in the Person of King James 1. and in so great an Interval it must needs be, that by the Intervention and Succession of new Laws, much of what was so ancient as the Times of Edw. 1. and Edw. 2. have received many Alterations: So that it is a great Evidence of the Excellency of our English Laws, that there remain to this Day so many of them in Force in that Part of Great Britain continuing to bear Witness, that once that excellent Prince Edw. 1. exercised Dominion and Jurisdiction there.

And thus far of the Communion of the Laws of England to Scotland, and of the Means whereby it was effected; from whence it may appear, That as in Wales, Ireland and Normandy, so also in Scotland, such Laws which in those Places have a Congruity or Similitude with the Laws of England, were derived from the Laws of England, as from their Fountain and Original, and were not derived from any of those Places to England.

XI

Touching the Course of Descents in England

Among the many Preferences that the Laws of England have above others, I shall single out Two particular Titles which are of Common Use, wherein their Preference is very visible, and the due Consideration of their Excellence therein, may give us a handsome Indication or Specimen of their Excellencies above other Laws in other Parts or Titles of the same also.

Those Titles, or *Capitula Legum,* which I shall single out for this Purpose, are these Two, *viz. 1st,* The hereditary Transmission of Lands from Ancestor to Heir, and the Certainty thereof: and *2dly,* The Manner of Trial by Jury, which, as it stands at this Day settled in England, together with the Circumstances and Appendixes thereof, is certainly the best Manner of Trial in the World; and I shall herein give an Account of the successive Progress of those *Capitula Legis,* and what Growth they have had in Succession of Time till they arriv'd so that State and Perfection which they have now obtain'd.

First, Then, touching Descents and hereditary Transmissions: It seems by the Laws of the Greeks and Romans, that the same Rule was held both in Relation to Lands and Goods, where they were not otherwise disposed of by the Ancestor, which the Romans therefore called *Successio ab intestato;* but the Customs of particular Countries, and especially here in England, do put a great Difference, and direct a several Method in the Transmission of Goods or Chattels, and that of the Inheritances of Lands.

Now as to hereditary Transmissions or Successions, commonly called with us Descents, I shall hold this Order in my Discourse, *viz.*

First, I shall give some short Account of the ancient Laws both of the Jews, the Greeks, and the Romans, touching this Matter.

Secondly, I shall observe some Things wherein it may appear, how the particular Customs or Municipal Laws of other Countries varied from those Laws, and the Laws here formerly used.

Thirdly, I shall give some Account of the Rules and Laws of Descents or hereditary Transmissions as they formerly stood, and as at this Day they stand in England, with the successive Alterations, that Process of Time, and the Wisdom of our Ancestors, and certain Customs grown up, tacitly, gradually, and successively have made therein.

And First, touching the Laws of Succession, as well of Descent of Inheritances of Lands, as also of Goods and Chattels, which among the Jews was the same in both.

Mr. Selden, in his Book *De Successionibus apud Hebræos,* has given us an excellent Account, as well out of the Holy Text as out of the Comments of the Rabins, or Jewish Lawyers, touching the same, which you may see at large in the 5th, 6th, 7th, 12th and 13th Chapters of that Book; and which, for so much thereof as concerns my present Purpose, I shall briefly comprise under the Eight following Heads, *viz.*

First, That in the Descending Line, the Descent or Succession was to all the Sons, only the eldest Son had a double Portion to any one of the rest, *viz.* If there were three Sons, the Estate was to be divided into four Parts, of which the eldest was to have two Fourth Parts, and the other two Sons were to have one Fourth Part each.

Secondly, If the Son died in his Father's Life-time, then the Grandson, and so *in Infinitum,* succeeded in the Portion of his Father, as if his Father had been in Possession of it, according to the *Jus Representationis* now in Use here.

Thirdly, The Daughter did not succeed in the Inheritance of the Father as long as there were Sons, or any Descendants from Sons in Being; but if any of the Sons died in the Life-time of his

Father having Daughters, but without Sons, the Daughters succeeded in his Part as if he himself had been Possessed.

Fourthly, And in Case the Father left only Daughters and no Sons, the Daughters equally succeeded to their Father as in Co-partnership, without any Prelation or Preference of the eldest Daughter to two Parts, or a double Portion.

Fifthly, But if the son had purchased an Inheritance and died without Issue, leaving a Father and Brothers, the Inheritance of such Son so dying did not descend to the Brothers, (unless in Case of the next Brother's taking to Wife the Deceased's Widow to raise up Children to his deceased Brother) but in such Case the Father inherited to such Son entirely.

Sixthly, But if the Father in that Case was dead, then it came to the Brothers, as it were as Heirs to the Father, in the same Manner as if the Father had been actually Possess'd thereof; and therefore the Father's other Sons and their Descendants *in Infinitum* succeeded; but yet especially, and without any double Portion to the eldest, because tho' in Truth the Brothers succeeded as it were in Right of Representation from the Father, yet if the Father died before the Son, the Descent was *de Facto* immediately from the Brother deceased to the other Brothers, in which Case their Law gave not a double Portion; and in Case the Father had no Sons or Descendants from them, then it descended to all the Sisters.

Seventhly, If the Son died without Issue, and his Father or any Descendants from him were extant, it went not to the Grandfather or his other Descendants; but if the Father was dead without Issue, then it descended to the Grandfather, and if he were dead, then it went to his Sons and their Descendants, and for want of them, then to his Daughters or their Descendants, as if the Grandfather himself had been actually possess'd and had died, and so *mutatis mutandis* to the *Proavus, Abavus, Atavus,* &c. and their Descendants.

Eighthly, But the Inheritance of the Son never resorted to the Mother, or to any of her Ancestors, but both she and they were totally excluded from the Succession.

The double Portion therefore that was *Jus Primogenituræ,* never took Place but in that Person that was the *Primogenitus,* of him from whom the inheritance immediately descended, or him that represented him; as if A. had two Sons, B. and C. and B. the eldest had two Sons, D. and E. and then B. died, whereas B. should have had a double Portion, *viz.* two Thirds in Case he had survived his Father; but now this double Portion shall be equally divided between D. and E. and D. shall not have two Thirds of the two Thirds that descended from A. to them. *Vide* Selden, *ut supra.*

Thus much of the Laws or Rules touching Descents among the Jews.

Among the Græcians, the Laws of Descents in some Sort resemble those of the Jews, and in some Things they differed. *Vide* Petit's *Leges Attica, Cap.* 1. *Tit.* 6. *De Testamentis & Hereditario Jure,* where the Text of their Law runs thus, *viz.*

> Omnes legitimi Filii Hæreditatem Paternam ex æquo inter se Hæriscunto, si quis intestatus moritur relictis Filiabus qui eas in Uxores ducunt hæredes sunto, si nullæ supersint, hi ab intestato hæreditatem cernunto: Et primo quidem Fratres defuncti Germani, & legitimi Fratrum Filii hæreditatem simil adeunto; si nulli Fratres aut Fratrum Filii supersint, iis geniti eadem Lege hæreditatem cernunto: Masculi autem iis geniti etiam si remotiori cognationis sint Gradu, præferuntor, si nulli supersint, Paterni proximi, ad sobrinorum usque Filios, Materni defuncti propinqui simili Lege Hæreditatem adeunto; si e neutra cognatione supersint intra definitum Gradum proximus cognatus Paternus, addito Notho Nothave; superstite Legitima Filia Nothus Hæreditatem Patris ne adito.

This Law is very obscure, but the Sense thereof seems to be briefly this, *viz.* That all the Sons equally shall inherit to the Father; but if he have no Sons, then the Husbands of the Daughters; and if he have no Children, then his Brothers and their Children; and if none, than his next Kindred on the Part of his Father, preferring the Males before the Females; and if none of the Father's Line, *ad Sobrinorum usque Filios,* then to descend to the Mother's Line. *Vide* Petit's Gloss thereon.

Among the Romans it appears, that the Laws of Successions or Descents did successively vary, for the Laws of the Twelve Tables did exclude the Females from Inheriting, and had many other Streightnesses and Hardships which were successively remedied:

First, by the Emperor Claudius, and after him by Adrian, in his *Senatus Consultus Tertullianus,* and after him by Justinian in his Third Institutes, *Tit. De Hæreditatibus quæ ab intestato deseruntur,* and the two ensuing Titles. And again, all this was further explained and settled by the Novel Constitutions of the said Justinian, stiled the *Authenticæ Novellæ, cap.* 18. *De Hæreditatibus ab intestato venientibus & agnatorum Jure sublato.* Therefore omitting the large Inquiry into the Successive Changes of the Roman Law in this particular, I shall only set down how, according to that Constitution, the Roman Law stands settled therein.

Descents or Successions from any Person are of Three Kinds, *viz. 1st,* In the Descending Line. *2dly,* The Ascending Line. *3dly,* The Collateral Line; and this latter is either *in Agnatos a Parte Patris,* or *in Cognatos a Parte Matris.*

1. *In the Descending Line,* These Rules are by the Roman Law directed, *viz.*

1. The Descending Line, (whether Male or Female, whether immediate or remote) takes Place, and prevents the Descent or Succession Ascending or Collateral *in infinitum.*

2. The remote Descents of the Descending Line succeed *in Stirpem, i.e.* in that Right which his Parent should have had.

3. This Descent or Succession is equal in all the Daughters, all the Sons, and all the Sons and Daughters, without preferring the Male before the Female; so that if the common Ancestor had three Sons and three Daughters, each of them had a sixth Part; and if one of them had died in the Life of the Father, having three Sons and three Daughters, the sixth Part that belonged to that Party should have been divided equally between his or her six Children, and so *in infinitum* in the Descending Line.

2. *In the Ascending Line,* there are these two Rules, *viz.*

1. If the Son dies without Issue, or any descending from him, having a Father and a Mother living, both of them shall equally succeed to the Son, and prevent all others in the Collateral Line, except Brothers and Sisters, and if only a Father, or only a Mother, he or she shall succeed alone.

2. But if the Deceased leaves a Father and a Mother, with a Brother and a Sister, *ex utrisque Parentibus conjuncti,* they all Four shall equally succeed to the Son by equal Parts without Preference of the Males.

3. *In the Collateral Line,* (*i.e.* where the Person dies without Father or Mother, Son or Daughter, or any descending from them in the Right Line) the Rules are these, *viz.*

1. The Brothers and Sisters, *ex utrisque Parentibus conjuncti,* and the immediate Children of them, shall exceed equally without Preference of either Sex, and the Children from them shall succeed *in stirpes;* as if there be a Brother and Sister, and the Sister dies in the Life of the Descendant leaving one or more Children, all such Children shall succeed in the Moiety that should have come to their deceased Mother, had she survived.

2. But if there be no Brothers or Sisters, *ex utrisque Parentibus conjuncti,* nor any of their immediate Children, then the Brothers and Sisters of the half Blood and their immediate Children shall succeed *in Stirpes* to the Deceased, without any Prerogative to the Male.

3. But if there be no Brothers or Sisters of the whole or half Blood, nor any of their immediate Children (for the Grandchildren are not provided for by the Law) then the next Kindred are called to the Inheritance.

(But by the Author's Leave, I think the Grandchildren are impliedly provided for, as they succeed their Father or Mother *Jure representationis.*)

4. And if the next Kindred be in an equal Degree, whether on the Part of the Father as *Agnati,* or on the Part of the Mother as *Cognati,* then they are equally called to the Inheritance, and succeeded *in Capita,* and not *in Stirpes.*

Thus far of the settled Laws of the Jews, Greeks, and Romans, but the Particular or Municipal Laws and Customs of almost every Country derogate from those Laws, and direct Successions in a much different Way. For Instance.

By the Customs of Lombardy, according to which the Rules of

the Feuds, both in their Descents and in other Things, are much directed; their Descents are in a much different Manner, *viz.* *Leges Feudarum, Lib.* 1. *Tit.* 1. If a Feud be granted to one Brother who dies without Issue, it descends not to his other Brother unless it be specially provided for in the first Infeudation: If the Donee dies, having Issue Sons and Daughters, it descends only to the Sons; whereas by the Roman Law it descends to both: The Brother succeeds not to the Brother unless specially provided for, & *Ibid. Tit.* 50. The Ascendants succeed not, but only the Descendants, neither does a Daughter succeed *nisi ex Pacto, vel nisi sit Feodum Fæmineum*

If we come nearer Home to the Laws of Normandy, Lands there are of Two Kinds, *viz.* Partible, and not Partible; the Lands that are partible, are Valvasories, Burgages, and such like, which are much of the Nature of our Socage Lands; these descend to all the Sons, or to all the Daughters: Lands not partible, are Fiefs and Dignities, they descend to the eldest Son, and not to all the Sons; but if there be no Sons, then to all the Daughters, and become partible.

The Rules and Directions of their Descents are as follow, *viz.*
1. For want of Sons or Nephews, it descends to the Daughters; if there be no Sons or Descendants from them, it goes to Brothers, and for want of Brothers, to Sisters, (observing as before the Difference between Lands partible and not partible) and accordingly the Descent runs to the Posterity of Brothers to the seventh Degree; and if there be no Brothers nor Sisters, nor any Descendants from them within the Seventh Degree, it descends to the Father, and if the Father be dead, then to the Uncles and Aunts and their Posterity, (as above is said in the Case of Brothers and Sisters) and if there be none, then to the Grandfather.

So that according to their Law, the Father is postponed to the Brother and Sister, and their Issues, but is preferred before the Uncle: Tho' according to the Jewish Law, the Father is preferred before the Brother; by the Roman Law, he succeeds together equally with the Brother; but by the English Law, the Father cannot take from his Son by an immediate Descent, *but may take as* Heir *to his Brother, who was* Heir *to his Son by* Collateral Descent.

2. If Lands descended from the Part of the Father, they could never resort by a Descent to the Line of the Mother; but in Case of Purchases by the Son who died without Issue, for want of Heirs of the Part of the Father, it descended to the Heirs of the Part of the Mother according to the Law of England.

3. The Son of the eldest Son dying in the Life of the Father, is preferred before a younger Son surviving his Father as the Law stands here now settled, tho' it had some Interruption, 4 *Johannis.*

4. On Equality of Degrees in Collateral Descents, the Male Line is preferred before the Female.

5. Altho' by the Civil Law, *Fratres ex utroque Parente conjuncti præferuntur Fratribus consanguineis tantum vel uterinis;* yet it should seem by the *Contumier* of Normandy, *Fratres consanguineis ei ex eodem Patre sed diversa Matre,* shall take by Descent together with the Brothers, *ex utroque conjuncti,* upon the Death of any such Brothers. But *Quere* hereof, for this seems a Mistake; for, as I take it, the half Blood hinders the Descent between Brothers and Sisters by their Laws as well as ours.

6. Leprosy was amongst them an Impediment of Succession, but then it seems it ought to be first solemnly adjudged so by the Sentence of the Church.

Upon all this, and much more that might be observed upon the Customs of several Countries, it appears, That the Rules of Successions, or hereditary Transmissions, have been various in several Countries according to their various Laws, Customs, and Usages.

And now, after this brief Survey of the Laws and Customs of other Countries, I come to the Laws and Usages of England in relation to Descents, and the Growth that those Customs successively have had, and whereunto they are now arrived.

First, Touching hereditary Successions: It seems, that according to the ancient British Laws, the eldest Son inherited their Earldoms and Baronies; for they had great Dignities and Jurisdictions annex'd to them, and were in Nature of Principalities, but that their ordinary Freeholds descended to all their Sons; and this Custom they carried with them into Wales, whither they were driven. This appears by *Statutum Walliæ* 12 E. 1. and which runs thus, *viz.*

Aliter usitatum est in Wallia quam in Anglia quoad Successionem hæreditatis; eo quod hæreditas partibilis est inter hæredes Masculos, & a tempore cujus non extiterit Memoria partibilis exitit. Dominus Rex non vult quod consuetudo illa abrogetur: sed quod hæreditates remaneant partibiles, inter consimiles hæredes sicut esse Consueverunt; & fiat partitio illius sicut fieri consuevit. Hoc excepto Bastardi non habeant de cætero hæreditates & etiam quod non habeant purpartes, cum legitimis nec sine legitimis.

Whereupon Three Things are observable, *viz. 1st,* That at this Time the hereditary Succession of the eldest Son was then known to be the common and usual Law in England. *2dly,* That the Succession of all the Sons was the ancient customary Law among the British in Wales, which by this Statute was continued to them. *3dly,* That before this Time, Bastards were admitted to inherit in Wales as well as the Legitimate Children, which Custom is thereby abrogated; and although we have but few Evidences touching the British Laws before their Expulsion hence into Wales, yet this Usage in Wales seems sufficiently to evidence this to have been the ancient British Law.

Secondly, As to the Times of the Saxons and Danes, their Laws collected by Brompton and Mr. Lambard, speak not much concerning the Course of Descents; yet it seems that commonly Descents of their ordinary Lands at least, except Baronies and Royal Inheritances, descended also to all the Sons: For amongst the Laws of King Canutus, in Mr. Lambard is the Law, *viz.* No. 68. "Sive quis incuria five Morte repentina fuerit intestato mortuus, Dominus tamen nullam rerum suarum Partem (præter eam quæ jure debetur Hereoti nomine) sibi assumito. Verum eas Judicio suo Uxori, Liberis & cognatione proximis juste (pro suo cuique jure) distributio."

Upon which Law, we may observe these five things, *viz.*

1st, That the Wife had a Share, as well of the Lands for her Dower, as of the Goods.

2dly, That in reference to hereditary Successions, there then seem'd to be little Difference between Lands and Goods, for this Law makes no Distinction.

3dly, That there was a Kind of settled Right of Succession, with Reference to Proximity and Remoteness of Blood, or Kin, *Et cognatione proximis pro suo cuique jure.*

4thly, That in Reference to Children, they all seem'd to succeed alike, without any Distinction between Males and Females.

5thly, That yet the Ancestor might dispose of by his Will as well Lands as Goods, which Usage seems to have obtained here unto the Time of Hen. 2. as will appear hereafter. *Vide* Glanville.

Thirdly, It seems that, until the Conquest, the Descent of Lands was at least to all the Sons alike, and for ought appears to all the Daughters also, and that there was no Difference in the hereditary Transmission of Lands and Goods, at least in Reference to the Children: This appears by the Laws of King Edward the Confessor, confirm'd by King William 1. and recited in Mr. Lambard, Folio 167. as also by Mr. Selden in his Notes upon *Eadmerus,* viz. *Lege 36 Tit. De Intestatorum Bonis;* Pag. 184. "Si quis Intestatus obierit, Liberi ejus Hæreditatem æqualiter divident."

But this equal Division of Inheritances among all the Children was found to be very inconvenient: For,

1st, It weakened the Strength of the Kingdom, for by frequent parcelling and subdividing of Inheritances, in Process of Time they became so divided and crumbled, that there were few Persons of able Estates left to undergo publick Charges and Offices.

2dly, It did by Degrees bring the Inhabitants to a low Kind of Country living, and Families were broken; and the younger Sons, which had they not had those little Parcels of Land to apply themselves to, would have betaken themselves to Trades, or to Civil or Military, or Ecclesiastical Employments, neglecting those Opportunities, wholly apply'd themselves to those small Divisions of Lands, whereby they neglected the Opportunities of greater Advantage of enriching themselves and the Kingdom.

And therefore King William 1. having by his Accession to the Crown gotten into his Hands the Possessions and Demesns of the Crown, and also very many and great Possessions of those that oppos'd him, or adhered to Harold, disposed of those Lands or

great Part of them to his Countrymen, and others that adhered
to him, and reserved certain honorary Tenures, either by Baronage, or in Knights-Service or Grand Serjeancy, for the Defence of
the Kingdom, and possibly also, even at the Desire of many of
the Owners, changed their former Tenures into Knights-Service,
which Introduction of new Tenures was nevertheless not done
without Consent of Parliament; as appears by the additional Laws
before mentioned, that King William made by Advice of Parliament, mentioned by Mr. Selden in his Notes on Eadmerus, Page
191. amongst which this was one, *viz.*

> Statuimus etiam & firmiter præcipimus ut omnes Comites
> Barones Milites & Servientes & universi liberi Homines totius
> Regni nostri habeant & teneant se semper in Armis & in Equis ut
> decet & oportet, & quod sint semper prompti & bene parati ad
> Servitium suum integrum nobis explendendum & peragendum,
> cum semper opus fuerit secundum quod nobis de Feodis debent
> & tenentur Tenementis suis de Jure facere & sicut illis statuimus
> per Commune Concilium totius Regni nostri, Et illis dedimus &
> concessimus in Feodo Jure hæreditario.

Whereby it appears, that there were two Kinds of Military
Provisions; one that was set upon all Freeholds by common Consent of Parliament, and which was usually called *Assisa Ar-
morum;* and another that was Conventional and by Tenure, upon
the Infeudation of the Tenant, and which was usually called
Knights Service, and sometimes Royal, sometimes Foreign
Service, and sometimes *Servitium Loricæ.*

And hence it came to pass, that not only by the Customs of
Normandy, but also according to the Customs of other Countries,
those honorary Fees, or Infeudations, became descendible to the
Eldest, and not to all the Males. And hence also it is, that in
Kent, where the Custom of all the Males taking by Descent generally prevails, and that pretend a Concession of all their Customs
by the Conqueror, to obtain a Submission to his Government, according to that Romantick Story of their Moving Wood: But
even in Kent itself, those ancient Tenements or Fees that are held
anciently by Knights Service, are descendible to the Eldest Son, as
Mr. Lambard has observed to my Hands in his *Perambulation,*
Page 533, 553. out of 9 H. 3. Fitz. Prescription 63. 26 H. 8.5.

and the Statute of 31 H. 8. *cap.* 3. And yet even in Kent, if Gavelkind Lands escheat, or come to the Crown by Attainder or Dissolution of Monasteries, and be granted to be held by Knights Service, or *per Baroniam,* the Customary Descent is not changed, neither can it be but by Act of Parliament, for it is a Custom fix'd to the Land.

But those honorary infeudations made in ancient Times, especially shortly after the conquest, did silently and suddenly assume the Rule of Descents to the Eldest, and accordingly held it; and so altho' possibly there were no Acts of Parliament of those Elder Times, at least none that are now known of, for altering the ancient Course of Descents from all the Sons to the Eldest, yet the Use of the Neighbouring Country might introduce the same Usage here as to those honorary Possessions.

And because those honorary Infeudations were many, and scattered almost through all the Kingdom, in a little Time they introduced a Parity in the Succession of Lands of other Tenures, as Socages, Valvasories, &c. So that without Question, by little and little, almost generally in all Counties of England (except Kent, who were most tenacious of their old Customs in which they gloried, and some particular Feuds and Places where a contrary Usage prevailed) the generality of Descents or Successions, by little and little, as well of Socage Lands as Knights Service, went to the eldest Son, according to the Declaration of King Edw. 1. in the Statute of Wales above mentioned, as will more fully appear by what follows.

In the Time of Hen. 1. as we find by his 70th Law, it seems that the whole Land did not Descend to the eldest Son, but begun to look a little that Way, *viz. Primum Patris Feudum, Primogenitus Filius habeat.* And as to *Collateral Descents,* that Law determines thus: "Si quis sine Liberis decesserit Pater aut Mater ejus in hæreditatem succedat vel Frater vel Soror si Pater & Mater desint, si nec hos, habeat Soror Patris vel Matris, & deinceps in Quintum Geniculum; qui cum propinquiores in parentela sint hæreditario jure succedant; & dum Virilis sexus extiterit & hæreditas ab inde sit, Fœminea non hæreditetur."

By this Law it seems to appear;

1. The eldest Son, tho' he had *Jus primogenituræ,* the principal Fee of his Father's Land, yet he had not all the Land.

2. That for want of Children, the Father or Mother inherited before the Brother or Sister.

3. That for want of Children, and Father, Mother, Brother, and Sister, the Land descended to the Uncles and Aunts to the fifth Generation.

4. That in Successions Collateral, Proximity of Blood was preferred.

5. That the Male was preferred before the Female, *i.e.* The Father's Line was preferred before the Mother's, unless the Land descended from the Mother, and then the Mother's Line was preferred.

How this Law was observed in the interval between Hen. 1. and Hen. 2. we can give no Account of; but the next Period that we come to is, the Time of Hen. 2. wherein Glanville gives us an Account how the Law stood at that Time: *Vide* Glanville, *Lib.* 7. Wherein, notwithstanding it will appear, that there was some Uncertainty and Unsettledness in the Business of Descents or Hereditary Successions, tho' it was much better polished then formerly, the Rules then of Succession were either in Reference to Goods, or Lands. *1st,* As to Goods, one Third Part thereof went to the Wife, another Third Part went to the Children, and the other Third was left to the Disposition of the Testator; but if he had no Wife, then a Moiety went to the Children, and the other Moiety was at the Deceased's Disposal. And the like Rule if he had left a Wife, but no Children. Glanv. *lib.* 7. *cap.* 5. & *Vide lib.* 2. *cap.* 29.

But as to the Succession of Lands, the Rules are these.

First, If the Lands were Knights Service, they generally went to the eldest Son; and in case of no Sons, then to all the Daughters; and in case of no Children, then to the eldest Brother.

Secondly, If the Lands were Socage, they descended to all the Sons to be divided; *Si feurit Soccagium* & *id antiquitus divisum;* only the Chief House was to be allotted to the Purparty of the Eldest, and a Compensation made to the rest in lieu thereof: "Si vero non fuerit antiquitus divisum, tunc Primogenitus secundum quorundam Consuetudinem totam Hæreditatem obtinebit, secundum autem quorundam Consuetudinem postnatus Filius

Hæres est." Glanville, *lib.* 7. *cap.* 3. So that altho' Custom directed the Descent variously, either to the eldest or youngest, or to all the Sons, yet it seems that at this Time, *Jus Commune,* or Common Right, spoke for the eldest Son to be Heir, no Custom intervening to the contrary.

Thirdly, As the Son or Daughter, so their Children *in infinitum,* are preferred in the Descent before the Collateral Line or Uncles.

Fourthly, But if a Man had two Sons, and the eldest Son died in the Life-time of his Father, having Issue a Son or Daughter, and then the Father dies; it was then controverted, whether the Son or Nephew should succeed to the Father, tho' the better Opinion seems to be for the Nephew, Glanvil. *lib.* 7. *cap.* 3.

Fifthly, A Bastard could not inherit, *Ibid. cap.* 13, or 17. And altho' by the Canon or Civil Law, if A. have a Son born of B. before Marriage, and after A. marries B. this Son shall be legitimate and heritable; yet according to the Laws of England then, and ever since used, he was not heritable, Glanvil. *lib.* 7. *cap.* 15.

Sixthly, In case the Purchaser died without Issue, the Land descended to the Brothers; and for want of Brothers, to the Sisters; and for want of them, to the Children of the Brothers or Sisters; and for want of them, to the Uncles; and so onward according to the Rules of Descents at this Day; and the Father or Mother were not to inherit to the Son, but the Brothers or Uncles, and their Children. *Ibid. cap.* 1. & 4.

And it seems, That in all Things else the Rules of Descents in reference to the Colateral Line were much the same as now; as namely, That if Lands descended of the Part of the Father, it should not resort to the Part of the Mother, or *e converso;* but in the Case of Purchasers, for want of Heirs of the Part of the Father, it resorted to the Line of the Mother, and the nearer and more worthy of Blood were preferred: So that if there were any of the Part of the Father, tho' never so far distant, it hindred the Descent to the Line of the Mother, though much nearer.

But in those Times it seems there were two Impediments of Descents or hereditary Successions which do not now obtain, *viz.*

First, Leprosy, if so adjudged by Sentence of the Church: This indeed I find not in Glanville; but I find it pleaded and allowed in the Time of King John, and thereupon the Land was adjudged from the Leprous Brother to the Sister. *Pasch.* 4 *Johannis.*

Secondly, There was another Curiosity in Law, and it was wonderful to see how much and how long it prevailed; for we find it in Use in Glanville, who wrote *Temp.* Hen. 2. in Bracton *Temp.* Hen. 3. in *Fleta Temp.* Edw. 1. and in the broken Year of 13 E. 1. Fitzh. Avowry 235. *Nemo potest esse Tenens* & *Dominus,* & *Homagium repellit Perquisitum:* And therefore if there had been three Brothers, and the eldest Brother had enfeoffed the second, reserving Homage, and had received Homage, and then the second had died without Issue, the Land should have descended to the youngest Brother and not to the eldest Brother, *Quia Homagium repellit perquisitum,* as 'tis here said, for he could not pay Homage to himself. *Vide* for this, Bracton, *Lib.* 2. *cap.* 30. Glanvil. *Lib.* 7. *cap.* 1. Fleta, *Lib.* 6. *cap.* 1.

But at this Day the Law is altered, and so it has been for ought I can find ever since 13 E. 1. Indeed, it is antiquated rather than altered, and the Fancy upon which it was grounded has appear'd trivial; for if the eldest Son enfeoff the second, reserving Homage, and that Homage paid, and then the second Son dies without Issue, it will descend to the Eldest as Heir, and the Seigniory is extinct. It might indeed have had some Color of Reason to have examined, whether he might not have waved the Descent, in case his Services had been more beneficial than the Land: But there could be little Reason from thence to exclude him from the Succession. I shall mention no more of this Impediment, nor of that of Leprosy, for that they both are vanished and antiquated long since; and, as the Law now is, neither of these are any Impediment of Descents.

And now passing over the Time of King John and Richard 1. because I find nothing of Moment therein on this Head, unless the Usurpation of King John upon his eldest Brother's Son, which he would fain have justified by introducing a Law of prefering the younger Son before the Nephew descended from the elder Brother: But this Pretention could no way justify his Usurpation, as has been already shewn in the Time of Hen. 2.

Next, I come to the Time of Hen. 3. in whose Time the Tractate of Bracton was written, and thereby in *Lib.* 2. *cap.* 30. & 31. and *Lib.* 5. *cap.* It appears, That there is so little Variance as to Point of Descents between the Law as it was taken when

Bracton wrote, and the Law as afterwards taken in Edw. 1's. Time, when Britton and Fleta wrote, that there is very little Difference between them, as may easily appear by comparing Bracton *ubi supra,* & Fleta, *Lib.* 5. *cap.* 9. *Lib.* 6. *cap.* 1, 2. that the latter seem to be only Transcripts or Abstracts of the former. Wherefore I shall set down the Substance of what both say, and thereby it will appear, that the Rules of Descents in Hen. 3. and Edw. 1's Time were very much one.

First, At this Time the Law seems to be unquestionably settled, that the eldest Son was of Common Right Heir, not only in Cases of Knight Service Lands, but also of Socage Lands, (unless there were a special Custom to the contrary, as in Kent and some other Places) and so that Point of the Common Law was fully settled.

Secondly, That all the Descendants *in infinitum,* from any Person that had been Heir, if living, were inheritable *Jure representationis;* as, the Descendants of the Son, of the Brother, of the Uncle, &c. And also,

Thirdly, That the eldest Son dying in the Life-time of the Father, his Son or Issue was to have the Preference as Heir to the Father before the younger Brother, and so the Doubt in Glanville's Time was settled, Glanvil. *Lib.* 7, *cap.* 3. "Cum quis autem moriatur habens Filium postnatum, & ex primogenito Filio præmortuo Nepotem, Magna quidem Juris dubitatio solet isse uter illorum preferendus fit alii in illa Successioni, scilicet, utrum Filius aut Nepos?"

Fourthly, The Father, or Grandfather, could not by Law inherit immediately to the Son.

Fifthly, Leprosy, Though it were an Exception to a Plaintiff, because he ought not to converse in the Courts of Law, as Bracton, *Lib.* 5. *cap.* 20 yet we no where find it to be an Impediment of a Descent.

So that upon the whole Matter, for any Thing I can observe in them, the Rules of Descents then stood settled in all Points as they are at this Day, except some few Matters (which yet soon after settled as they now stand) *viz.*

First, That Impediment or Hindrance of a Descent from him that did Homage to him that received it, seems to have been yet in Use, at least till 13 E. 1. and in Fleta's Time, for he puts the Case and admits it.

Secondly, Whereas both Bracton and Fleta agree, that half Blood to him that is a Purchaser is an Impediment of a Descent from the Common Ancestor, half Blood is no Impediment. As for Instance; A. has Issue B. a Son and C. a Daughter by one *Venter,* and D. a Son by another *Venter:* If B. purchases in Fee and dies without Issue, it shall descend to the Sister, and not to the Brother of the half Blood; but if the Land had descended from A. to B. and he had entred and died without Issue, it was a Doubt in Bracton and Britton's Time, whether it should go to the younger Son, or to the Daughter? But the Law is since settled, that in both Cases it descends to the Daughter, *Et. seisina facit Stipitem* & *primum Gradum. Et Possessio Fratris de Feodo simplici facit Sororem esse hæredem.*

Thus upon the whole it seems, That abating those small and inconsiderable Variances, the States and Rules of Descents as they stood in the Time of Hen. 3. or at least in the Time of Edw. 1. were reduced to their full Complement and Perfection, and vary nothing considerably from what they are at this Day, and have continued ever since that Time.

I shall therefore set down the State and Rule of Descents in Fee-Simple as it stands at this Day, without meddling with Particular Limitations of Entails of Estates, which vary the Course of Descents in some Cases from the Common Rules of Descents of hereditary Successions; and herein we shall see what the Law has been and continued touching the same ever since Bracton's Time, who wrote in the Time of Hen. 3. now above 400 Years since, and by that we shall see what Alterations the Succession of Time has made therein.

And now to give a short Scheme of the Rules of Descents, or hereditary Successions, of the Lands of Subjects as the Law stands at this Day, and has stood for above four hundred Years past, *viz.*

All possible hereditary Successions may be distinguished into these 3 Kinds, *viz.* either,

1st, In the Descending Line, as from Father to Son or Daughter, Nephew or Niece, *i.e.* Grandson or Grandaughter. Or,

2dly, In the Collateral Line, as from Brother to Brother or Sister, and so to Brother and Sisters Children. Or,

3dly, In an Ascending Line, either direct, as from Son to Father or Grandfather, (which is not admitted by the Law of England) or in the transversal Line, as to the Uncle or Aunt, Great-Uncle or Great-Aunt, &c. And because this Line is again divided into the Line of the Father, or the Line of the Mother, this transverse ascending Succession is either in the Line of the Father, Grandfather, &c. on the Blood of the Father; or in the Line of the Mother, Grandmother, &c. on the Blood of the Mother: The former are called *Agnati,* the latter *Cognati:* I shall therefore set down a Scheme of Pedigrees as high as Great-Grandfather and Great-Grandmothers Grandsires, and as low as Great-Grandchild; which nevertheless will be applicable to more remote Successions with a little Variation, and will explain the whole Nature of Descents or hereditary Successions.

This Pedigree, with its Application, will give a plain Account of all Hereditary Successions under their several Cases and Limitations, as will appear by the following Rules, taking our Mark or Epocha from the FATHER and MOTHER.

But first, I shall premise certain general Rules, which will direct us much in the Course of Descents as they stand here in England: (*Viz.*)

First. In Descents, the Law prefers the Worthiest of Blood: As,

1st, In all Descents immediate, the Male is preferred before the Female, whether in Successions Descending, Ascending, or Collateral: Therefore in Descents, the Son inherits and excludes the Daughter, the Brother is preferred before the Sister, the Uncle before the Aunt.

2dly, In all Descents immediate, the Descendants from Males are to be preferred before the Descendants from Females: And hence it is, That the Daughter of the eldest Son is preferred in Descents from the Father before the Son of the younger Son; and the Daughter of the eldest Brother, or Uncle, is preferred before the Son of the younger; and the Uncle, nay, the Great-Uncle, *i.e.* the Grandfather's Brother, shall inherit before the Uncle of the Mothers Side.

Secondly, In Descents, the next of Blood is preferred before the more remote, tho' equally or more worthy. And hence it is,

The PATERNAL Line.

The MATERNAL Line.

Tritavus, or Great-Grandfather's Great-Grandfather

Tritavia, or Great-Grandmother's Great-Grandmother

Atavus, or Great-Grandfather's Grandfather

Atavia, or Great-Grandmother's Grandmother

Abavus, or Great-Grandfather's Father

Abavia, or Great Grandmother's Mother

Proamita Magna Great-Great-Aunt   *Propatruus Magnus* Gr. Great-Uncle   *Proavus* Gr. Grandfather

Proavia, or Gr. Grandmother   *Proavunculus* Gr. Great-Uncle   *Promatertera Magna* Great Great-Aunt

Amita Magna Great-Aunt   *Patruus Magnus* Great-Uncle   *Avus*, or Grandfather

Avia, or Grandmother   *Avunculus Mag.* Great-Uncle   *Matertera Magna* Great-Aunt

Amita, or Aunt   *Patruus*, or Uncle   *Pater*, or FATHER

Mater, or MOTHER   *Avunculus* Mother's Brother   *Matertera* Mother's Sister

Consobrinus A Mother's Sister

Consobrina A Mother's Sister's Daughter

Consobrinus A Mother's Brother's Son

Consobrina A Mother's Brother's Daughter

Soror, his Sister   *Frater*, his Brother   *Filius Primus* Eldest Son

Neptis, or Granddaughter

Nepos Nephew   *Neptis* Niece   *Nepos* Nephew   *Neptis* Niece   *Nepos*, or Grandson

Nepos Nephew   *Neptis* Niece

Note: The Descendants from all these Six in the next Degree, if Male, is called *Pronepos*, if Female, *Proneptis*, i.e. Great Grandson, or Great Grandaughter.

1st, The Sister of the whole Blood is preferred in Descents before the Brother of the half Blood, because she is more strictly joined to the Brother of the whole Blood (*viz.* by Father and by Mother) than the half Brother, though otherwise he is the more worthy.

2dly, Because the Son or Daughter being nearer than the Brother, and the Brother or Sister than the Uncle, the Son or Daughter shall inherit before the Brother or Sister, and they before the Uncle.

3dly, That yet the Father or Grandfather, or Mother or Grandmother, in a direct ascending Line, shall never succeed immediately the Son or Grandchild; but the Father's Brother (or Sisters) shall be preferred before the Father himself; and the Grandfather's Brother (or Sisters) before the Grandfather: And yet upon a strict Account, the Father is nearer of Blood to the Son than the Uncle, yea than the Brother; for the Brother is therefore of the Blood of the Brother, because both derive from the same Parent, the Common Fountain of both their Blood. And therefore the Father at this Day is preferred in the Administration of the Goods before the Son's Brother of the whole Blood, and a Remainder limited *Proximo de Sanguine* of the Son shall vest in the Father before it shall vest in the Uncle. *Vide* Littleton, *Lib.* 1. fol. 8, 10.

Thirdly, That all the Descendants from such a Person as by the Laws of England might have been Heir to another, hold the same Right by Representation as that Common Root from whence they are derived; and therefore,

1st, They are in Law in the same Right of Worthiness and Proximity of Blood, as their Root that might have been Heir was, in case he had been living: And hence it is, that the Son or Grandchild, whether Son or Daughter of the eldest Son, succeeds before the younger Son; and the Son or Grandchild of the eldest Brother, before the youngest Brother; and so through all the Degrees of Succession, by the Right of Representation, the Right of Proximity is transferred from the Root to the Branches, and gives them the same Preference as the next and worthiest of Blood.

2dly, This Right transferred by Representation is infinite and unlimited in the Degrees of those that descend from the Represented; for *Filius* the Son, the *Nepos* the Grandson, the *Abnepos* the Great-Grandson, and so *in infinitum* enjoy the same Privilege of Representation as those from whom they derive their Pedigree have, whether it be in Descents Lineal, or Transversal; and therefore the Great-Grandchild of the eldest Brother, whether it be Son or Daughter, shall be preferred before the younger Brother, because tho' the Female be less worthy than the Male, yet she stands in Right of Representation of the eldest Brother, who was more worthy than the younger. And upon this Account it is,

3dly, That if a Man have two Daughters, and the eldest dies in the Life of the Father, leaving six Daughters, and then the Father dies; the youngest Daughter shall have an equal Share with the other six Daughters, because they stand in Representation and Stead of their Mother, who could have had but a Moiety.

Fourthly, That by the Law of England, without a special Custom to the contrary, the eldest Son, or Brother, or Uncle, excludes the younger; and the Males in an equal Degree do not all inherit: But all the Daughters, whether by the same or divers *Venters,* do inherit together to the Father, and all the Sisters by the same *Venter* do inherit to the Brother.

Fifthly, That the last Seisin in any Ancestor, makes him, as it were the Root of the Descent equally to many Intents as if he had been a Purchaser; and therefore he that cannot, according to the Rules of Descents, derive his Succession from him that was left actually seised, tho' he might have derived it from some precedent Ancestor, shall not inherit. And hence it is, That where Lands descend to the eldest Son from the Father, and the Son enters and dies without Issue, his Sister of the whole Blood shall inherit as Heir to the Brother, and not the younger Son of the half Blood, because he cannot be Heir to the Brother of the half Blood: But if the eldest Son had survived the Father and died before Entry, the youngest Son should inherit as Heir to the Father, and not the Sister, because he is Heir to the Father that was last actually seised. And hence it is, That tho' the Uncle is preferred before the Father in Descents to the Son; yet if the

Uncle enter after the Death of the Son, and die without Issue, the Father shall inherit to the Uncle, *quia Seisina facit Stipitem.*

Sixthly, That whosoever derives a Title to any Land, must be of the Blood to him that first purchased it: And this is the Reason why, if the Son purchase Lands and dies without Issue, it shall descend to the Heirs of the Part of the Father; and if he has none, then to the Heirs on the Part of the Mother; because, tho' the Son has both the Blood of the Father and of the Mother in him, yet he is of the whole Blood of the Mother, and the Consanguinity of the Mother are *Consanguinei Cognati* of the Son.

And of the other Side, if the Father had purchased Lands, and it had descended to the Son, and the Son had died without Issue, and without any Heir of the Part of the Father, it should never have descended in the Line of the Mother, but escheated: For tho' the *Consanguinei* of the Mother were the *Consanguinei* of the Son, yet they were not of Consanguinity to the Father, who was the Purchaser; but if there had been none of the Blood of the Grandfather, yet it might have resorted to the Line of the Grandmother, because her *Consanguinei* were as well of the Blood of the Father, as the Mother's Consanguinity is of the Blood of the Son: And consequently also, if the Grandfather had purchased Lands, and they had descended to the Father, and from him to the Son; if the Son had entred and died without Issue, his Father's Brothers or Sisters, or their Descendants, or, for want of them, his Great-Grandfather's Brothers or Sisters, or their Descendants, or, for want of them, any of the Consanguinity of the Great-Grandfather, or Brothers or Sisters of the Great-Grandmother, or their Descendants, might have inherited, for the Consanguinity of the Great-Grandmother was the Consanguinity of the Grandfather; but none of the Line of the Mother, or Grandmother, *viz.* the Grandfather's Wife, should have inherited, for that they were not of the Blood of the first Purchaser. And the same Rule *e converso* holds in Purchases in the Line of the Mother or Grandmother, they shall always keep in the same Line that the first Purchaser settled them in.

But it is not necessary, That he that inherits be always Heir to the Purchaser; it is sufficient if he be of his Blood, and Heir to him that was last seised. The Father purchases Lands which descended to the Son, who dies without Issue, they shall never descend to the Heir of the Part of the Son's Mother; but if the Son's Grandmother has a Brother, and the Son's Great-Grandmother hath a Brother, and there are no other Kindred, they shall descend to the Grandmother's Brother; and yet if the Father had died without Issue, his Grandmother's Brother should have been preferred before his Mother's Brother, because the former was Heir of the Part of his Father tho' a Female, and the latter was only Heir of the Part of his Mother; but where the Son is once seized and dies without Issue, his Grandmother's Brother is to him Heir of the Part of his Father, and being nearer than his Great Grandmother's Brother, is preferred in the Descent.

But *Note,* This is always intended so long as the Line of Descent is not broken; for if the Son alien those Lands, and then repurchase them again in Fee, now the Rules of Descents are to be observ'd as if he were the original Purchaser, and as if it had been in the Line of the Father or Mother.

Seventhly, In all Successions, as well in the *Line Descending, Transversal, or Ascending,* the Line that is first derived from a Male Root has always the Preference.

Instances whereof in the *Line Descending,* &c. *viz.*

A. has Issue two Sons B. and C. B. has Issue a Son and a Daughter D. and E. D. the Son has Issue a Daughter F. and E. the Daughter has Issue a Son G. Neither C. nor any of his Descendants, shall inherit so long as there are any Descendants from D. and E. and neither E. the Daughter, nor any of her Descendants, shall inherit so long as there are any Descendants from D. the Son, whether they be Male or Female.

So in Descents Collateral, as Brothers and Sisters, the same Instances apply'd thereto, evidence the same Conclusions.

But in Successions in the Line Ascending, there must be a fuller Explication; because it is darker and more obscure, I shall therefore set forth the whole Method of *Transversal Ascending Descents* under the Eight ensuing Rules, *viz.*

First, If the Son purchases Lands in Fee-Simple, and dies without Issue, those of the Male Line ascending, *usque infinitum* shall be preferred in the Descent, according to their Proximity of Degree to the Son; and therefore the Father's Brothers and Sisters and their Descendants shall be preferred before the Brothers, of the Grandfather and their Descendants; and if the Father had no Brothers nor Sisters, the Grandfather's Brothers and their Descendants, and for want of Brothers, his Sisters and their Descendants, shall be preferr'd before the Brothers of the Great Grandfather: For altho' by the Law of England the Father or Grandfather cannot immediately inherit to the Son, yet the Direction of the Descent to the *Collateral Ascending Line,* is as much as if the Father or Grandfather had been by Law inheritable; and therefore as in Case the Father had been inheritable, and should have inherited to the Son before the Grandfather, and the Grandfather, before the Great-Grandfather, and consequently if the Father had inherited and died without Issue, his eldest Brother and his Descendants should have inherited before the younger Brother and his Descendants; and if he had no Brothers but Sisters, the Sisters and their Descendants should have inherited before his Uncles or the Grandfather's Brothers and their Descendants. So though the Law of England excludes the Father from inheriting, yet it substitutes and directs the Descent as it should have been, had the Father inherited, *viz.* It lets in those first that are in the next Degree to him.

Secondly, The second Rule is this: That the Line of the Part of the Mother shall never inherit as long as there are any, tho' never so remote, of the Line of the Part of the Father; and therefore, tho' the Mother has a Brother, yet if the *Atavus* or *Atavia Patris* (*i. e.* the Great-Great-Great-Grandfather, or Great-Great-Great-Grandmother of the Father) has a Brother or a Sister, he or she shall be preferred, and exclude the Mother's Bother, though he is much nearer.

Thirdly, But yet further. The Male Line of the Part of the Father ascending, shall *in Æternum* exclude the Female Line of the Part of the Father ascending; and therefore in the Case proposed of the Son's purchasing Lands and dying without Issue, the Sister of the Father's Grandfather, or of his Great-Grandfather, and so *in infinitum* shall be preferred before the Father's Mother's Brother, tho' the Father's Mother's Brother be a Male, and the Father's Grandfather or Great-Grandfather's Sister be a Female, and more remote, because she is of the Male Line, which is more worthy than the Female Line, though the Female Line, be also of the Blood of the Father.

Fourthly, But as in the Male Line ascending, the more near is preferred before the more remote; so in the Female Line descending, so it be of the Blood of the Father, it is preferred before the more remote. The Son, therefore purchasing Lands, and dying without Issue, and the Father, Grandfather, and Great-Grandfather, and so upward, all the Male Line being dead without any Brother or Sister, or any descending from them; but the Father's Mother has a Sister or Brother, and also the Father's Grandmother has a Brother, and likewise the Father's Great-Grandmother has a Brother: Tho' it is true, that all these are of the Blood of the Father; and tho' the very remotest of them, shall exclude the Son's Mother's Brother; and tho' it be also true, that the Great-Grandmother's Blood has passed through more Males of the Father's Blood than the Blood of the Grandmother or Mother of the Father; yet in this Case, the Father's Mother's Sister shall be preferred before the Father's Grandmother's Brother, or the Great Grandmother's Brother, because they are all in the Female Line, *viz. Cognati* (and not *Agnati*), and the Father's Mother's Sister is the nearest, and therefore shall have the Preference as well as in the Male Line ascending, the Father's Brother or his Sister shall be preferred before the Grandfather's Brother.

Fifthly, But yet in the last Case, where the Son purchases Lands and dies without Issue, and without any Heir on the Part of the Grandfather, the Lands shall descend to the Grandmother's Brother or Sister, as Heir on the Part of his Father; yet if the Father had purchased this Land and died, and it descended to his Son who died without Issue, the Lands should not have descended to the Father's Mother's Brother or Sister, for the Reasons before given in the *Third Rule:* But for want of Brothers or Sisters of the Grandfather, Great-Grandfather, and so upwards in the Male ascending Line, it should descend to the Father's Grandmother's Brother or Sister which is his Heir of the Part of his Father, who should be preferred before the Father's Mother's Brother, who is in Truth the Heir of the Part of the Mother of the Purchaser, tho' the next Heir of the Part of the Father of him that last died seized; and therefore, as if the Father that was the Purchaser had died without Issue, the Heirs of the Part of the Father, whether of the Male or Female Line, should have been preferred before the Heirs of the Part of the Mother; so the Son, who stands now in the Place of the Father, and inherits to him primarily, in his Father's Line, dying without Issue, the same Devolution and hereditary Succession should have been as if his Father had immediately died without Issue, which should have been to his Grandmother's Brother, as Heir of the Part of the Father, though by the Female Line, and not to his Mother's Brother, who was only Heir of the Part of his Mother, and who is not to take till the Father's Line both Male and Female be spent.

Sixthly, If the Son purchases Lands and died without Issue, and it descends to any Heir of the Part of the Father, and then if the Line of the Father (after Entry and Possession) fail, it shall never return to the Line of the Mother; tho' in the first Instance, or first Descent from the Son, it might have descended to the Heir of the Part of the Mother; for now by this Descent and Seisin it is lodged in the Father's Line, to whom the Heir of the Part of the Mother can never derive a Title as Heir, but it shall rather escheat: But if the Heir of the Part of the Father had not entred, and then that Line had failed, it might have descended to the Heir of the Part of the Mother as Heir to the Son, to whom immediately, for want of Heirs of the Part of the Father, it might have descended.

Seventhly, And upon the same Reason, if it had once descended to the Heir of the Part of the Father of the Grandfather's Line, and that Heir had entred, it should never descend to the Heir of the Part of the Father of the Grandmother's Line, because the Line of the Grandmother was not of the Blood or Consanguinity of the Line of the Grandfather's Side.

Eighthly, If for Default of Heirs of the Purchaser of the Part of the Father, the Lands descend to the Line of the Mother, the Heirs of the Mother of the Part of her Father's Side, shall be preferred in the Succession before her Heirs of the Part of her Mother's Side, because they are the more worthy.

And thus the Law stands in Point of Descents or Hereditary Successions in England at this Day, and has so stood and continued for above four Hundred Years past, as by what has before been said, may easily appear. And *Note,* The most Part of the Eight Rules and Differences above specified and explained, may be collected out of the Resolutions in the Case of Clare versus Brook, &c. in Plowden's *Commentaries,* Folio 444.

XII

Touching Trials by Jury

Having in the former Chapter somewhat largely treated of the Course of Descents, I shall now with more Brevity consider that other Title of our Law which I before propounded (in order to evidence the Excellency of the Laws of England above those of other Nations,) *viz. The Trial by a Jury of Twelve Men;* which upon all Accounts, as it is settled here in this Kingdom, seems to be the best Trial in the World: I shall therefore give a short Account of the Method and Manner of that Trial, *viz.*

First, The Writ to return a Jury, issues to the Sheriff of the County: And,

1st, He is to be a Person of Worth and Value, that so he may be responsible for any Defaults, either of himself or his Officers. And, *2dly, Is sworn,* faithfully and honestly to execute his Office. This Officer is entrusted to elect and return the Jury, which he is obliged to do in this Manner: 1. Without the Nomination of either Party. 2. They are to be such Persons as for Estate and Quality are fit to serve upon that Employment. 3. They are to be of the Neighbourhood of the Fact to be inquired, or at least of the County or Bailywick. And, 4. Anciently Four, and now Two of them at least are to be of the Hundred. *But Note, This is now in great Measure altered by Statute.*

Secondly, Touching the Number and Qualifications of the Jury.

1st, As to their Number, though only Twelve are sworn, yet

Twenty-four are to be returned to supply the Defects or Want of Appearance of those that are challenged off, or make Default. *2dly,* Their Qualifications are many, and are generally set down in the Writ that summons them, *viz.* 1. They are to be *Probi* & *legales Homines.* 2. Of sufficient Freeholds, according to several Provisions of Acts of Parliament. 3. Not Convict of any notorious Crime that may render them unfit for that Employment. 4. They are not to be of the Kindred or Alliance of any of the Parties. And, 5. Not to be such as are prepossed or prejudiced before they hear their Evidence.

Thirdly, The Time of their Return.

Indeed, in Assizes, the Jury is to be ready at the Bar the first Day of the Return of the Writ: But in other Cases, the Pannel is first returned upon the *Venire Facias,* or ought to be so, and the Proofs or Witnesses are to be brought or summoned by *Distringas* or *Habeas Corpora* for their Appearance at the Trial, whereby the Parties may have Notice of the Jurors, and of their Sufficiency and Indifferency, that so they may make their Challenges upon the Appearance of the Jurors if there be just Cause.

Fourthly, The Place of their Appearance.

If it be in Cases of such Weight and Consequence as by the Judgment of the Court is fit to be tried at the Bar, then their Appearance is directed to be there; but in ordinary Cases, the Place of Appearance is in the Country at the Assizes, or *Nisi Prius,* in the County where the Issue to be tried arises: And certainly this is an excellent Constitution. The great Charge of Suits is the Attendance of the Parties, the Jury-Men and Witnesses: And therefore tho' the Preparation of the Causes in Point of pleading to Issue, and the Judgment, is for the most Part in the Courts at Westminster, whereby there is kept a great Order and Uniformity of Proceedings in the whole Kingdom, to prevent Multiplicity of Laws and Forms; yet those are but of small Charge, or Trouble, or Attendance, one Attorney being able to dispatch forty Mens Business with the same Ease, and no greater Attendance than one Man would dispatch his own Business: But the great Charge and Attendance is at the Trial, which is therefore brought Home to the Parties in the Countries, and for the most Part near where they live.

Fifthly, The Persons before whom they are to appear.

If the Trial be at the Bar, it is to be before that Court where the Trial is; if in the Country, then before the Justices of Assizes, or *Nisi Prius,* who are Persons well acquainted with the Common Law, and for the most Part are Two of those Twelve ordinary Justices who are appointed for the Common Dispensation of Justice in the Three great Courts at Westminster. And this certainly was a most wise Constitution: For

1st, It prevents Factions and Parties in the Carriage of Business, which would soon appear in every Cause of Moment, were the Trial only before Men residing in the Counties, as Justices of the Peace, or the like, or before Men of little or no Place, Countenance or Preheminence above others; and the more to prevent Partiality in this Kind, those Judges are by Law prohibited to hold their Sessions in Counties where they were born or dwell.

2dly, As it prevents Factions and Part-takings, so it keeps both the Rule and the Administration of the Laws of the Kingdom uniform; for those Men are employed as Justices, who as they have had a Common Education in the Study of the Law, so they daily in Term-time converse and consult with one another; acquaint one another with their Judgments, sit near one another in Westminster-Hall, whereby their Judgments and Decisions are necessarily communicated to one another, either immediately or by Relations of others, and by this Means their Judgments and their Administrations of Common Justice carry a Consonancy, Congruity and Uniformity one to another, whereby both the Laws and the Administrations thereof are preserved from that Confusion and Disparity that would unavoidably ensue, if the Administration was by several incommunicating Hands, or by provincial Establishments: And besides all this, all those Judges are solemnly sworn to observe and judge according to the Laws of the Kingdom, according to the best of their Knowledge and Understanding.

Sixthly, When the Jurors appear, and are called, each Party has Liberty to take his Challenge to the Array itself, if unduly or partially made by the Sheriff; or if the Sheriff be of Kin to either Party, or to the Polls, either for Insufficiency of Freehold, or Kindred or Alliance to the other Party, or such other Challenges, either Principal, or to the Favour, as renders the Juror unfit and incompetent to try the Cause, and the Challenge being confess'd or found true by some of the rest of the Jury, that particular incompetent Person is withdrawn.

Seventhly, Then Twelve, and no less, of such as are indifferent and are return'd upon the principal Pannel, or the Tales, are sworn to try the same according to their Evidence.

Eighthly, Being thus sworn, the Evidence on either Part is given in upon the Oath of Witnesses, or other Evidence by Law allowed, (as Records and ancient Deeds, but later Deeds and Copies of Records must be attested by the Oaths of Witnesses) and other Evidence in the open Court, and in the Presence of the Parties, their Attornies, Council and all By-standers, and before the Judge and Jury, where each Party has Liberty of excepting, either to the Competency of the Evidence, or the Competency or Credit of the Witnesses, which Exceptions are publickly stated, and by the Judges openly or publickly allowed or disallowed, wherein if the Judge be partial, his Partiality and Injustice will be evident to all By-standers; and if in his Direction or Decision he mistake the Law, either through Partiality, Ignorance, or Inadvertency, either Party may require him to seal a Bill of Exception, thereby to deduce the Error of the Judge (if any were) to a due Ratification or Reversal by Writ of Error.

Ninthly, The Excellency of this open Course of Evidence to the Jury in Presence of the Judge, Jury, Parties and Council, and even of the adverse Witnesses, appears in these Particulars:

1st, That it is openly; and not in private before a Commissioner or Two, and a couple of Clerks, where oftentimes Witnesses will deliver that which they will be ashamed to testify publickly.

2dly, That it is *Ore Tenus* personally, and not in Writing, wherein oftentimes, yea too often, a crafty Clerk, Commissioner, or Examiner, will make a Witness speak what he truly never meant, by his dressing of it up in his own Terms, Phrases, and Expressions; whereas on the other Hand, many times the very Manner of a Witness's delivering his Testimony will give a probable Indication whether he speaks truly or falsly; and by this Means also he has Opportunity to correct, amend, or explain his Testimony upon further Questioning with him, which he can never have after a Deposition is set down in Writing.

3dly, That by this Course of personal and open Examination, there is Opportunity for all Persons concern'd, *viz.* The Judge, or any of the Jury, or Parties, or their Council or Attornies, to propound occasional Questions, which beats and boults out the Truth much better than when the Witness only delivers a formal Series of his Knowledge without being interrogated; and on the other Side, preparatory, limited, and formal Interrogatories in Writing, preclude this Way of occasional Interrogations, and the best Method of searching and sifting out the Truth is choak'd and suppress'd.

4thly, Also by this personal Appearance and Testimony of Witnesses, there is Opportunity of confronting the adverse Witnesses, of observing the Contradiction of Witnesses sometimes of the same Side, and by this Means great Opportunities are gained for the true and clear Discovery of the Truth.

5thly, And further, The very Quality, Carriage, Age, Condition, Education, and Place of Commorance of Witnesses, is by this Means plainly and evidently set forth to the Court and the Jury, whereby the Judge and Jurors may have a full Information of them, and the Jurors, as they see Cause, may give the more or less Credit to their Testimony, for the Jurors are not only Judges of the Fact, but many Times of the Truth of Evidence; and if there be just Cause to disbelieve what a Witness swears, they are not bound to give their Verdict according to the Evidence or Testimony of that Witness; and they may sometimes give Credit to one Witness, tho' oppos'd by more than one. And indeed, it is one of the Excellencies of this Trial above the Trial by Witnesses, that altho' the Jury ought to give a great Regard to Witnesses and their Testimony, yet they are not always bound by it, but may either upon reasonable Circumstances, inducing a Blemish upon their Credibility, tho' otherwise in themselves in Strictness of Law they are to be heard, pronounce a Verdict contrary to such Testimonies, the Truth whereof they have just Cause to suspect, and may and do often pronounce their Verdict upon one single Testimony, which Thing the Civil Law admits not of.

Tenthly, Another Excellency of this Trial is this; That the Judge is always present at the Time of the Evidence given in it: Herein he is able in Matters of Law emerging upon the Evidence to direct them; and also, in Matters of Fact, to give them a great Light and Assistance by his weighing the Evidence before them, and observing where the Question and Knot of the Business lies, and by shewing them his Opinion even in Matter of Fact, which is a great Advantage and Light to Lay-Men: And thus, as the Jury assists the Judge in determining the Matter of Fact, so the Judge assists the Jury in determining Points of Law, and also very much in investigating and enlightning the Matter of Fact, whereof the Jury are Judges.

Eleventhly, When the Evidence is fully given, the Jurors withdraw to a private Place, and are kept from all Speech with either of the Parties till their Verdict is delivered up, and from receiving any Evidence other than in open Court, where it may be search'd into, discuss'd and examin'd. In this Recess of the Jury they are to consider their Evidence, and if any Writings under Seal were given in Evidence, they are to have with them; they are to weigh the Credibility of Witnesses, and the Force and Efficacy of their Testimonies, wherein (as I before said) they are not precisely bound to the Rules of the Civil Law, *viz.* To have two Witnesses to prove every Fact, unless it be in Cases of Treason, nor to reject one Witness because he is single, or always to believe Two Witnesses if the Probability of the Fact does upon other Circumstances reasonably encounter them; for the Trial is not here simply by Witnesses, but by Jury; nay, it may so fall out, that the Jury upon their own Knowledge may know a Thing to be false that a Witness swore to be true, or may know a Witness to be incompetent or incredible, tho' nothing be objected against him, and may give their Verdict accordingly.

Twelfthly, When the whole Twelve Men are agreed, then, and not till then, is their Verdict to be received; and therefore the Majority of Assentors does not conclude the Minority, as is done in some Countries where Trials by Jury are admitted: But if any one of the Twelve dissent, it is no Verdict, nor ought to be received. It is true, That in ancient Times, as Hen. 2. and Hen. 3.'s Time, yea, and by Fleta in the Beginning of Edw. 1.'s Time, if the Jurors dissented, sometimes there was added a Number equal to the greater Party, and they were then to give up their Verdict by Twelve of the old Jurors, and the Jurors so added; but this Method has been long Time antiquated, notwithstanding the Practice in Bracton's Time, *lib.* 4. *cap.* 9. and Fleta, *lib.* 4. *cap.* 9. for at this Day the entire Number first empanell'd and sworn are to give up an unanimous Verdict, otherwise it is none. And indeed this gives a great Weight, Value and Credit to such a Verdict, wherein Twelve Men must unanimously agree in a Matter of Fact, and none dissent; though it must be agreed, that an ignorant Parcel of Men are sometimes governed by a few that are more knowing, or of greater Interest or Reputation than the rest.

Thirteenthly, But if there be Matter of Law that carries in it any Difficulty, the Jury may, to deliver themselves from the Danger of an Attaint, find it specially, that so it may be decided in that Court where the Verdict is returnable; and if the Judge overrule the Point of Law contrary to Law, whereby the Jury are perswaded to find a general Verdict (which yet they are not bound to do, if they doubt it,) then the Judge, upon the Request of the Party desiring it, is bound by Law in convenient Time to seal a Bill of Exceptions, containing the whole Matter excepted to; that so the Party grieved, by such Indiscretion or Error of the Judge, may have Relief by Writ of Error on the Statute of Westminster 2.

Fourteenthly, Altho' upon general Verdicts given at the Bar in the Courts at Westminster, the Judgment is given within Four Days, in Presumption that there cannot be any considerable Surprize in so solemn a Trial, or at least it may be soon espied; yet upon Trials by *Nisi prius* in the Country, the Judgment is not given presently by the Judge of *Nisi prius,* unless in Cases of *Quare Impedits:* But the Verdict is returned after Trial into that Court from whence the Cause issued, that thereby, if any Surprize happened either through much Business of the Court, or through Inadvertency of the Attorney or Council, or through any Miscarriage of the Jury, or through any other Casualty, the Party may have his Redress in that Court from whence the Record issued.

And thus stands this excellent Order of Trial by Jury, which is far beyond the Trial by Witnesses according to the Proceedings of the Civil Law, and of the Courts of Equity, both for the Certainty, the Dispatch, and the Cheapness thereof: It has all the

Helps to investigate the Truth that the Civil Law has, and many more. For as to Certainty,

1st, It has the Testimony of Witnesses, as well as the Civil Law and Equity Courts.

2dly, It has this Testimony in a much more advantageous Way than those Courts for Discovery of Truth.

3dly, It has the Advantage of the Judge's Observation, Attention, and Assistance, in Point of Law by way of Decision, and in Point of Fact by way of Direction to the Jury.

4thly, It has the Advantage of the Jury, and of their being *de Vicineto,* who oftentimes know the Witnesses and the Parties: And,

5thly, It has the unanimous Suffrage and Opinion of Twelve Men, which carries in itself a much greater Weight and Preponderation to discover the Truth of a Fact, than any other Trial whatsoever.

And as this Method is more certain, so it is much more expeditious and cheap; for oftentimes the Session of one Commission for the Examination of Witnesses for one Cause in the Ecclesiastical Courts, or Courts of Equity, lasts as long as a whole Session of *Nisi prius,* where a Hundred Causes are examined and tried.

And thus much concerning Trials in Civil Causes. As for Trials in Causes Criminal, they have this further Advantage, That regularly the Accusation, as preparatory to the Trial, is by a Grand Jury: So that as no Man's Interest, according to the Course of the Common Law, is to be tried or determined without the Oaths of a Jury of twelve Men; so no Man's Life is to be tried but by the Oaths of Twelve Men, and by the Preparatory Accusation or Indictment by Twelve Men or more precedent to his Trial, unless it be in the Case of an Appeal at the Suit of the Party.

Index

Magna Carta (Charta), xxv, 7, 12,
33, 36, 91, 95, 96, 99,
100–103, 124, 126
Maitland, F. W., viii, xi
Man, Isle of, 117–18
Matilda (Maud), Empress, 88
Memory, legal, 3–5, 6, 13, 45
Mirror of Justices, 106
Mortgages, 81
Murder fine, 69

Nepos, Cornelius, xiii, xiv, xv
Nisi Prius, 109, 161, 162, 166, 167
Normandy. *See* Law, Norman;
Conquest, Norman
Novae Narrationes, 106

Odo, Bishop, 65
Oyer and *Terminer,* 109

Paris, Matthew, 6, 7, 57, 68, 74, 75,
88, 94, 95
Parliament, xxv, xxviii, xxix, xxxi,
xxxii, 3, 4, 5, 6, 7, 8, 16, 19,
27, 31–36, 39, 40, 48, 69, 72,
83, 99, 100, 101, 105, 118,
127, 143, 144; Oxford, 15;
Irish, 115, 117; records, 9–15.
See also Legislation; Statutes
Patent Rolls, 105
Petition of Right, 27
Pipe Rolls, 88, 89, 94, 98
Pleading, xxxv, 96, 101, 105, 108,
111–12; of statutes, 11–12
Plowden, Edmund, 46, 159
Pocock, J. G. A., viii, xiii, xxvii
Prerogative, 18, 76, 107–8
Puritanism, xvi, xvii, xxx

Real actions, xxv, xxxvi, 109–10,
110–11
Reeves, John, xi
Relief, 77
Richard I, 4, 5, 6, 7, 13, 73–85
passim, 93–96, 107, 122, 147
Richard II, 12, 26, 35, 73, 109
Robert, Duke of Normandy, 57

Robert Curthose, 86
Rolle, Henry (*Abridgment*),
xxxviii

Scotland, 57, 118, 122–32
Selden, John, xvii, 5, 20, 21, 62,
69–71, 94, 134, 136, 142,
143
Serjeanty, 77, 143
Shapiro, Barbara J., xxxvii
Sheriff, 76, 96, 114, 115, 160
Spelman, Henry, xvii, 37, 62, 64,
66
Stare decisis, 46
Statutes, 3–13, 28, 45; ancient,
12–14; of limitation, 4, 80;
penal, 1–2, 113. *See also*
Parliament; Legislation
Acton Burnel, 103
Articuli cleri, 102
Articuli super cartas, 36, 102–4
Carlisle, 102
Circumspecte agatis, 102
Confirmation of Charters, 102
De Donis, xxiv
De Mercatoribus, 103
De modo levandi fines, 103
De Prerogativa Regis, 107
De tallagio non concedendo, 103
Dictum of Kenilworth, 8, 101
of Edward III, 33, 36, 67
of Elizabeth I, 23
Gloucester, 9
of Henry IV, 33
of Henry VII, 104
of Henry VIII, 20, 21, 24, 104
Marlebridge, 100, 124
Merton, 8, 36, 76, 80, 100, 116,
126
Mortmain, 126
Quia emptores, 103
Quo Warranto, 9, 36
of Richard II, 24, 25
Rutland, 104, 117
of Uses, xxiv
Walliae, 141, 144